# EVERYDAY RELIGIOSITY AND THE POLITICS OF BELONGING IN UKRAINE

# EVERYDAY RELIGIOSITY AND THE POLITICS OF BELONGING IN UKRAINE

Catherine Wanner

CORNELL UNIVERSITY PRESS   ITHACA AND LONDON

First published 2022 by Cornell University Press

Library of Congress Cataloging-in-Publication Data

Names: Wanner, Catherine, 1960– author.
Title: Everyday religiosity and the politics of belonging in Ukraine / Catherine Wanner.
Description: Ithaca [New York] : Cornell University Press, 2022. | Includes bibliographical references and index.
Identifiers: LCCN 2021060342 (print) | LCCN 2021060343 (ebook) | ISBN 9781501764950 (hardcover) | ISBN 9781501764981 (paperback) | ISBN 9781501764967 (pdf) | ISBN 9781501764974 (epub)
Subjects: LCSH: Orthodox Eastern Church—Ukraine—History—21st century. | Christianity and politics—Ukraine—History—21st century. | Church and state—Ukraine—History—21st century. | Christianity and politics—Orthodox Eastern Church—History—21st century. | Ukraine—Religion—21st century. | Ukraine—Church history—21st century. | Ukraine—Politics and government—21st century.
Classification: LCC BR1050.U45 W36 2022 (print) | LCC BR1050.U45 (ebook) | DDC 280/.209477—dc23/eng/20220215
LC record available at https://lccn.loc.gov/2021060342
LC ebook record available at https://lccn.loc.gov/2021060343

DOI: https://doi.org/10.7298/scv8-f015

For Adrian, Elizabeth, Nicholas, and Katrina

# Contents

# Acknowledgments

One of the sweetest moments of completing a book is the opportunity it provides to acknowledge the kindness and generosity of so many along the way. This book was many years in the making. Extraordinary events were so fast breaking that for years it was in a state of perpetual revision. My greatest debt in writing this book is to the many people in Ukraine who, once again, have shared their time, thoughts, and experiences by opening up their hearts to talk candidly about their dreams, fears, joys, and sorrows. This willingness to trust and be patient with an overly curious American and her strange and endless questions never ceases to amaze me.

In addition to those I interviewed, many people have provided years of inspiring conversation and friendship for which I remain immensely grateful. I would like to thank Liudmyla Asmalovska and the entire Ornatsky extended family, Olha Filippova, Lada Kolomiyets, Anna Kuks and her entire family, the multigenerational Lapchyk family, Natalia Kovalchuk, Valentyna Pavlenko, Alla Perminova, the Patlay family, Olena Yahodovska and all members of her family. Svitlana Shlipchenko and Yurii Mykytenko deserve extra special mention for their years of hospitality, generosity, and sustaining inspiration.

Several colleagues have been insightful readers of this manuscript. I thank them for their encouragement and critical feedback, often at much needed moments. Olena Bohdan, Nicholas Denysenko, Kate Dudley, Gertrud Hülemeier, Tetiana Kalenychenko, Neringa Klumbyte, Jeanne Kormina, Julia Lerner, Sonja Luehrmann, Vlad Naumescu, Nancy Ries, Michele Rivkin-Fish, Joel Robbins, and Viktor Yelensky all read parts of this manuscript and improved it immeasurably. Julia Buyskykh, Bruce Grant, Valentyna Pavlenko and Oxana Shevel, read this manuscript in its entirety and offered many helpful suggestions and necessary improvements. Bruce Grant has been a steady and engaging conversation partner since my days in graduate school. I am deeply appreciative of his sharp critical eye, which is exceeded only by his deep sense of humanity. He has read every monograph I have ever written and has always been forthright with criticism gently delivered. I am grateful to Joel Robbins and Birgit Meyer for conversation and their provocative scholarship on religion, which I have found inspiring on numerous occasions.

The research for this book was partly funded by a grant from the Fulbright Scholar Program that allowed me to benefit from the rich intellectual atmosphere at the Ukrainian Catholic University in 2019–20. At UCU, I benefited from scholarly exchanges with Svitlana Hurkina, Natalia Kovalchuk, Myroslav Marynovych, Oleh Turiy, Andriy Oliinyk, and UCU's many gifted students. I owe thanks to Trudi Hülemeier for inviting me to be a visiting scholar at the Institute of European Ethnology of Humboldt University in Berlin in 2016–17. This afforded me the company of exceptional scholars, such as Tsypylma Darieva, Regina Elsner, and Jens Adam. The Center for Governance and Culture of the University of St. Gallen, Switzerland funded many of my research trips to Ukraine and I am grateful for the ongoing support shown to me by my adopted country. I thank Ulrich Schmid for being such an impressively generous and visionary scholar. Others in Switzerland who have my thanks for years of encouragement and more assistance than they will ever know include Oksana Myshlovska, Sandra King-Savic, and Carmen Scheide.

I have presented parts of this book to engaged and thoughtful audiences at numerous universities. Their questions inevitably stimulated new ideas, and I am grateful for the critical feedback I have received at Humboldt University, the Center for East European and International Studies (ZOiS), and the Wissenschaftskolleg, all in Berlin; Ben-Gurion University of the Negev; Cambridge University; National Research Institute of Ukrainian Studies; Princeton University; the Ukrainian Catholic University; Universität Passau; University of Pennsylvania, and the State Research University Higher School of Economics, St. Petersburg, Russia.

I have been fortunate to have been included in several multiyear research projects over the course of writing this book. The interaction with scholars from different disciplines working on a variety of issues in a multitude of places has sharpened my thinking immeasurably. I would like to acknowledge the Region, Nation, and Beyond project (2012–15) and Transnational Contact Zones in Ukraine (2015 and ongoing) and Ulrich Schmid; the series of conferences and events of the Hidden Galleries Research Project based at the University of Cork, Ireland, organized by James Kapaló and Tatiana Vagramenko (2016–21); the New Arts of Persuasion Research Initiative, University of Toronto, especially Victoria Fomina and Simon Coleman (2020–21); and the Pew Research Center's Religious Belief and National Belonging in Central and Eastern Europe research initiative (2017).

I owe a particular debt to all the members of the Working Group on Lived Religion in Eastern Europe and Eurasia. Viktor Yelensky and I convened this research group in the immediate aftermath of the Maidan in 2014. Since then, it has evolved into an ongoing Working Group that meets for an annual conference and monthly seminars. The members of this Group have been a consistent source of inspiration and enthusiasm, shaping my research, thinking, and interests in countless ways. Specifically regarding research for this book, I thank Tetiana Kalenychenko and Julia Buyskykh, as well as Denis Brylov, Mykhailo Cherenkov, Andriy Fert, Oleg Kyselov, Olena Soboleva, Alla Marchenko, Viktor Yelensky, and Yuliya Yurchuk. Other colleagues in Ukraine who have shared their knowledge and insight over the years and in other ways have supported my efforts to understand religion in Ukraine include Dmytro Volk, Constantin Sigov, Olena Bogdan, Liudmyla Fylypovych, and Oksana Yurkova.

I benefited from the critical feedback of editors and reviewers of journals that published parts of this research over the years. Portions of chapter 2 appeared in "An Affective Atmosphere of Religiosity: Animated Places, Public Spaces and the Politics of Attachment in Ukraine and Beyond," *Comparative Studies in Society and History* 62, no. 1 (January 2020): 68–105, https://doi.org/10.1017/S0010417519000410; portions of chapter 4 in "Commemoration and the New Frontiers of War in Ukraine," *Slavic Review* 78, no. 2 (Summer 2019): 328–35, https://doi.org/10.1017/slr.2019.88; and portions of chapter 5 in "Empathic Care and Healing the Wounds of War in Ukraine," *Emotions and Society* 3, no. 1 (May 2021): 155–70, https://doi.org/10.1332/263169021X16139626598365. At Cornell University Press, I thank Roger Haydon and Jim Lance for their early interest in this manuscript and for helping bring it to fruition. Clare Jones ensured the quality of images and maps, and Mary Gendron reviewed the text with care and great patience. And once again, I am fortunate to have the photographic talents of Tania D'Avignon illustrating many of the facets of life in Ukraine I depict. Tania has never failed to share the wealth of spectacular images she has made that illustrate why Ukraine is such a magnetic place.

Finally, I offer my heartfelt thanks to the four people in my life who make everything worth it. My husband, Adrian Wanner, and our three children, Elizabeth, Nicholas, and Katrina, have always provided the sustaining joy that makes all else possible. It is to them that I dedicate this book.

# Abbreviations

| | |
|---|---|
| ATO | Anti-Terrorist Operation |
| EP | Ecumenical Patriarch |
| KP | Kyiv Patriarch |
| MP | Moscow Patriarch |
| OCU | Orthodox Church of Ukraine |
| ROC | Russian Orthodox Church |
| UAOC | Ukrainian Autocephalous Orthodox Church |
| UGCC | Ukrainian Greek Catholic Church |
| ULA | Ukrainian Leadership Academy |
| UOC-KP | Ukrainian Orthodox Church-Kyiv Patriarchate |
| UOC-MP | Ukrainian Orthodox Church-Moscow Patriarchate |

## Note on Transliteration and Translation

I have followed a slightly modified Library of Congress system for transliterating Cyrillic. Both Ukrainian and Russian are spoken in Ukraine. I have translated and transliterated speech from the language in which it was spoken or written. Some names used in this book are pseudonyms. In those instances, I have used names transliterated from the language the person primarily uses. When an individual is a public figure or a published author, I have used his or her real name. Place names are rendered in Ukrainian if the place is in Ukraine (Kyiv, not Kiev; Donbas, not Donbass; Odesa, not Odessa) and in Russian if the place is in Russia. All translations are my own unless otherwise noted.

# Preface

This book analyzes how religion connects people(s) and forges attachments to place, and how this creates motivations to act. The war over the political orientation and geopolitical fate of Ukraine, which, by extension, lays the groundwork for the orientation and fate of Russia, plays out on a parallel level involving religion. This gives the full-scale Russian invasion of Ukraine that began on February 24, 2022, a significant religious dimension. The stakes for religious institutions are equally as high as they are for the states and political regimes involved. The ethnographic material presented here on informal religious practices reveals why and how religion has become something of a proxy war to the Russian aggression in Ukraine and why each side strives to capitalize on the use of religion as a political resource.

The power of Orthodoxy lies in its pervasive influence on social and political life through the affective atmosphere it creates in societies where it predominates. Its naturalized presence in Ukraine is a key factor that has allowed vernacular religious practices to flourish and to permeate public space and public institutions. These religious practices, as well as the sacred qualities of the spaces in which they take place, augment an atmosphere of religiosity. This has put in place an upward spiral that gives religious institutions growing influence. They are politically relevant because religious practices enact bonds of relatedness among the living and between the living and dead, which carry obligations of reciprocity. This is why history, and historical commemorations in particular, have become so politically fraught in both Ukraine and Russia, and why ecclesiastical and political leaders are so invested in defining and performing them. Both the Ukrainian and Russian states have weaponized religion and politicized historical events and figures to provoke certain geopolitical outcomes and to advance domestic political agendas. They mobilize religion to shape collective and self-perceptions to trigger action and reaction. Vernacular religious practices, be they oriented toward prior sacrifice and past glory or forthcoming empowerment and future glory, are anchored in particular places. These practices create attachments to those places, which even the harshest critics of religion wish to keep accessible. This gives religiosity unrivaled powers of persuasion, albeit ones that are often volatile and create unpredictable consequences.

In Ukraine, persuasive efforts to engender loyalty to a particular religious leader, a corresponding political vision, and a version of history to justify those choices center on the so-called Just Orthodox, or *prosto Pravoslavni*. The term refers to Ukrainians who decline to express allegiance to a particular patriarch and religious institution while still identifying as Orthodox. This book focuses on this rather large sector of Ukrainian society, including how they came into being and the dynamics influencing their choices of allegiance. The Just Orthodox are an amorphous group of sympathizers to Eastern Christianity. They do not form any kind of stable, identifiable community, nor do they have leaders. They maintain a commitment to a faith tradition along with a guarded distance from religious institutions. As swing voters in the competition for allegiance, they play a pivotal role in defining the Orthodox religious landscape in Ukraine, and by extension in Russia as well, given how embedded and entwined Orthodoxy is in both countries. They will play a key role in determining the balance of power between Kyiv and Moscow, between the Ecumenical Patriarch and the Moscow Patriarch, and in terms of determining which city is the "Third Rome."

The Revolution of Dignity in 2013–14 validated the cultural dexterity exhibited by the Just Orthodox when it married civic understandings of what it means to be Ukrainian and to belong in Ukraine with shared radical hope for a vision of a revitalized collective future. The project to realize that vision was soon compromised by the obligation to contend with challenges to Ukraine's sovereignty as Russia annexed Crimea and fueled a separatist insurgency in Eastern Ukraine. The deaths of protesters and soldiers triggered grief and expressions of mourning—and eventually that grief morphed into rage.

The seismic changes to the religious landscape in Ukraine since then are in response to the challenges to Ukrainian state sovereignty. These changes are one of the many factors that accelerated the tensions between Russia and Ukraine. Seeking geopolitical and religious dominance over Ukraine and Ukrainians, the Putin regime launched a full-scale invasion of Ukraine. The typesetting of this book was complete on February 24, 2022, the exact day Russian forces crossed the border into Ukraine and began expanding the damage that had been inflicted on the Donbas since 2014 to major urban centers, towns, and villages across Ukraine. I did not alter the original text.

The ethnographic descriptions in this book of religiosity and the rhythms of everyday life in Ukraine now serve comparative purposes. They depict the fluid, informal, vernacular religious practices and novel forms of identity, which are often found in borderland areas, that existed in Ukraine prior to the 2022 Russian invasion. I once heard it said that good ethnography follows the standards of a courtroom: it should present material that is beyond a reasonable doubt. When a final inventory is taken of all that has been destroyed in Ukraine as a result of the Russian invasion, we will find that the religious and cultural landscape, like all else, has been transformed by the trauma of war. The Ukrainian ability to mesh historical legacies with elastic, adaptive cultural practices, epitomized by the Just Orthodox and their informal religious practices and the atmosphere of religiosity those practices created, will change once again. As we take stock of all that was lost and all that could have been, if not for massive displacement, destruction, and the senseless loss of human life due to war, I hope this book will serve as a testimony to the future that Ukrainians had once envisioned for themselves.

# EVERYDAY RELIGIOSITY AND THE POLITICS OF BELONGING IN UKRAINE

**MAP 0.1.** Map of Ukraine before 2022 with the disputed Donbas territories and the annexed Crimean Peninsula.

# INTRODUCTION
## Together and Apart

Religion and politics intersect in powerful and sometimes unusual ways. On occasion this serves the common good. Other times, it is to everyone's detriment. For centuries, Ukrainians and Russians were part of the same Orthodox Church headed by the Moscow Patriarch. Commemorating certain historic events, such as the advent of Christianity in Kyivan Rus' in 988 or the contribution of the Soviet Red Army to victory during World War II, provides an opportunity for some to recall this common religious and civilizational heritage and the relationship between Russians and Ukrainians that it bore in order to influence the future direction of politics. In July 2021 Russian President Vladimir Putin penned a widely publicized, lengthy historical essay, which he titled "On the Historical Unity of Russians and Ukrainians." No longer just "fraternal nations," as Soviet rhetoric posited, Putin asserts that Ukrainians and Russians are "one people." He laments, as he has in prior speeches, the divisions that have emerged within "what is essentially the same historical and spiritual space."[1] Putin concludes his survey of the entangled historical experience Russians and Ukrainians share by asserting that the "sovereignty of Ukraine is possible only in partnership with Russia."[2] After the speech, 41 percent of Ukrainians agreed that Russians and Ukrainians share a common past in a single historical and spiritual space.[3] Does it follow then that they share a common future? If religion is the source of their common heritage, what role might it play in forging the unity or the divisions that could characterize that future? This book considers how Ukrainians use religion to respond to these questions. The answers will determine their collective future and the prospects for stability in the region. Religion has become a force shaping geopolitics as well as a vehicle individuals use to express how they aspire to live and the identities and allegiances they are willing to embrace.

Every Ukrainian knows the word *tomos*. It refers to a *"tomos* of autocephaly,"* which the Ecumenical Patriarch of Constantinople grants to establish a new Orthodox Church. After much anticipation, the Ecumenical Patriarch (EP) granted a *tomos* on January 6, 2019, following persistent requests from Ukrainian state and ecclesiastical authorities.[4] The creation of an independent Orthodox Church of Ukraine (OCU), with its own patriarchate, that could potentially rival the Russian Orthodox Church (ROC), was initially hailed as the greatest schism in Christianity since the Protestant Reformation 500 years ago. Some feared—and others hoped—that it would be the beginning of at least two Orthodoxies developing that would bring an end to a universal Eastern Christianity that extends from Eastern Europe to the Middle East and, thanks to migration, into Southeast Asia, Africa, and the Americas. The tensions over whether to grant institutional independence to the OCU, over the objections of the ROC, provoked a standoff that involved the Moscow Patriarch, the Ecumenical Patriarch in Constantinople, and Orthodox churches across Europe, with disagreements threatening to create lasting divisions within Eastern Christianity.[5]

Ukrainians, regardless of religious affiliation or persuasion, keenly followed the campaign to receive a *tomos* because it had become embedded in efforts to secure Ukrainian borders while fighting a hybrid war of guns and disinformation. With serious challenges to Ukraine's sovereignty underway, creating an independent church was a means to reduce Russian influence in Ukraine and deal a blow to the standing of the ROC, and by extension to President Putin, in retaliation for annexing Ukrainian territory and sparking and supporting armed separatism in Eastern Ukraine. For the ROC, Ukrainian autocephaly threatens to transfer several key monasteries and numerous parishes, clergy, and believers away to another jurisdiction, opening up the possibility that the dominance of the ROC and its influence in the region might eventually be eclipsed by either Constantinople or Kyiv. In this way, the *tomos* hardened the soft power of religion in the region.

Efforts to establish ecclesiastical independence from Russia to strengthen Ukrainian state independence have been in the making in some form since the Russian Empire collapsed in 1917 (Denysenko 2018; Plokhy and Sysyn 2003; Shestopalets 2021; Wanner and Yelensky 2019). Since the fall of the Soviet Union in 1991, most presidents of Ukraine tried to some extent to create an independent church to buttress the nascent state and advance nation-building. However, no single leader made it the priority that President Petro Poroshenko did. He and his administration worked tirelessly to secure the *tomos* and establish a local church, and this became his signature accomplishment.

His predecessor, Viktor Yanukovych, used Orthodoxy to bring Ukraine more firmly into Moscow's orbit. Elites in the Donbas region of Eastern Ukraine relied on the Ukrainian Orthodox Church of the Moscow Patriarchate (UOC-MP), which is what the Orthodox Church in Ukraine integrated into the Russian Orthodox Church is called, to articulate a regional identity that fused elements of an all-Russian, Soviet, and Cossack past. To strengthen the presence of the UOC-MP in the region, oligarchs sponsored the construction of churches, and some even insisted employees attend liturgies (Wanner and Yelensky 2019, 274–77).[6] These diametrically opposed efforts reflect the interpenetration of religious and political authorities and the import of religion for sovereignty, borders, and belonging, especially in predominantly Orthodox societies.

A series of cascading events decisively turned the tide of political and popular will toward securing a *tomos*. In November 2013, then President Yanukovych refused to sign an Association Agreement with the European Union in favor of integrating Ukraine more firmly into the Eurasian Customs Union. This decision provoked mass protests, which Yanukovych ordered violently suppressed in February 2014. One month later, Russia annexed Crimea from Ukraine. One month after that, Russian-backed separatists ignited armed conflict on Ukraine's eastern border with Russia. Once the war began, not only the politicization but the weaponization of religion in the region intensified. Establishing a separate and independent Orthodox Church of Ukraine through a *tomos* by breaking over three centuries of institutional connections to the Russian Orthodox Church had broad, popular support in most regions of Ukraine.

The atmosphere of the moment prompted political views to find expression in terms of religion. Consider how Yurii Byriukov framed his political convictions. He was a Maidan activist, turned volunteer fighter in Eastern Ukraine, and controversial fundraiser for the war effort before he became an adviser to President Poroshenko. On August 31, 2018, before the *tomos* was granted, he posted in Russian on Facebook, "Well, I am really an atheist. Entirely. All the way. But I am, without a doubt, an atheist of the Kyiv Patriarchate. I have watched the whole story of the *tomos* unfold but not because it would somehow affect me. The whole country needs it."[7] This sense of "being an atheist of the Kyiv Patriarchate" was a sentiment shared by many nonbelievers and sympathizers (*prykhylnyky* in Ukrainian), or people who are favorably inclined toward Orthodoxy although they might not consider themselves religious. Muslim communities in Ukraine, who mostly are made up of Crimean Tatars, immigrants, and some Ukrainians, also adopted the slogan, "I am a Muslim of the Kyiv Patriarchate" to signal their ardent support for a Ukrainian church independent from Moscow. Endorsement for the *tomos* came from many unlikely quarters because it became synonymous with a political endorsement of Ukrainian sovereignty.

This is why there was such intense interest in the *tomos*, such pronounced support for it, and why political leaders worked so steadfastly to secure it. Ukrainian independence seemed to be at stake.

The ROC offered stiff resistance to the prospect of a Ukrainian Church. It considers its canonical domain to be the historical territory of the Russian Empire. Since 1686, control over religious life in Ukraine has been officially directed by the Moscow Patriarch, who ordained the metropolitan of Kyiv. The ROC began to promote itself as the leader of the "Russian World" (*Russkii Mir*), an evolving concept that has come to position the ROC as the protector of traditional values. The ROC posits that certain things are eternal and unchanging, such as gender, heterosexuality, nationality, and power. The Russian World concept is also used by Russian state officials to justify the righteousness of the imperial vision of all Eastern Slavs (Russians, Ukrainians, and Belarussians) under one church led by the Moscow patriarch. Some separatist soldiers in eastern Ukraine politically loyal to Moscow initially called themselves an "Orthodox Army" in recognition of this social fact.

Yet making religious institutions a secondary battlefield has not panned out as expected. Within three months of an independent church forming, about 500 parishes left the Moscow Patriarchate and reaffiliated to the OCU. Although many government officials who were initiators of autocephaly expected this to be just the beginning, reaffiliations quickly slowed and now only trickle in. One year after its creation, the OCU had over 1,000 parishes, but this paled in comparison to the over 12,000 of the UOC-MP. By 2020, it had become obvious that significant numbers of UOC-MP clergy and believers had little inclination or possibility to reaffiliate, even when they supported the OCU in principle. Growth in the number of OCU communities comes primarily from building new churches, which number over 7,000.

Despite President Poroshenko's *tomos* victory, he was voted out of office in a landslide in the spring of 2019. The new leader, Volodymyr Zelensky, a secular Jew, proclaimed his disinterest in religious affairs and lack of intention to meddle. Still, upon assuming office, he was promptly handed a list of "red lines" signed by leaders of nongovernmental organizations (NGOs) and unions, journalists, writers, policymakers, and celebrities. The signatories claimed to be "actively defending Ukraine's sovereignty and national interests."[8] Among the lines not to be crossed was "implementing any actions aimed at undermining or discrediting the Orthodox Church of Ukraine or supporting the Russian Orthodox Church in Ukraine." This statement makes no mention of religious conviction, practice, or affiliation, but speaks volumes about fiercely held views on institutional religion, even among atheists, sympathizers, and the nonreligious. The signatories threatened political instability should any of the red lines be crossed and the Ukrainian Church weakened. Why do they care? Why are they willing to take to the streets again if the state sides with the wrong Orthodox church? The reason is as personal as it is political.

## Everyday Religiosity

The armed conflict over the political orientation and geopolitical fate of Ukraine which, by extension, begins to sketch out the orientation and fate of Russia, finds a parallel in terms of religion. Religion is ripe for politicization, and yet its potential is volatile and unpredictable. After mounting extraordinary efforts to create or resist the Orthodox Church of Ukraine, few of the anticipated consequences for either side have materialized. Outside Ukraine, other Orthodox churches have tacitly or implicitly accepted the OCU, muting the threat of any kind of lasting split within Orthodoxy. Within Ukraine, the *tomos* and the Orthodox Church of Ukraine thus far have shifted the terms of religious pluralism by widening the spectrum of Orthodox churches on offer. The ethnographic material presented here unpacks the paradox of why the keen interest among Ukrainians to establish an independent church has been slow to translate into engaged support and yet why and how religious institutions nonetheless remain a formidable political resource.

Even though the ardent endorsement of ecclesiastical independence has thus far not generated a thriving institution nor yielded cataclysmic divisions within Eastern Christianity, it would be a mistake to assume that religion is unimportant. The power of Orthodoxy lies in its pervasive influence on social and political life through the affective atmosphere it creates. Its naturalized presence is a key factor that has allowed a plethora of vernacular religious practices to flourish and to permeate public space and public institutions with little resistance. These religious practices, as well as the sacred qualities of the spaces in which they take place, augment an atmosphere of religiosity, putting in place an upward spiral that gives religious institutions great influence. Vernacular religious practices draw on an Eastern Christian faith tradition for validation and authentication, more so than on a particular denomination or specific Orthodox Church. They are politically relevant because they articulate bonds of relatedness, which carry obligations of reciprocity, among the living and between the living and dead. This is why history, and historical commemorations in particular, have become so politically fraught and why ecclesiastical and political leaders are so invested in defining them. Both the Ukrainian and Russian states, as well as many others, mobilize religion to provoke certain geopolitical outcomes and to advance domestic political agendas by influencing self and collective perceptions such that they trigger action or reaction. Vernacular religious practices, be they oriented toward prior sacrifice and past glory or forthcoming empowerment and future grandeur, are anchored in particular places (monasteries, graves, monuments, and the like). These practices create attachments to those places, which even the harshest critics of religion wish to keep accessible, bound as they are by borders that religious institutions can help fortify. This gives Orthodox churches powers of persuasion that are unrivaled.

Vernacular religious practices in Ukraine, and in other Orthodox societies, are often born of institutional disaffection and are widely visible alongside institutional forms of religion, but not necessarily within them. These forms of lived religion, however, are pervasive. The vernacular, as applied to the analysis of social practices, is rooted in the Annales school of social history and the rise of Alltagsgeschichte, both of which emphasize the importance of local variations on historical patterns in the daily lives of nonelites. The term was originally popularized in Scandinavia and North America in folklore studies (Bowman and Valk 2012, 4–6). I use the term vernacular religious practices to indicate the culturally patterned variation that results from the dynamic blending of institutionally prescribed religious practices oriented toward the transcendent and individual spiritual innovation. By drawing on a common faith tradition, these vernacular practices retain shared meanings. Although they are often tailored to individual circumstances and idiosyncrasies, they are often readily recognizable to others and therefore have a social character. Even though individuals might turn to vernacular practices to escape institutional confines and the judgment of others, this does not mean that they discredit religion per se.

Vernacular religious practices accommodate belief, doubt, and nonbelief, along with the desire to belong and the refusal to be coerced by institutions (Wanner 2014, 435). This yields responsiveness to religiosity and openness to religious sentiment while acknowledging a cynical suspicion of persons in authority, including clergy, and the institutions they command. This ultimately serves to expand the ways the political and religious can be melded together to greater effect. Vernacular religious practices, as forms of everyday religiosity, allow for the integration of religion into other domains of social life, including politics, health care, the urban landscape, and so on, and thereby cloud the boundaries between the religious and the nonreligious, the sacred and the secular.

These practices invoke institutional forms of religion for the purposes of validation and legitimation, which is what makes them symbiotically interdependent on religious institutions. Such practices become religion, as opposed to superstitions, folk practices, New Age fads, and the like, when they are performed at sites where institutionalized religion, state authorities, and the political visions they promulgate intersect. In other words, emplacement in particular sites makes religion out of vernacular religious practices. As Jonathan Z. Smith famously noted, "Inside the house it's dirt; outside, it's earth" (1978, 291). The site can change the meaning, sacred qualities, and reactions to rites and the objects, signs, and symbols used in performing them. By emplacing idiosyncratic popular practices in relation to religious institutions, they become lived forms of religion.

Most studies of religion in Orthodox countries, contemporary or historical, focus on either institutional religion or on forms of popular religion that go beyond what is authorized by the institutional church.[9] Such conceptualizations undervalue the relational interplay between institutional religion and vernacular forms of religious practice (Ammerman 2014; Orsi 2002; Tweed 2015). One of the goals I have for this book is to illustrate the extent to which these practices impose themselves on institutions, even as they are constrained by them, and how institutions are complicit in bringing everyday religiosity into public space and public institutions. I depict the interrelational, mutually constituting nature of vernacular religious practices and how they both serve to fortify lived religious practices and enhance an affective atmosphere of religiosity.

Vernacular religious practices merit our attention because, in appealing to higher powers, they trade on shared norms and rhythms of communal practice, horizontal bonds of solidarity as well as vertical intergenerational connections, and inform ethical and moral convictions. This reveals the agency religious institutions have as political actors in shaping identities and social integration, as well as the agency vernacular religious practices bequeath to individuals through their ability to engage in daily micropolitical acts, sometimes in concert with and other times independent of religious institutions. Both contribute to the politics of belonging and social (dis)integration as they play out in everyday religiosity.

When the study of religion is not situated within oppositional frameworks of institutional/popular, high/low, agency/nonagency, and so on, the conceptual nature of religion as an object of study changes. Defining religion is notoriously difficult, given its situational, local, and instrumental nature. The nuances of everyday religiosity compound those difficulties by resisting clear divides between the sacred and the profane, the religious and the secular, and illustrate how permeable the lines dividing them are. Vernacular religious practices exist on a sliding continuum between these binaries (Meyer 2020; Tweed 2006, 29–53; Wanner 2020). They reveal how icons can become decorative objects as easily as objects of veneration; how an ordinary city street can become the site of shrines and ritualized mourning; and health-care facilities, replete with chapels and chaplains, can supplant officially consecrated places by offering healing through prayer and other acts of devotion.

The vibrancy of vernacular religiosity in Ukraine and elsewhere is both an outgrowth of and a contributor to the deinstitutionalization of religion.

Deinstitutionalization as a process should not be confused with a rise in secularism, deprivatization, or the strengthening of a nontranscendent way of thinking.[10] Rather, vernacular religious practices have contributed to emplacing religion in public space and public institutions, which intensifies an affective atmosphere of religion by multiplying the sites of religious practice to include those related to consecrated places, rather than directly within them. This serves to normativize the presence and power of religion. Ultimately, deinstitutionalizing religiosity makes the binary distinction between the religious and the secular no longer a sharp analytic tool for understanding social change. Once objects, practices, and visions of the past are emplaced in certain sites within an affective atmosphere of religiosity, they can "pivot to the sacred" and take on transcendent qualities (Smith 1972). The practices they inspire recognize the sacredness, transcendence, or otherwise extraordinary nature of the site. Religious innovation, be it from above in the form of institutional creation or from below in the form of vernacular religious practices, reveals the dexterity with which religiosity can create a sense of place, project sacred qualities on to it, and enable attachments to that place such that people feel they belong there. This is why religion can become such a valuable political resource. This suggests a reconsideration of the secular in terms of how easily it can be transformed and a recognition of the limits of profane means of creating allegiance and feelings of belonging.

Such an amorphous conceptualization of religion courts a certain "messiness" to use David Hall's (1997, x) characterization of lived religion. Yet to fully understand the relevance of religion for individuals and societies, especially those with a predominant faith tradition, a broad understanding of religiosity must be deployed. Robert Orsi proposes "direct attention to institutions *and* persons, text *and* rituals, practice *and* theology, things *and* ideas—all as media of making and unmaking worlds" (2002, xix). He rightfully insists that a focus on lived religion should not simply reverse hierarchical binaries that previously privileged institutional forms of practice as true and real and relegated vernacular practices in homes, on the street, or in nature as superstitions of the ignorant. The relationship between the two is symbiotic and not necessarily hierarchical. Moreover, both are constrained by power relations that impose themselves on both institutions and vernacular practices. Everyday religiosity integrates these diverse elements, and yet hones in on how they relate to the "sacred, transcendent or beyond the ordinary" (Ammerman 2007, 225).

Although it is impossible to isolate a distinct phenomenon that can neatly be called "religion" and separate it from other aspects of social, cultural, and political life, concepts must be defined enough so that they can be useful analytically. Birgit Meyer encourages us to conceive of religion as a "generalizing concept" that facilitates comparison and analysis (2020, 2). She conceives of religious phenomena as "practices of mediation" between the immanent and the transcendent. Mediation involves the use of "practices, ideas and things" to make real and tangible a sense of the "beyond." I use religiosity as a "generalizing concept" to select, group, and compare practices oriented toward the transcendent, and specifically practices situated beyond the threshold of official religious sites. By casting such a wide net, I do not posit certain practices as "religion" and others as "not religion" to be eliminated from consideration. Rather, I include vernacular religious practices that yield transcendent experiences, even among people who are agnostics, doubters, or nonbelievers, because otherworldly experiences emerge in relationship with the realities of everyday life (Orsi 1997, 7).

The study of lived religion and the vernacular practices that characterize it instantly situate religiosity within the everyday and its commonplace routines (Ammerman 2007; Engelke 2013; Henig 2020; Knibbe and Kupari 2020; Tweed 2015). A focus on everyday religiosity highlights the habitualness, domesticity, and mundaneness in which transcendent bonds of social solidarity are embedded. Everyday life is often juxtaposed to the extraordinary, understood as miraculous, magical, or sacred. When a crisis or an extraordinary event punctuates the routines of everyday life, such as the Maidan protests, it ruptures the fabric and flow of everyday life by generating new routines, rhythms, sites, and smells in everyday life. Indeed, the war constitutes an extraordinary event, which has shaped the ordinary in new ways. Religiosity also connects the ordinary to the extraordinary and makes communal experiences from individual death and loss. In this way, as Nancy Ries writes, "almost everywhere, ritual—that realm of the extraordinary, liminal, upside-down, carnivalesque, transcendent—in fact enshrines nothing as much as the local practices of the everyday" (2002, 733). In other words, the ordinary, everyday is shot through with the extraordinary.

The materiality of public space (aesthetic styles and architecture), in which everyday religiosity takes place, forms an atmosphere that serves as an ecology of experience. An atmosphere of religiosity fosters dispositions, inclinations, orientations, and convictions, religious and political, that affect indifferent agnostics, committed atheists, and pious believers alike. The atmosphere of religiosity that exists in Ukraine forms the backdrop to everyday experiences and extraordinary events that characterize the lifeworlds of Ukrainians. The power of atmosphere lies in its ability to either intensify or mute sensations that inform experiences. When an atmosphere becomes affective, it influences how experiences are understood and the reactions they ignite. A particular atmosphere that permeates everyday life can generate sensations and vistas such that indifferent agnostics become no longer so indifferent, committed atheists no longer so committed, and believers more pious. The reverse is equally as true. The frequency and intensity of transcendent experiences can also diminish and even vanish.

The key point is that a particular atmosphere can provoke and persuade people to feel, think, and act differently.

## The Just Orthodox

An analysis of vernacular religious practices explains why some Ukrainians self-define as Just Orthodox (*prosto Pravoslavni* in Ukrainian), preferring to eschew allegiance to a particular denomination and yet maintain a commitment to a faith tradition. The Just Orthodox, much like the so-called nones elsewhere, do not necessarily reflect a reduction in religious practices or diminished appeals to otherworldly forces. Nonaffiliation and the deinstitutionalization of religiosity are not necessarily reliable indicators of secularism. They should not be equated with indifference to a transcendent realm or to a reduction in the political power of religiosity to shape ethical and moral beliefs and drive collective, directed action. Rather, I argue that nonaffiliation and the deinstitutionalization of religiosity have yielded a group that prefers to self-identify as Just Orthodox.

Religious attitudes and behaviors are reflected in language. Only 12 percent of Ukrainians attend church with any regularity.[11] *Parafiiany* is the Ukrainian word for parishioners, but the Russian, *prikhozhane*, reveals actual practice. It literally means those who arrive. Scholars who study religious behavior, and even the Russian Orthodox Church itself, also use the word *zakhozhane* (from the verb *zakhodit'*) to signify those who drop in. *Zakhozhane* is usually rendered in English as "casual believers."[12] Interestingly, there is no equivalent word in Ukrainian for *zakhozane*. Moreover, the word *zakhozhane* is neither used nor even widely known in Ukraine, although the pattern of dropping in is common in Ukraine as well. People drop in to light a candle or pray before an icon or relic, but not to participate in a liturgy (see figure I.1). *Prykhylnyky*, or sympathizers, is the Ukrainian word used to describe equally episodic forms of practice. Here we have the important caveat that *prykhylnyky* connotes positively inclined emotional engagement. Another phrase that is used somewhat tongue in cheek in both languages is "atheists with traditions" to indicate those who partake in religious practices without subscribing to higher forms of otherworldly power and authority.

Using metrics of belief and institutional participation, as is common to measure religiosity in predominantly Christian societies, a paradoxical picture emerges in Eastern Christian societies. Surveys after the Maidan that inquire if respondents are believers or nonbelievers will learn that under 7 percent of Ukrainians say they are nonbelievers.[13] However, if given a wider spectrum of possibilities to indicate attitudes toward belief, such as "waiver between belief

**FIGURE I.1.**   Women in St. Nicholas Church of the UOC-KP in Western Ukraine in 2017 who have dropped in to church for the purposes of lighting a candle, prayer, meditation, or to rest. Photo by the author.

and nonbelief," "indifferent," "convinced atheist," or "hard to say," we learn that in late 2020 only two-thirds claim to be "believers." Agnosticism and antipathy color the often culturally motivated reasons to engage in religious practice. In 2020, 62 percent of the 44 million Ukrainians claimed to be Orthodox and an additional 9 percent claimed to be "Just Christian." Of those who claimed to be Orthodox, 30 percent indicated a preference for the recently created OCU and 22 percent chose the Orthodox church under the Moscow Patriarchate. However, the greatest number of all, 43.1 percent, claimed to be "Just Orthodox," and declined to declare an allegiance or preference for a particular Orthodox church. If measured by region, in 2020 60 percent of Orthodox in Eastern Ukraine said they were Just Orthodox. Twenty years earlier, 55 percent of all Ukrainians identified as Just Orthodox.[14] Although gradually some allegiances are firming up, there is still evidence of significant soft confessionalism.

While conducting research on religion in Ukraine among those who consider themselves Just Orthodox, many I spoke with deny that they are religious. Few enter a church, and fewer still for the purposes of attending a liturgy. Some do not know basic doctrines, such as the Ten Commandments, and they do not partici- pate in church-based rituals, including communion. Yet, when I see them ac- tively practicing their faith in pervasive and public ways and note the enormous political influence religious institutions wield, I find nothing nominal about it. People indeed believe, but not always in religion, and they practice to belong, but not always to a church. Their allegiance is to a faith tradition, not a specific insti- tutional structure; to moral authorities who might be clergy as easily as they could be spiritual advisers, poets, or writers; and to honoring the sacred, which they might find in cemeteries, nature, or at monuments far more often than in a church. This shapes practice and political orientations in decisive ways.

Some anthropologists have tried to capture, what might be for some, the counterintuitive nature of religiosity in Orthodox societies by remaking Grace Davie's succinct depiction of English attitudes toward religion as "believing with- out belonging." Jeanne Kormina (2010, 280) suggests that "belonging without believing" is more appropriate for Russians who are part of a "church of the un- churched" (Kormina and Luehrmann 2017). Mikhail Epstein refers to "mini- mal religion" to depict the Russian blending of mysticism, theosophy, "faith pure and simple," and estrangement from religious institutions (1999, 378).

In Ukraine, the Just Orthodox, as casual believers, sympathizers, and atheists with traditions, engage in religiosity as a form of self-help, in response to the beat of cultural and political rhythms, or out of a desire for cultural belonging, but they do it on their own terms. The vernacular qualities of this lived, everyday re- ligiosity simultaneously accommodate a guarded distance and an active attach- ment to institutional structures, a refusal to be coerced by them, and the desire to belong to something greater than themselves. Vernacular religiosity is a vehicle to overcome institutional disaffection and suspicion of clergy while capitalizing on the validation and authentication of sacred status and correct practice those in- stitutions and their leaders offer to sites, objects, and people.

Often the category *prosto Pravoslavni* is mistranslated as "simply Orthodox." People who so self-describe are setting a limit. To identify as Just Orthodox is to withhold allegiance to a particular Orthodox Church but claim allegiance to an Eastern Christian tradition. They are not "undecided" nor "unprepared for de- nominational choice" (Casanova 2020). They deliberately reject selecting a de- nomination in part because of the political implications with which they are freighted, as pro-Ukrainian (Orthodox Church of Ukraine, and previously Ukrainian Orthodox Church-Kyiv Patriarchate), pro-Russian (Ukrainian Or- thodox Church-Moscow Patriarchate), or in an earlier era, pro-diaspora and pro- Ukrainian (Ukrainian Autocephalous Orthodox Church). They are Orthodox because they embrace a confessional tradition and recognize its contribution to Ukrainian art, architecture, and other facets of culture and history. This makes for important differences between the Just Orthodox and the growing number of "nones" in the United States and Europe, who decline allegiance to a particular denomination and faith tradition on the grounds that they are "spiritual but not religious" (Ammerman 2013; Litonjua 2015). I focus specifically on people who refuse to commit to a particular Orthodox institution, not because they are unable to choose, but because they are unwilling. Their allegiance is to a faith tradition to which their everyday religiosity connects them, all the while maintaining a measured distance from the religious institutions that indirectly validate their vernacular practices. While their attachment to Orthodoxy draws on a sense of cultural heritage and patrimony, it is not nostalgic or purely sentimental. Rather, it allows them to reaffirm or negate relatedness, morally validate those relationships, and maintain the affective atmosphere of religiosity that colors their everyday lives.

An affective atmosphere of religiosity is one of the most important factors that create this large contingency of Just Orthodox sympathizers and casual believers. Their religiosity exists in the spaces between institutional religion and the places where everyday life unfurls. The Just Orthodox are important politically because they constitute swing voters when it comes to a multitude of issues. They are nonpracticing only in the sense of formal religious rituals but often highly active when it comes to engaging in vernacular religious practices. They are not engaged in religious affairs, but they are also not indifferent. They can be detached enough to stay at home when conflicts flare or politically mobilized enough to fight with a zeal that can only be described as religious. They care that a *tomos* has been granted and an independent Ukrainian Church has been created, but they do not care enough to actively participate in institutional religious life.

There is an imperfect parallel with American Jews. In a similar vein, scholars struggle to come up with categories to characterize the cross-cutting religious and cultural beliefs, practices, and political behaviors among some Jews in the United States. A 2020 Pew survey found that the Jewish "nones," or as they are also sometimes called "Jews with no religion," "cultural Jews," and "ethnic Jews," might not believe in a deity, but they host or attend seders, fast on Yom Kippur, have Hebrew-language prayer books, are committed to commemorating the Holocaust, and care about Israel.[15] In other words, their expressions of Judaism and of being Jewish are neither purely cultural, political, nor strictly religious. Rather, their religiosity orients—not determines—their understandings of the past and their present actions, but is of little help when envisioning the future, including the afterlife.

There are several key differences in the ways religious and cultural expressions intersect among mostly nonobservant American Jews and the Just Orthodox. A guarded attitude toward clergy and religious institutions is usually the primary reason the Just Orthodox decline to practice religion within institutional confines. The Just Orthodox are far less dismissive of God, spirits, soul, miracles, and other divine apparitions. Often nonobservant American Jews, by contrast, have shed belief in God and a worldview that gives otherworldly forces a central role in directing their lives. They do not claim to avoid organized religion because of a generalized wariness towards clergy or religious institutions per se. What members of both groups share, however, is a recognition of religion as fundamental to defining who they are as a person and to forming the people with whom they identify and feel allegiance.

Therefore investigating how religious practices and concepts create relatedness by linking individuals to each other, to groups, to the dead, to the divine, and to a civilizational-aesthetic tradition is often a far more productive approach to assessing the meaning and relevance of religion in the lives of individuals or a particular group than questions regarding belief, participation in formal religious rituals, and institutional affiliation. These relationships color an atmosphere that shapes lifeworlds, or the context in which perceptions, orientations, and political behaviors form. In short, for the Just Orthodox, nonobservant American Jews, and the growing number of "nones" worldwide, using understandings of being religious, as defined by monotheistic belief and active participation in a particular religious community, especially when embedded in survey instruments, could produce misleading results. Religiosity has moved into a spectrum of intimate, private, and public spheres and, depending on the local context, transformed the types of sites that are recognized as sacred and the practices that appeal to otherworldly forces associated with them. This obliges us to expand what constitutes religion, why and where people might practice it, and what the consequences of these practices could be.

Religion provides a lens to see the extent to which a place is embedded in entangled histories that interweave institutional understandings as to what constitutes religion with customary practices grounded in localized knowledges. By focusing on how religion entangles people together, we are able to think beyond the narrow nation-state model. No nation or state, and especially not one like Ukraine that is situated in a borderland region that has been the site of volatile political struggle over the course of the twentieth century, can be considered a self-contained unit. Connections matter not only to the place in question but to the peoples who become linked in history, aesthetic sensibility, and understandings of morality.

The existence of these entanglements is evidenced in the interlocking pasts and the present everyday lives of peoples and places that inform hierarchies of space, colonial reflexes, and institutional frameworks that all serve as legacies of these past encounters. Global flows do not just bring peoples, ideas, and goods together. They order the hierarchies, and power relations that inform the conditions of how spaces and peoples are interconnected (Gupta and Ferguson 1992, 8). The lands now known as Ukraine and Russia have always been interconnected. They are just increasingly interconnected in different ways. Religion is a driving force in this regard.

# Religion and Politically Defining Space: The Russian World and the Kyivan Tradition

Orthodoxy, unlike most other Christian faiths, has a prominent nation-state orientation that links a person to a group and the place where that group lives via a state and its practices of governing. This is why we have the Greek Orthodox Church, Romanian Orthodox Church, and, now after many attempts, the Orthodox Church of Ukraine. One prominent exception to the nation-state model of Orthodox denominational organization is the Russian Orthodox Church. It mirrors the former contours of the Russian Empire in a contemporary entity it calls the "Russian World." The Russian World, as a proposed canonical territory, a conceptual "Großraum," as Mikhail Suslov (2016) calls it, substitutes for state borders and was used by Putin in his historical essay to justify the unification of Russians, Ukrainians, and Belarussians in a single spiritual space led by the Moscow Patriarch. The Russia World concept also seeks to include the multitude of Russian speakers who are now dispersed throughout the world thanks to massive out-migration from the former USSR. Since the second half of the nineteenth century, the All-Russian (*obshcherusskii* in Russian) and Ukrainian nation-building projects have clashed (Miller 2003, 249). The concept of a Russian World, as an imagined community based on the Russian language, culture, and Orthodoxy, categorically denies the very possibility of an independent, autonomous Ukrainian nation and church.

Ukraine is the only majority Orthodox country with multiple Orthodox jurisdictions. Others might have Old Believer communities, but in Ukraine there are multiple Eastern Christian churches that have national aspirations. Although an institutional history of these churches is beyond the scope of this book, suffice it to say that theologically, doctrinally, and liturgically they all draw on an Eastern Christian Byzantine tradition and therefore have a great deal in common liturgically, doctrinally, and in terms of their aesthetic traditions. They do, however, have vastly different political visions and bases of support, some within Ukraine and some beyond, which is manifest in terms of how they interpret the past. Different understandings of the past stand in for tangible theological or ritual differences to distinguish these churches from each other and are used to justify their different visions for the political future of the country.

The OCU resulted from the *tomos* and is the newest, canonically recognized church led by Metropolitan of Kyiv and All Ukraine Epiphanius (Dumenko). The OCU formed from the merger of the UOC-KP, UAOC, and two bishops of the UOC-MP at Kyiv's Saint Sophia's Cathedral on December 15, 2018. A schism in 1992 after Ukrainian independence led to the creation of the UOC-KP, which was not canonically recognized. The patriarch of this church, Filaret (Denysenko), who was born in 1929, had been metropolitan of Kyiv in the ROC during the Soviet period. He later withdrew his support for the OCU after multiple disagreements over his own leadership role in the new church. Prior to 2018, the UOC-KP had the greatest number of declared supporters. The UAOC was created in 1921, outlawed in the USSR in the 1930s, but thrived in diaspora communities. It was reestablished in Ukraine in 1990 and later incorporated into the OCU. At the end of 2020, the OCU had approximately 7,000 parishes and its strongest base of support is in central Ukraine.[16]

The UOC-MP is the Orthodox church in Ukraine affiliated with the Russian Orthodox Church. The UOC-MP has the greatest number of parish communities, over 12,000 in late 2020, and is led by Metropolitan of Kyiv and All Ukraine Onufrii (Berezovsky), who was born in 1944 in Chernivtsi in Western Ukraine. Three of the five most important monasteries for Eastern Slavs are located in Ukraine and are affiliated with the UOC-MP.

Lastly, the Ukrainian Greek Catholic Church (UGCC) is especially prevalent in Western Ukraine and among diaspora communities. It was created in 1596 when churches in the Polish-Lithuanian Commonwealth entered into communion with Rome. It was outlawed in the USSR in 1946. Approximately 9 percent of the Ukrainian population is affiliated with the UGCC, making it the largest Eastern rite Catholic church in the world. Although it follows a Byzantine rite, it recognizes the authority of the pope and is part of the Holy See. In 2005, to augment the national standing of the UGCC and to expand its base beyond several Western Ukrainian provinces, the Archepiscopal See moved from Lviv to Kyiv.[17]

The Kyivan Tradition, Ukraine's response to the Russian World, celebrates Ukraine for the European borderland it is and the crossroads of confessions it has been and could revive. The UGCC positions itself as uniquely poised to promote the Kyivan Tradition as a model of interconfessional cooperation. The UGCC has remained a distinctly Ukrainian church, not subsumed by either Polish Catholicism or Russian Orthodoxy, and bridges Eastern and Roman Christianity by incorporating aesthetic, liturgical, and institutional-organizational elements of both. The Kyivan Tradition is a unifying concept, an all-Ukrainian umbrella, that allows for all Eastern Christian churches in Ukraine to be considered national and for a spectrum of churches to find enough common ground to pursue shared goals. Individuals exercise their own agency in response to the political jockeying of religious institutions for power and privilege by considering themselves Just Orthodox.

There is great anticipation as to whether the new Orthodox Church of Ukraine will take the lead from its northern neighbor and maintain a close alliance with the state. This is a distinct possibility, given the pronounced role Ukrainian President Petro Poroshenko played in securing the *tomos* that allowed for a Ukrainian Church in the first place. Moreover, many European countries also have state churches. A second option would be the OCU continuing the role churches played during the Maidan protests of 2013–14, when they were both useful and a thorn in the side of the state. The churches had enough independence to criticize the state, even as they enjoyed the benefits of its protection. Recalibrating power dynamics to be mutually beneficial, instead of hierarchical with the church subservient to state needs, is referred to as the national church option. Even this orientation would represent a sea change in Eastern Slavic Orthodoxy. A third option draws on church-state relations that have been particularly germane in French-speaking Catholic regions where the Catholic Church is considered patrimonial and its religious buildings, objects, and art as manifestations of cultural heritage. In this way, Orthodoxy as patrimony usefully creates a sense of cultural heritage which is parallel to, and yet distinct from, processes of nation- and state-building (Hervieu-Lèger 2004; Knell 2021; Yurchuk 2021; Zubrzycki 2016).

Beyond these possibilities, I argue that the most decisive factor will be the extent to which the new church will be able to assume an affective presence in Ukrainian society by hosting vernacular religious practices that constitute a meaningful form of everyday religiosity (see figure I.2). I base this claim on long-term ethnographic research in Ukraine, which has demonstrated to me that ongoing affinities to a particular church, monastery, or other religious site are not primarily based on the political orientation espoused by the site's jurisdiction. Rather, allegiances have everything to do with the meaningfulness of religious practices that occur in those sites and the attachments and feelings of relatedness they cultivate. After extensive ethnographic research, I focus on these informal, vernacular practices because this is how religion is lived for many Ukrainians. Whether or not the OCU becomes the host of meaningful vernacular practices is the most reliable indicator of its fate. Moreover, these informal practices contribute to an affective atmosphere of religiosity, which is essential to creating a confessional state, a state church, or governing principles in the form of political theology. Therefore, they are a factor driving the intersection of religion, politics, and belonging.

**FIGURE I.2.**    Entering a church to light a candle is a common practice. People do this to remember someone who has passed away, to mark a special occasion, or as part of a prayer request. Photo by Tania Mychajlyshyn-D'Avignon.

## Slow Ethnography

One week after the Soviet Army invaded Afghanistan, I entered an Orthodox Church for the first time. It was January 1980, and the brightness of the snow-covered Moscow streets dimmed after the sun went down, making subzero temperatures drop even further and prompting Moscovites to press on in their journeys into the warmth. Back in those days, foreigners were assigned guides who accompanied them in their travels around the city. I didn't know it at the time, but the American professor who accompanied this group of American students to the USSR was Orthodox. One day, our guide, whose name I don't remember, but I can still see her stout body wrapped in a green wool coat topped with a pristine white fur collar, took us on an excursion to a church. Wasn't religious practice supposed to be forbidden in the USSR? I thought so, but as an irreverent teenager, I wasn't much interested in religion, so I didn't give the seeming paradox much thought.

I had, however, become interested in warming my feet. So whereas other students chose to stay outside on the street, I went into the church for warmth. I was stunned at what I saw: a thick air, visible to the eye, laden with smoke from candles, steamy breath, and the sweat of bundled-up people who had been in the church too long. Glittering, golden icons of saints with wide eyes and elongated noses, starring down in dizzying intimacy, rose above those who leaned in to kiss them in acts of adoration. The incense created a peculiar but pleasant smell that was totally unfamiliar. And then there were the voices. Beautiful, melodic voices wafting down, seemingly from on high. I spun in circles in search of the source of such sublime sound. I did not know then that choirs are often deliberately hidden above so that their voices are heard, but they are not seen. The sounds, the smells, the beauty of glittering icons, and, most of all, the sight of elderly women, some carrying babies and others in dresses kneeling on a hard, cold stone floor, all reciting prayers with pious devotion meant that every sense of my body had been activated upon entrance to this place.[18] It was almost a relief, a feeling of fleeing, when I felt the cold rush of air hit my face on the street again. I never forgot that moment and thereafter entered many Orthodox churches as an amateur anthropologist in observance of the natives during this period of undergraduate study of Russian literature in the USSR. Years passed before I began to think critically and analytically about religion at all, and about Orthodoxy in particular.

When I began conducting ethnographic research on religion in Ukraine in the late 1990s, I first focused on Baptist and Pentecostal communities as well as a variety of other New Religious Movements of Western origin, such as Charismatics, Jehovah's Witnesses, Mormons, and Adventists. Like many such groups in the West, they follow patterns of communal organization that include formal membership, regular church attendance, hierarchical leadership, and an emphasis on textually grounded belief and conviction. Unlike in the West, these groups in most regions of Eurasia, including Ukraine, were frequently considered "totalitarian sects" and accused of "brainwashing" and "zombifying" members. Discovering the motivation to convert and join such a stigmatized, minority religious group intrigued me.

I realize now, retrospectively, how much easier it was to study these persecuted, marginalized groups than it is to study widely accepted, ambient Orthodox practices. These groups had a specific location in which they gathered to do organized, collective activities with a stunning degree of predictability. They gathered several times a week for services, holiday celebrations, rites of passage rituals, musical training, volunteer work, and missionizing. Communities coordinated with each other to provide charitable and social services. There were specific places to go, people to talk to, and activities to observe. The greatest boon of all to an anthropologist were the so-called Bible study groups that met weekly in people's homes. They were, in essence, group therapy sessions over tea and cookies. The members poured out their hearts, revealing their fears, joys, anxieties, hopes, and struggles to make sense of it all morally, logistically, and emotionally, with occasional references to the Bible. These places offered clear perches from which to see how religion could impact individual lives, social orders, and form lifeworlds.

By contrast, when I began more systematically interviewing nonreligious, nonaffiliated people who self-identify as Just Orthodox, as opposed to Orthodox of a particular patriarchate, I quickly realized that very few of the established categories and concepts used to study religion apply. Some were even outright misleading. The word "religion" itself was problematic. When I posed questions concerning religion (*relihia* in Ukrainian), as opposed to faith (*vira* in Ukrainian), I received different answers. Questions regarding religion usually elicited either blank stares, evasiveness, or charges of arrogant, distant clergy and the self-serving, coercive institutions of which they are a part. Most who self-identify as Just Orthodox do not form an allegiance to a church community or particular denomination. Aside from funerals, few partake in rituals. They might, however, participate in various forms of "nomadic Orthodoxy," as Jeanne Kormina (2019) calls pilgrimages, processions, and other religiously inspired movement. These practices offer temporary communities that are quickly assembled for specific purposes and, once fulfilled, quickly dissolved. Finding such people, observing their activities, and most of all comparing them was far more difficult.

Vernacular practices are not just the result of Soviet antireligious policies which, I have argued elsewhere, primarily produced ignorance of formalized aspects of institutional religion more so than upending belief by seeding doubt, let alone atheism (Wanner 2012). This lack of familiarity with formal religious practices, doctrine, and history, which often manifests as indifference among the Just Orthodox, is what has prompted scholars to refer to Eastern Slavs as "nominally Orthodox" or "Orthodox in name only" (Billington 2007). This is the conventional wisdom that I seek to challenge. The concept of nominalism suggests that religion is not important. Wavering commitments to an institution and critical attitudes toward religious leadership should not be equated with nominalism, aversion, or even fossilized indifference.

I make this assertion after questions concerning faith, with no mention of the word religion, often brought forth references among the Just Orthodox to a spiritual adviser (*dukhovnyk* in Ukrainian) and the meaningfulness of this relationship. When speaking of faith, people made references to the illustrious role Orthodoxy has played in enriching and defining Eastern Slavic civilization and to its numerous accomplishments in the domains of art, architecture, and learning rather than criticizing the profiteering, power-driven nature of religious institutions. Although few attend church services, many pray regularly, often go to church to light a candle, participate in pilgrimages, and attend exhibits, concerts, and performances with religious themes. In short, to learn about Orthodox religious practices and beliefs, it became clear to me that it is best not to mention religion, and church is not the best place to go.[19]

Some states claim secular governance over deeply religious citizenries, such as the United States. In parts of Europe, we have states that mobilize religion, sometimes in the form of state churches, for the purposes of governing populations that are deeply secular. Being religious or embracing secularism as a political principle of governance in these contexts differs because the enabling conditions that animate religiosity have shaped them differently. Many people I have spoken with over the years in Ukraine are like Ivan, a fifty-four-year-old small business owner in Chernivtsi in Western Ukraine. Shortly after insisting that he was an atheist, he volunteered, "I can't call myself a strong believer. But somewhere, deep down in our souls we are all believers. If we believe it will be better, that means we have already become believers." I am not arguing that religion is a universal human trait or that it is inherently good or bad. Rather, I am interested in the enabling conditions that make religiosity meaningful to individuals and, by extension, political useful to governing authorities. Since the collapse of the USSR, there has been a deepening of religiosity at the same time that the processes driving secularization continue unabated. In Ukraine, this leaves in its wake a society that is simultaneously increasingly religious and enduringly secular. One of the goals of this book is to explain why this is so by analyzing the sociohistorical processes that have produced dynamics, events, and conditions that enable everyday religiosity and its political utility for governance. The atmosphere that has emerged in Ukraine, and the dispositions, sensibilities, and temperaments that stem from it, have allowed religion to enter the public sphere, public institutions, and politics in significant ways. When an atmosphere enhances a transcendent, forward-looking hope for a better future "deep down in our souls," it primes the persuasive power of religiosity and makes it a political resource. The religious practices I observed, the inclinations to engage in them, and the interpretations of their meaning are idiosyncratic. Yet because they are so pervasive and draw from a common Eastern Christian faith tradition, they amount to a collective expression of faith that feeds an affective atmosphere of religiosity.

## About This Book

Much as one interprets a historical event or literary text, I have interpreted the experiences people related to me in interviews, conversations, encounters, or as they were written in memoirs, essays, and articles. What the event and documents in the archives or biography and literary texts are to other scholars, the words and practices of specific people are to me. My anthropological approach to religion is based on immersive, long-term fieldwork that now spans three decades and is cross-checked with interlocutors, colleagues, friends, and a variety of other written and oral sources accrued through life histories, interviews, and simply being there and bearing witness to the convulsive changes that have beset the region since the collapse of the USSR and which continue today. I first conducted ethnographic research in Kyiv and Lviv in 1990. Since then, I have returned to Ukraine almost every year, with many stays lasting for months and one for over one year. I have spent over thirty-four nonconsecutive months engaged in fieldwork in Ukraine. Most of the data presented here were gathered from 2014 to 2020 during the Maidan and post-Maidan periods. Social media, Skype, What's App, and now Zoom have transformed fieldwork. It is now far easier to plan and organize trips to coincide with specific events and interviews. Conversations with some interlocutors these days never really end even as revolutions, war, and global pandemics erupt. It is possible to maintain contact and trust over time and distances, which changes for the better the encounters and exchanges that take place onsite.

To come to some understanding of the meaning and role of religiosity in the everyday lives of Ukrainians during a particularly turbulent and transformative period, I conducted seventy-four formal interviews with individuals who claim to have an affinity with Orthodoxy, but not an affiliation to an Orthodox church. I also interviewed clergy, leaders of NGOs, and academics. In addition, I recorded nine life histories and conducted nine interviews with chaplains. Each interview was tape recorded and transcribed. Formal interviews were complemented by countless informal conversations with a wide spectrum of individuals during which I handwrote notes that were later formalized as fieldnotes. Many of the interviews and much of the participant observation took place in Kharkiv, a city in Eastern Ukraine in close proximity to the Russian border and the war zone, where the majority of those who claim to be Orthodox are Just Orthodox. I also conducted fieldwork in Lviv in Western Ukraine and in the capital, Kyiv. In selecting which profiles, encounters, or quotations to include, I have chosen those patterned responses that were related to me by many, and I believe to be representative and broadly illustrative of commonly held attitudes, values, and experiences. Frequently witnessed patterns of behavior and repeated assertions and retellings of experiences coalesced to inform the issues I have pursued and illustrate here ethnographically.

Almost all of my research over the years has been inspired by something puzzling I experienced or observed in the field, and this book is no exception. I am continually amazed by two long-standing observations. First, a great number of people act as if religion is so important that it cannot possibly be left to the church. This applies to government officials who seek to harness religion's powers to persuade and motivate as well as to individuals, whose ardent devotion is so sincere that it cannot be contained in a church. Second, I have spent enough time in Ukraine to have seen friends' parents die as well as some of their grown children pass away too. Death and loss are towering tropes of daily life, along with remembering and commemorating the dead. In trying to make sense of how these two might be related, I have not approached fieldwork with a particular conceptual, theoretical, or methodological agenda. Nor have I cherry-picked examples to support a theory or a pre-formulated hypothesis. Rather, approaching events and conversations with a sense of openness and without preconceived notions has allowed me to be surprised, enchanted, and at times stupefied by what I have heard, seen, and experienced. I have then tried to understand and relate these dynamics in all their complexity.

How can one study idiosyncratic vernacular religious practices, let alone the atmosphere to which I claim they contribute? Depicting an affective atmosphere of religiosity in writing is particularly challenging because it triggers visceral sensations that are of the moment and yet evoke relationships that have existed over time. It is seemingly ubiquitous and yet embedded in certain spaces. It is something one easily feels, senses, and experiences but is difficult to describe, especially as does not remain static but continually fluctuates. The virtue of ethnographic research is that its thick description reveals the genealogy of values, moods, and even atmospheres and how and why they inform behavior. Through comparison and concept translation and formation, ethnography illustrates how categories, such as Just Orthodox, vernacular religious practices, and even religion itself, are understood on the ground and how they contribute to shaping the direction of social and political change. They merit our attention because they reveal aspirations for *how* one would like to live, rather than *who* one is as reflected in categories of identity (Henig 2020).

Over the years, while conducting fieldwork, I have tried to occupy the militant middle ground as an empathic observer and listener to the rhythms of life in Ukraine. I am not of Slavic origin, and I am not religious. I am, however, interested in a person's lifeworld, their innermost convictions, and what is so deeply meaningful to them that it eludes articulation and yet is unshakeable. All of this is what brought me to religion and to the Just Orthodox.

I begin in chapter 1 with an analysis of the religious landscape in Ukraine and how and why a group of Just Orthodox might emerge. Chapter 2 details how an atmosphere of religiosity forms and shapes the lifeworlds, practices, and experiences of those who circulate in its spaces before considering its political potential. A plethora of vernacular religious practices allows individuals to seize agency from religious institutions and keep an affective atmosphere of religiosity vibrant and, by extension, the political power of religion formidable.

This atmosphere provided the backdrop for the Revolution of Dignity, the subject of chapter 3. I consider these protests a historic event because they yielded a period of rupture in which the society moved into a state of "no longer" and "not yet," trying to possess the past as opposed to being possessed by it. Religious sentiment, symbolism, and clergy played a role in engendering this transformation of individual and collective consciousness and setting the stage for an intensification of the affective qualities of an atmosphere of religiosity.

Chapters 4 and 5 consider how public space and public institutions, respectively, have been transformed by religious practices, which makes religion more legible and influential. The central square of the capital, where the protests took place, became the site of shrines and other commemorative practices, first to grieve for lost lives, and later to channel anger as a response to the annexation of Crimea, the eruption of armed conflict in eastern Ukrainian provinces, and the shattering of personal and professional networks of family, friends, and colleagues. This transformation of public space is complemented by the expansion of religiosity into secular public institutions led by military chaplains, which is analyzed in chapter 5. One of the direct consequences of the Maidan was the professionalization and rapid expansion of the military chaplaincy into public secular state institutions.

Taken together, I conclude by considering the role of religion, and specifically vernacular religious practices, in making or breaking relationships in conflict situations and analyzing when and how they serve to enflame tensions, rendering reconciliation ever more elusive, and when they might advance peace. Ultimately, the ability of religious leaders to cultivate empathy for others beyond their own group—or not—by using the power of religious practices to foster relatedness to others is a pivotal factor determining whether religion will use its potential to resolve or entrench conflicts.

# "FREEDOM IS OUR RELIGION"

The Religious Dimensions of Political Life

"Freedom Is Our Religion!" proclaimed the enormous panels covering the soot and grim of a burned-out building in the heart of downtown Kyiv. This was a slogan of the former Ukrainian President Petro Poroshenko. It was meant to reflect the ideals that spurred the popular Maidan uprising in 2013–14 that forced the pro-Russian oligarchic president of Ukraine to flee in the night, which gave Poroshenko the reins of power. The chains painted on each panel dynamically shatter as they meet, illustrating the release from colonial bondage that newfound salvation in "our religion" has delivered. These panels also illustrate how religion fundamentally integrates into politics and public space and comes to stand in for a collective sense of self. Written in Ukrainian and English, they were hung by the city administration, in consultation with a PR firm, prior to Kyiv hosting the televised Eurovision song contest in May 2017. They remained for over a year until the building was fully renovated. Many people with whom I spoke did not object to the banners. They explained the endorsement of "freedom" in terms of "our religion" to signal a commitment to freedom through independent statehood that was not just widely shared but fervently shared (see figure 1.1).

Although it evokes religion, this slogan is clearly a political statement. God, Jesus, the saints, and other biblical and institutionally recognized elements constitute religion, not secular political values, and many clergy pointed this out. Yet state and city authorities use religion to comment on political events, and to conjure up solidarity and a vision of future salvation, as symbolized by an end to colonial bondage with Russia. Mobilizing religion in this way underscores its political importance in popular consciousness.

**FIGURE 1.1.** "FREEDOM IS OUR RELIGION!" panels hung over buildings burned during the Maidan while those buildings were being renovated. This was a political slogan of Ukrainian president Petro Poroshenko, whose administration played a key role in creating the first independent Orthodox Church. Photo by Katrina Wanner.

These panels, with their expression of political goals in terms of religion, allow religion and politics to interpenetrate. Yet, if freedom is our religion, why would we need a church? Such political appeals serve to secularize the concept of religion to the extent that they shore it of any transcendent qualities and replace them with instrumental, transactional interests. Simultaneously, the victorious tone of the slogan also downplays the fact that the Maidan protests resulted in over one hundred people being shot dead in the streets and were followed by the loss of the coveted Crimean Peninsula and an undeclared war with Russia that grinds on after having taken the lives of over thirteen thousand civilians and produced over 1.5 million refugees.[1]

Most scholarship on religion has focused on groups that sway the agendas of key social and political institutions. Orthodoxy in Ukraine demonstrates other ways in which religion can be influential. An unquestioning acceptance of the organic presence of religion wields political power by becoming akin to second nature. By equating religion with freedom, the religious dimensions of political life elude recognition and critique. Rather than focusing on the ways religion challenges political agendas, religion can also unobtrusively integrate into public space and public institutions by accommodating itself to the secular, as these panels do. The visual and verbal articulation of key nationalizing political goals in terms of our religion allows religious institutions to exercise significant yet often unexamined influence, even over nonbelievers, by creating emotional attachments to specific people and places. Attachments articulated and experienced as our religion begin to explain religion's persuasive and motivational force.

Not all religious groups are allowed to be present in public space to the same degree and command the same powerful, uncontested proclamation of shared ideals. Historically dominant confessions can be quietly present even as they retain an authoritative and audible voice on a variety of social and foreign policy initiatives (Engelke 2012; Grzymała-Busse 2015; Olphiant 2021; Zubrzycki 2016). The voices of minority religious groups, by contrast, are often pressured to remain silent, and their heightened visibility makes them subject to greater scrutiny. Just as whiteness in the United States is not always recognized as a racial category because it positions itself as unmarked, and yet has a powerful presence and speaks with a forceful voice, the normative power and privilege of historically dominant faith traditions in states that claim to be secular often go unexamined and, by extension, unchecked. The same normative, unmarked status is granted to heterosexuality, the family, and a host of other identities and institutions that position themselves as organically natural, social facts.

Political proclamations can be made from the scaffolding of burned-out buildings in the capital in terms of "our religion" precisely because a single, dominant faith tradition is recognized as culturally embedded and naturally belonging. In Ukraine the ongoing, unchallenged acceptance of a public presence for religion is supported by a plethora of spiritualized practices that are place-based. This has fostered an affective atmosphere of religiosity, which informs inclinations to understand individual experiences and even political events in otherworldly terms. When religious institutions endorse these interpretations, they remain present in the lives of individuals who might otherwise be indifferent or even hostile to organized religion. This further naturalizes and renders normative the presence of religion in public space. This presence can be a form of power for religious institutions and for secular governing authorities because the ability to incite emotions that prompt actions and reactions makes religiosity politically useful.

Rather than directly challenging a secular worldview and pluralist governing principles, in many instances, the political power of religious institutions is strengthened by simply expanding their presence in an accommodationist mode. In countries with a dominant faith tradition, there are many possibilities that allow for religion to be inserted into public life and remain present. This potentially gives religion the power to provoke people to act across a broad spectrum, from the indifferent and disengaged to the pious and devout.

Peter Berger, the noted sociologist of religion, reversed his earlier deleterious predictions of the withering of religion. In assessing the dynamics of religion in contemporary public life, he said, "But it's not the challenge of secularity; it's a different challenge. The problem with modernity is not that God is dead, as some people hoped and other people feared. There are too many gods, which is a challenge, but a different one" (Thuswaldner 2014, 16). There are a multitude of ways to show homage to God, gods, ancestors, spirits, forces, ghosts, and a burgeoning number of places where other otherworldly manifestations of divine power and wrath can be experienced. Each has distinct political implications. To come to a clearer understanding of them, Hent de Vries advocates attending to "the visible and tangible, the living and enabling conditions of 'the religious'" (2008, 66). In this chapter, I consider the enabling conditions that have widened the spectrum of practices that address a variety of otherworldly forces in a variety of places and how these practices might simultaneously feed religious pluralism, the deinstitutionalization of religion through everyday religiosity, and feelings of belonging.

## The Legibility of Religion

Ukraine and Russia share a long history and a common Eastern Christian faith tradition. The political and cultural landscapes of both are colored by widespread vernacular religious practices, multiconfessional populations, the challenges of pluralism, and modes of secularity. However, religion has been politicized differently in each country. As a result, religious organizations have reacted in divergent ways, demonstrating once again that, although the similarities and contrasts brought to light through comparison can yield insight, the study of religion is always local (Orsi 2005,167). A particular historical context shapes the enabling conditions of religiosity and produces discontinuities and discrepancies, even among regions that have a long, shared historical experience and common faith tradition. As we will see, although I focus on atmosphere as a distinguishing feature, Cyril Hovorun (2018) refers to "political Orthodoxies" emerging in Ukraine, whereas John Burgess to "lived theology" in Russia (2017). All bespeak an embedded, practice-driven understanding of religion.

In other European countries, especially those with a dominant Orthodox Church, there is a degree of reliable cooperation between secular political and clerical authorities in pursuit of what they both deem the "common good," even if this assessment is popularly disputed (Boguzmil and Yurchuk 2021; Metreveli 2020). Exploring the interplay of these alliances beyond predominantly Catholic and Protestant countries helps to move discussions of pluralism, secularism, and confessionalism to consider a fuller spectrum of possibilities as to how the politicization of religion and the fusion of national and religious identities might occur such that they shape the forms of lived religion that emerge.

In analyzing secularism in Catholic and Protestant Europe, José Casanova (2013) suggests that a series of secularizations have occurred there that involved a shift from a territorial anchoring of religion in confessional states to states that fostered a public sphere (more or less) characterized by a supposed neutral valence toward religion. As a by-product of this shift, confessional identities gradually diminished in meaning. In essence, processes of secularization in Europe centered on deconfessionalizing states by disestablishing state churches. However, this process never really occurred in the Russian Empire. The Imperial Russian state celebrated the triad of Orthodoxy-Autocracy-Nationality to the end.

Even on the eve of the Russian Revolution, Orthodox practice had fractured into "intensely particularistic" and "kaleidoscopic variations" on informal practices (Freeze 1998, 213; see also Chulos 2003; Kivelson and Greene 2003). These vernacular practices often traded on elements recognized within institutional religion. The persistence of these vernacular practices and the forms of piety they generated made the implementation of secularism as a political principle in the Soviet Union incomplete at best (Luehrmann 2011: 6–12; Smolkin 2018: 31–45; Wanner 2012: 7–2). My point is not that religion is a universal inevitability, rather to note the historical roots of an atmosphere of religiosity in this region.

Religion has historically played a prominent role in categorizing and organizing populations in Eastern Europe. The propensity of the Russian Imperial state to use religious-based identities to offer or deny services according to religious group membership, as well as the Soviet penchant for making an assessment of political reliability in religious terms (believer versus nonbeliever; church versus sect), has given religious identifications tremendous meaning—albeit a meaning that inevitably carries a significant political component. Believers in the USSR arrested for visibly practicing religion were usually considered political prisoners. This is why, especially in the 1960s, embracing religion was a means for believers and secular intelligentsia alike to express anti-Soviet sentiment (Hurkina 2014; Shlikhta 2014).

Although the USSR implemented governing practices designed to diminish belief in the supernatural and eradicate the social and political capital of religious institutions, this symbiotic church-nation-state relationship was not eradicated. It merely fluctuated in intensity. The political power of an atmosphere of religiosity rests on the fact that it is something that is already there, already integrated into public and private spaces, and often unquestioningly so. Testifying to the tenacity of the presence of Orthodoxy in the public sphere, the Soviet state did not merely adopt secularism as a governing principle, as other European states did. Rather, it advocated militant atheism to suppress the Orthodox Church and impede it from assuming any political or persuasive power. To block the legible practice of religion in public, Soviet leaders were obliged to dynamite monasteries and cathedrals, monitor cemeteries, execute clergy, and teach atheism. This occurred even as the Soviet state itself developed its own sacred sites, eschatology, political rituals, and cult of the dead, blurring the lines delineating the religious from the secular as modes of being and governing (Bernstein 2013, 2019; Etkind 2013; Halfin 2000; Slezkine 2017).

Karl Marx's contention that the "spiritual aroma" of religion had to be extinguished provided the motivation to heavily repress the Russian Orthodox Church. Victoria Smolkin recalls the Russian proverb, "A sacred space is never empty," which implies that sacred spaces carry a sacred residue that yearns to be filled (2018). Soviet leaders understood that spiritual atheism had to fill the spiritual aroma left in empty sacred spaces with communist content that would include "morality, emotions, aesthetics, rituals, and community experience" if they were to truly be "caretakers of the Soviet soul" (2018, 19). Once the church's political power was neutralized, Smolkin analyzes how the Soviet state's efforts shifted from promoting militant atheism to scientific atheism. Their intention was to eradicate the residual forms of lived religion, which remained embedded in worldviews and ways of life.

The ROC functioned with the least onerous restrictions of all religious institutions in the USSR. It engaged in a kind of accommodation and adaptation to state demands in exchange for maintaining a presence to serve the religiously inclined. Tamara Dragadze (1993) uses the phrase "domestication of religion" to characterize the use of coercive measures in the USSR to drive religion into a sphere where it was no longer legible to the state and therefore not as threatening. Most notably, during World War II, under the strain of wartime conditions and given the advantages to be gained by mobilizing the population to respond to the Nazi invasion in 1941, Stalin allowed the reopening of Orthodox churches and otherwise relaxed repressive measures against those who visibly practiced religion. This period renewed the links between Orthodoxy and ethnonational belonging and reinvigorated the mission of the ROC to be a protector of its people and the state that governs them. By contrast, the Ukrainian Autocephalous Orthodox Church and the Ukrainian Greek-Catholic Church were repressed and driven underground during the Soviet period in the 1930s and 1946, respectively. The postwar period, with its annexation of territories from Poland, Slovakia, Hungary, and Romania, all countries bordering Ukraine to the West, saw the addition of numerous, active religious communities to Soviet Ukraine. These Ukrainian religious institutions and communities were often antagonistic to state structures, which they perceived as imperial, oppressive, and connected to a seat of power in Russia.

The collapse of the Soviet Union coincided with a religious revival that bred religious pluralism and orchestrated attempts at religiously infused nation-building across the former USSR. In Ukraine, this sharpened the politicization of religion even as it made the presence of religiosity more pervasive. The post-Soviet independent Ukrainian state was weak and unable and unwilling to impose restrictions on religious organizations. This meant that the religious landscape became remarkably open and unrestricted, which allowed minority faith groups to flourish and even make Ukraine a base from which to establish additional communities across the former Soviet Union. Innovation in Orthodoxy produced a religious field that became splintered, contested, and deeply political. Ukraine became the first predominantly Orthodox country to host multiple Orthodox churches. The Ukrainian Orthodox Church-Kyiv Patriarchate (UOC-KP) was created in 1992 and the Ukrainian Autocephalous Orthodox Church (UAOC) returned to Ukraine in 1990 after having been outlawed in the USSR decades earlier.

After independence and a reevaluation of the Soviet narrative of twentieth-century history, religious symbolism began to be fundamentally integrated into monuments and other renditions of the Ukrainian nation. The Holodomor, or the Famine of 1932–33, became a defining event in the newly crafted Ukrainian national narrative. One of the most emblematic monuments to the Holodomor, a mother and child within a cross, is strategically placed before St. Michael's Monastery, which was destroyed by Soviet authorities in the 1930s and reconstructed by the Ukrainian state.[2] In this way, monasteries and other religious buildings provide an auspicious means to harness religion for political and nationalizing purposes. The buildings themselves, as we will see, define and relate political spaces to one another, revealing the evolving place of religion in public space.

# Articulating Relatedness

The Ecumenical Patriarch, as head of the "mother church," establishes "daughter churches," or autonomous Orthodox jurisdictions. However, the birth of a daughter church is far more complicated when fraternal nations are involved. When state and ecclesiastical authorities use kinship terms to characterize institutional relatedness, they do so to signal unbreakable familial bonds, which makes innovation and change that much more difficult. The EP had previously established autonomous Orthodox churches in territories that had once been part of the Russian Empire but are now beyond Russian borders. Enclave Orthodox denominations have been canonically recognized in a wide spectrum of predominantly non-Orthodox societies, as close by as the Estonian Apostolic Orthodox Church and the Polish Autocephalous Orthodox Church and as far away as the Syrian Orthodox Church in India and the Ethiopian Orthodox Tewahedo Church (Bandak and Boylston 2014; Boylston 2018; Engelhardt 2015; Naumescu 2019). However, on January 6, 2019, the Ecumenical Patriarch followed the other well-established organizational pattern within Eastern Christianity of one nation-one church when he formally granted a *tomos* of autocephaly to the Orthodox Church of Ukraine (OCU) on Orthodox Christmas, according to the Julian calendar. As of February 3, 2019, the leader of the new Ukrainian church became Epiphanius Metropolitan of Kyiv and all Ukraine. (He could not be made patriarch because he was only thirty-seven years old at the time.)

The creation of the OCU was meant to end the splintering of Orthodoxy in Ukraine into competing denominations and recalibrate the presence and influence of the Russian Orthodox Church, via the UOC-MP, in Ukraine after the war broke out in 2014.[3] However, the new Ukrainian church introduced the prospect of significantly weakening the standing of the ROC. There are over 12,000 UOC-MP parishes in Ukraine, almost one-third the total number of the ROC. Three of the five most important Orthodox monasteries for Eastern Slavs are located in Ukraine. Now that there is an Orthodox Church of Ukraine, to whom do these valuable properties and buildings belong? This was the first issue that arose that eluded an easy answer. A slew of others followed.

Among the most controversial of initiatives to fortify the OCU to arise was Law 5309, which was adopted on December 20, 2018. The law was specifically tailored to Russia, the UOC-MP, and to the immediate circumstances at hand. It takes aim at the name of religious organizations "whose governing center is in the state which, according to the Law of Ukraine, is recognized as carrying out military aggression against Ukraine and/or temporarily occupying part of the territory of Ukraine." This law was designed to bluntly oblige the UOC-MP to state in its name that it is really the Russian Orthodox Church. The law also bars UOC-MP clergy from formally serving as chaplains in the Ukrainian Army and elsewhere because its governing center is in an aggressor state. This brought charges that the Ukrainian state placed the UOC-MP in an officially sanctioned disadvantaged position to privilege the standing of the OCU as the national church, the very actions for which Ukrainian officials criticized the Russian government in its promotion and protection of the ROC (Vovk 2020: 45–47).

Minority faith groups were always present in Ukraine, but now they are part of a pluralist cultural and religious citizenry with an internationally approved human rights discourse to draw on. International condemnation of Ukrainian law was swift. Secularism, as a political principle, is meant to forge a religiously neutral public sphere that neither favors nor discriminates against a particular group or groups. However, when borders change and new states emerge, as was the case when the USSR dissolved in 1991, conflicts accompany the changing contours of religiosity even when they are conceptualized in kinship terms. Are Russian-speakers in Ukraine ethnic Russians (*russkie* in Russian) and therefore compatriots who are part of the Russian World and should be part of the Moscow Patriarchate, as the Moscow Patriarch and President Putin contend? Or are they simply Russian-speaking Ukrainians, as Ukrainians assert, who are entitled to their own church now that Ukrainian statehood has existed for over three decades given the nation-state organizational model of many Orthodox churches? These positions tip institutional religious belonging in diametrically opposed directions. They reveal the divergent paths Orthodoxy is taking in Ukraine and Russia, and how it is increasingly separating, not only Russians and Ukrainians through their embrace of a common faith, but Ukrainians from each other as well. Differences are already abundant between the OCU and UOC-MP in terms of expressions of political dissent and historical understanding. It is likely a matter of time before differences in theological interpretation emerge as well.

The ROC's vast initiative of "in-churching" (*votserkovlenie* in Russian), which John Burgess describes as nothing short of re-Christianization, of creating a mission field that encompasses "all of society, indeed the whole of creation" (2017, 10), finds no Ukrainian counterpart in Ukraine. Nor does the 200 Churches program, a companion project to build two hundred new churches in Moscow so that a church is within walking distance of every Moscovite. Scott Kenworthy and Alexander Agadjanian note the "striking visibility" of the Russian Orthodox Church in the form of "multiplying churches, news references, religiously staged political ceremonies, and the omnipresence of religious symbolism" (2021, 262). A key goal of the Russian World concept has become the promotion and institutionalization of anti-Western, Orthodox conservatism, which celebrates traditional values, especially as they relate to gender, including sex roles and identities, through a variety of ROC-sponsored family, sport, and militarized youth programs (Fomina 2017; Knorre and Zygmont 2020; Stoeckl and Medvedeva 2018). These are means by which church and state leaders work in concert to craft a militarized-religious aesthetic and institutionalize certain ethical and moral practices to shape social and political life. Those who might wish there was a similar degree of church-state cooperation in Ukraine have to contend with multiple Eastern Christian churches that have different regional bases of support, highly active religious minorities, and a robust civil society.

Additionally, the peril courted by the Russian state's instrumentalization of the ROC and the church's cooperative attitude toward state authorities means that critical attitudes towards one bleed into the other.[4] The Pussy Riot punk performers chose Moscow's Cathedral of Christ the Savior, the symbol of the New Russia, as the site of their "punk prayer" to implore the Mother of God to take away Putin (Bernstein 2016; Steinholdt 2013; Storch 2013). An indictment of political power in Russia easily slips into a critique of the Russian Orthodox Church. The state's response to this political protest was to charge the performers with hooliganism motivated by religious hatred.

The protests in St. Petersburg in 2017 over the city administration's decision to give St. Isaac's Cathedral back to the Russian Orthodox Church to be used as a place of worship reveal other tensions. The cathedral previously had been a museum, concert hall, and art gallery. To many residents of St. Petersburg, the cathedral was so historically and culturally important that the church could not be trusted with it. They preferred secular "experts," such as museum curators, archivists, and city officials, to be the stewards of this valuable property (Kormina 2020). These experts and their supporters could be described as patrimonial Orthodox because their ardent investment in the church centered on its value in defining Russia's cultural heritage. Protesters who objected to returning the building to the ROC argued that should St. Isaac's become a church, this would effectively "reduce access to objects of cultural heritage" (Kenworthy and Agadjanian 2021, 256). In the end, the disagreement over whether this important landmark should revert to its original purpose as a church or remain a state museum and monument was so contested that the process of restitution was halted.

Across the former Soviet Union, not just in Russia and Ukraine, the public sphere, politics, and everyday life cannot be understood without taking stock of religion. The needs, tribulations, and demands of these post-Soviet states structure the context in which religiosity is practiced and the extent to which religious institutions can intervene to furnish legitimizing narratives or condemnatory proclamations. The plethora of indirect means to renew the political and cultural prominence of religion in Ukraine, Russia, and beyond cannot simply be explained as a postsecular rediscovery of religion or greater processes of de-Sovietization or desecularization, from above or below. Even though we tend to equate secularization with a curtailing of religious presence and power, quite the opposite can occur when religion itself is appropriated as culture or cultural heritage and allowed to confessionalize public space. This emotionally draws in the nonbelieving and nonpracticing and gives them reasons to care, sometimes intensely, about landmarks with religious and historical value, objects of religious and artistic significance, and traditions of a politicized, religious nature that are recognized as national. The current instrumental use of religious sentiment and transcendent symbolism on the part of politicians, their citizenry, and clerical leaders reflects the emergence of conditions in which religion is capable of playing a galvanizing role in forging a new governing and moral order. Religious institutions, their property, and their leadership become the recipient of endorsement as easily as they become the target of fury.

## Confessionalizing Space: What Religion Does

Maurice Bloch argues for the centrality of imagination as an element in religion (2008, 2056). He conceptualizes religion as a form of human sociality that encompasses aspects of the "transcendental social" and "transactional social."[5] The first refers to essentialized roles that inform individual and communal self-perceptions that are often so deeply embedded that they become unremarkable, or, as Bloch puts it, "nothing special." He makes this argument after historically tracing the coterminous evolution of the state and religion and noting the enduring relevance of elders, ancestors, and historical figures, who continue to garner respect and devotion by serving as ideal types to be imitated. After their transactional social roles, meaning their usefulness in a purely instrumental sense, have ended, they assume a transcendent role (Bloch 2008, 2057).

I sharpen Bloch's assertion to argue that the centrality of the transcendent social rests on its ability to imagine relatedness, actual or desired. Religion and religious rituals provide a means to enact and make visible this relatedness, making it experiential. This is what often sparks motivations to partake in vernacular religious practices among the Just Orthodox. Through ritual and ritualized behaviors, the transcendent social is uniquely capable of bringing together the living, the dead, and the divine in an ordered, performative fashion. It ascribes rights and obligations to transactional social roles that articulate not just a sense of timeless, enduring relatedness in the form of transcendent social roles but also a mechanism for validating proper fulfillment of the obligations these relationships carry (being a good parent, child, or descendant). This is how and why history, the sacralization of the past, and the extraordinary events and people who characterize it (the Baptism of Kyivan Rus' and World War II, for example), as we will see, are central to religion in Ukraine and to the politics of belonging in the region.[6] The transcendent social slides easily into the transactional social, and historical figures become useful for advancing current interests. "Everything in Ukraine," as an older man in Lviv said to me, "begins with the past." The connections transcendent figures generate can be harnessed politically to advance purely transactional causes.

This suggests a refinement of how we understand the emotional and spiritual experiences that result from engagement in everyday religiosity and the motivations and rewards for doing so. The transcendent social bequeathed from the past is central to forming attachments and feelings of belonging in the present. Sharp distinctions between the religious and the secular, which in some cases impose themselves on law and forms of governance, are not always apparent in the workings of social life. An ongoing blending of the transcendent and the transactional in everyday life begins to suggest why in societies where there has been a growing deinstitutionalization of religious practices and a slow and gradual disengagement with institutionalized religion, we do not see a corresponding diminution of belief in otherworldly forces nor a reduction in practices that appeal to them. Rather, we see the ongoing influence and permutation of religiosity into social and political life as the transcendent social, which connects the living to ancestors and to future generations. As such, it shapes lifeworlds in a way that, as Bloch (2008) suggests, is "nothing special," because these processes are rarely recognized and discussed, "but very central" because they inform the atmosphere within which events unfold, practices occur, and ideal type figures deemed worthy of veneration emerge.

What then are we to make of religion? What is the object of study when the focus is on everyday religiosity? As a generalizing concept, religion incorporates the transcendent as a distinguishing referent. Religious experiences differ from other embodied, sensual experiences that might also be generated by an atmosphere because they involve appeals to otherworldly forces. Art and music also create atmospheres and are great motivators of behavior and feelings, which is why they are so germane to religious practice. Religion, however, has the capacity to function, as Tweed (2007) notes, as "watch and compass," meaning it situates a person or group in time and space, including a timelessness and omnipresence. Tweed comes close to my framing of the importance of atmosphere as a translocative and transtemporal carrier of religious sentiment that nonetheless creates specific places out of amorphous space when he evokes aquatic metaphors to describe the flow and motion of religion. He defines religion as "confluences of organic-cultural flows that intensify joy and confront suffering by drawing on human and suprahuman forces to make homes and cross boundaries" (2007, 54). We agree that religion keenly delineates space and marks and crosses "the ultimate horizon of human life" (Tweed 2007, 54). An atmosphere, however, unlike the aquatic metaphors Tweed uses, can cease to heighten emotion and can dampen agentive proclivities when it becomes bland or neutral. By ceasing to generate sensorial experiences, an atmosphere fosters passivity and indifference, an option that is not foreseen in the flow Tweed depicts. Moreover, an atmosphere is "already there," although it is neither given nor static (de Vries 2008, 74). I argue

**FIGURE 1.2.**   These banners hang on the Palace of Sports in the center of Kyiv. The top banner announces a National Day of Prayer for Ukraine on May 27 and reads, "We are praying for you, Ukraine!" Photo by Katrina Wanner.

that it is created by vernacular religious practices and the sacrality they bequeath to certain spaces (see figure 1.2). An atmosphere, when it assumes translocative and transtemporal qualities, matters because it can merge individual interests into common public interests by engendering connections, dependencies, and attachments such that a political community forms.

This was in evidence when Moscow Patriarch Kirill addressed the Fifteenth World Russian People's Sobor held in Moscow on May 25, 2011. He included a promotion of the political implications of the Russian World concept and stressed that the nations inhabiting the area of historical Rus', which primarily includes Ukraine, Belarus and Russia, should:

> realize that they are part of the same civilization and see the Russian World as a common supranational project. . . . We need to continue to be aware of the uniqueness of the Russian way of living and reproduce it not only in the countries where Russian culture predominates but also to attest to it far beyond our boundaries. . . . No country in the Russian World can act on the international stage totally alone. The principle of unity should be respected here as well. . . . Only a united Russian World can become a strong subject of international law.

This vision of the Russian World was fundamentally incorporated into the self-proclaimed "Donetsk People's Republic" (DPR). Its constitution, penned in 2014, states that "Recognizing itself to be an integral part of the Russian World as well as of Russian civilization confessing to the Orthodox faith (the Faith of Christian Orthodox Catholic Eastern Confession), the Russian Orthodox Church of the Moscow Patriarchate recognizes its base in the Russian World . . . and accepts the present constitution." Orthodoxy thereby situates its adherents in a translocal, transtemporal realm, the vastness of which is still clearly defined and even policed. Asserting that Orthodoxy of the Moscow Patriarchate is irreconcilable with all other religions, the leaders of DPR have heavily repressed non-Orthodox believers as apostates.[7] Orthodoxy, as the antithesis to the West and the bulwark against a "Gayropa" agenda, has become part of the official political doctrine of Russia, and therefore, it has been embraced in the separatist regions of Ukraine as a means to secure a place in the Russian World.

A stark rendition of cultural intimacy that vacillates between transactionalism and appeals to the transcendent is offered in a speech Putin delivered to the Russian Duma on March 19, 2014, following the annexation of Crimea. He began by saying, "It pains our hearts to see the suffering in Ukraine . . . we are not simply close neighbors but, as I have said many times already, we are one people. Kiev is the mother of Russian cities. Ancient Rus is our common source and we cannot live without each other." Evoking the transactional value of transcendent figures and places, Putin refers to "ancient Khersones, where Prince Vladimir was baptized. His spiritual feat of adopting Orthodoxy predetermined the overall basis of the culture, civilization and human values that unite the peoples of Russia, Ukraine and Belarus." Putin went on to insist that, because the graves of Russian soldiers who laid down their lives so that Crimea could become part of the Russian empire are so meaningful, access to them must be retained.[8] Religion therefore not only defines certain places. It also defines the relationships among peoples who share the meaning of those places. For Putin, Kyivan Rus' and Crimea are religiously meaningful sites to both Ukrainians and Russians. Therefore, Russians and Ukrainians are one people, they are both part of the Russian World, and this calls for a single political-religious space, whose seat of power is, of course, in Moscow.

Rooting Orthodoxy in particular places to achieve specific political goals works in multiple directions. In 2004, when Viktor Yanukovych was prime minister, he strove to elevate the status of the Sviatohirsk Monastery in the Donbas, which is affiliated with the UOC-MP, to the rank of *lavra*. This is a special status, modeled after the Mount Athos Monastery in Greece. It is bequeathed to a monastery that also has cells, or caves, for hermits. This designation indicates the highest degree of sacredness. The last monastery to be proclaimed a *lavra* was in 1833, when the Pochaiv Monastery in Western Ukraine, which is also affiliated with the UOC-MP, received this distinction. The relatively unknown Sviatohirsk Monastery became the fifth *lavra* in the history of the ROC and the third to be located in Ukraine, along with the Kyiv Pechersk Lavra and Pochaiv. Yanukovych used the new status of the Sviatohirsk Lavra to augment his standing politically and underline the growing regional, spiritual and cultural importance of the Donbas under his leadership.[9]

Given the established pattern in the region of church-state partnership, to the extent that there are differences in statecraft, political technologies, and geopolitical alliances emerging between the Russian and Ukrainian states, inevitable political differences manifest as ecclesiastical and other differences among Orthodox churches. As the OCU and the UOC-MP compete with one another, political and clerical leaders attempt to sway public opinion in their favor by using religion to make or unmake relatedness to render a particular denomination more authentically attractive. Such efforts color the context in which informal practices as forms of everyday lived religion unfurl and contribute to an affective atmosphere of religiosity.

## Places as Bearers of History

While state borders and state churches contribute to politicized feelings of belonging, other corollary, but equally important, extra-institutional devotional practices link believers to nonstate defined places. Place and affect are interacting components of religious experience and emotionalized place-making that cultivate "affective interiors of the body and mind" (Sarbadhikary 2015, 8). Practices that we have come to think of as standard indicators of religiosity, such as attendance at weekly liturgies, participation in formal clergy-led rituals, and other doctrinally related practices, in Ukraine and elsewhere, pale in meaning and frequency when compared to the roster of informal, somewhat impromptu, devotional practices that often occur in particular places considered sacred, spiritual, or otherwise inhabited by higher forces.

Experiencing sacred places involves an understanding of who has a right to govern them. Contested understandings provide an impetus for divisions and separations of all kinds, the most brutal of which we see playing out on the Russo-Ukrainian border. Ritualized practices emplace practitioners in a particular location by drawing on the materiality of place, including the buildings and ritual objects located there, to conjure up the sacred in the form of visions, insights, and sensations, which not only evoke the past but make the physical presence of the past palpable. More than just a trigger for the recall of certain historical memories, the emplacement of religious rituals in particular sites

generates an encounter with the past, evidenced by the tangible affective sensations experienced in the bodies of practitioners. In this way, religious practices
have enormous political utility. They are able to serve as vehicles to experience
and validate particular historical interpretations that can potentially serve political goals in the present.

Meaningful, extra-institutional devotional practices, such as processions to
honor those killed in war, pilgrimages to sacred places (natural, monumental,
or monasterial), burial rituals, and a variety of home-based practices, all create
inclinations, orientations, and allegiances. Informal practices done communally
bespeak the extraordinary elasticity of Orthodoxy and its openness to religious
innovation, including digital innovation, and the emergence of charismatic figures. They also suggest a comparatively limited institutional ability to accommodate pressures to reform. This openness creates a wide spectrum of practices
born of the same faith tradition, which also makes compromise over denominational differences more difficult.

The role of emplacing religious practices, including vernacular religious practices, in certain state structures, and its corollary consequences for the experience of affect, are key elements that provide the extraordinary openness and a
legible definition that characterizes Orthodoxy. In its national and transnational
dimensions, Orthodoxy fosters religious practices and identities that are ambient, pronounced, and inherited. They emplace individuals within a particular
group and locate that group in a space that is usually demarcated by a relationship to a state governing structure. This inherited, axiomatic church-state relationship means that Eastern Christian societies are ripe for the politicization of
religion and the confessionalization of politics.

Despite perennial proposals to form a national version of Islam (Keane 2018a)
or Catholicism (Grzymała-Busse 2015), Islam and Catholicism maintain a certain universalism in spite of tensions between "great" and "little" traditions
(Darieva 2018; Marsden 2005; Orsi 2002, 1996; Schmoller 2020). In addition to
a similar universalism in Eastern Christianity and an analogous toggle between
officially sanctioned practices and popular variations on the same, an additional
layer in the form of a national church is inserted that structures the feelings the
institution creates. In countries with a predominantly Orthodox population,
a sense of national religion is fundamentally integrated into political power structures, concepts of state sovereignty, and the contours of nationhood, giving it a
pronounced territorial dimension. Territory in the form of statehood is a factor
that distinguishes Orthodoxy from other confessions when it comes to the familiar tensions between vernacular religious practices and institutionally-based
forms of practice. Embedding Orthodoxy in politically delineated spaces gives

it a national cast that impedes its portability, especially compared to other Christian faiths that have creeds and modes of missionizing that can be inserted in almost any context.[10] The sharp differentiation of political and religious spheres, which characterizes the post-Enlightenment normative version of modern governance, is absent in Ukraine, and many other Orthodox countries, leaving the ideal of a national church serving citizens of a sovereign state visibly interwoven into the social and political fabric.[11]

Rather than offering institutional histories, analyses of inter-confessional conflicts, and sparing among religious leaders, a rarely examined source of power that shapes the religious landscape is a particular atmosphere that religiosity can cultivate when it is positioned as germane to cultural heritage, historical experience, and the practices of everyday life. When vernacular religiosity seeps into secular public institutions and sacralizes public space, it can turn a space into a place. Practices forge attachments to those places, to Khersones where Prince Vladimir was first baptized, to a monastery that creates regional prestige, and to the people who live there. This can play a role in fashioning the inclination to bond together as one people across state borders. Conversely, depending on the atmosphere, the same practices can also inspire antipathy and the impulse to fight and defend.

Beyond creating relationships, religiosity can be used to create—or destroy—relatedness. Religion is a powerful vehicle capable of expressing and enacting the commitments that bind individuals to each other, to faith, to divine powers, and I suggest here, to a particular place as well. The social and communal aspects of religion can dynamically connect people to each other by providing a set of practices, vocabulary, and means of moral validation to either affirm or deny relatedness. The fulfillment of moral obligations embedded in relationships is often realized through religion. Giving a proper burial to one's parents, caring for a sick child by praying for their recovery, or commemorating the sacrifices of fellow citizens in dedicated sacred spaces are all means to affirm relatedness. Religion offers guidance as to how to be a virtuous son/daughter, mother/father, and co-national and, if followed, a shared means of validation. When a form of otherworldly presence is experienced, the bonding can include past and future generations as well. Ritual actively stimulates connections across generations by making the presence of the dead feel palpable and puts links to future generations within reach. In this way, networks of relationships of a horizontal (across space) and vertical (over time) nature serve to create meaningful connections enacted and reaffirmed in everyday religiosity. Experiences understood in spiritual and religious terms are sometimes colored by elements of nonbelief and doubt. When doubt-filled experiences fuse with a desire to belong and overlap with political

**FIGURE 1.3.**    Graffiti in a village in Western Ukraine that reads in Russian "Regardless of how sick you might be, find yourself an atheist." The broken heart suggests that the writer regrets having to offer this advice. Photo by the author.

convictions, they can become meaningful and motivational nonetheless (see figure 1.3).

# Belonging and the Bonds of Solidarity

Relatedness articulates who belongs and who does not. Even neighbors and compatriots can be othered, and the connections to them severed. This is why the moral obligation to "Love thy neighbor" states in other terms another well-known commandment, "Thou shall not kill." Especially in conflict situations, if religious institutions use their moral authority to create—or withhold—empathy for others, they can exercise an outsized role in cultivating tolerance and inclusiveness or in fomenting violence and prolonging simmering tensions.[12] By propagating shared understandings of relatedness, values, and causal agency of divine origin, religious institutions have the potential to promote in-group solidarity as easily as they can spur the exclusion of others. Each of these dynamics is vibrantly in play in Ukraine.

Moral commitments anchored in relationships intersect with the religious in governing but add consideration of the role of place and affective experiences in forging the interlocking connections among them. The organizational structure of Orthodox denominations adds important dimensions of state sovereignty as well, which is an additional reason why religion has become so intensely political in Ukraine and gone straight to redrawing the country's borders. An affective atmosphere of faith is an outgrowth of the political and cultural history of the region and yields certain sensibilities and dispositions that can be mobilized to political ends by transforming group membership into an identity with its requisite moral obligations. Most important, fostering an affective atmosphere of religiosity is an essential first step toward creating a confessional state, mobilizing religious nationalism, and implementing forms of political theology, and therefore it merits our attention.

# GOLD DOMED KYIV
## The Power of Atmosphere

Teresa Brennan begins her study of affect by asking if there is anyone who has not, at least once, walked into a room and "felt the atmosphere" (2004, 1). She could have just as easily asked if there is anyone who, after arriving in another country, has not "felt the atmosphere." An atmosphere distinguishes one context from another and, in doing so, makes places. Gold domed cupolas define landscapes across Ukraine and contribute to an atmosphere of religiosity. When the material and spatial merge with the sensual to create experiences, an atmosphere forms. This means that the material environment can yield its own immaterial form as atmosphere. This is one source of its agency. When an atmosphere is not just felt, but, as Brennan says, begins "getting into the individual" and transmitting the feelings and inclinations of people who circulate in those spaces, then that atmosphere has become affective and both intimate and impersonal.

After years of conversation and observation, I came to appreciate the power and persuasiveness of an affective atmosphere of religiosity and how it shapes the ways people see the world and their place in it. I was always puzzled by what seemed like a paradox: many in Ukraine claim to be nonreligious, nonpracticing, nonbelieving, and yet, they feel a strong emotional attachment to Orthodoxy.[1] What exactly is it that they care about, and why? Slow ethnography over many years has brought into view the "social-aesthetic-material-political worlding" that affect creates (Stewart 2017, 193). This atmosphere forges a collective capacity among the people who live in this place to feel and react in certain ways.

I use this to explain the disgust and respect religion inspires along with the harsh criticism and heartfelt allegiance the church commands. Even though sensational experiences are felt on the individual level, when the sources for those experiences are in the public sphere, they begin to lay the fundamental groundwork, not only for lifeworlds, but also for political orientations and inclinations that are collective and often unshakable.

Before analyzing how vernacular religious practices contribute to an affective atmosphere of religiosity and how this can become politically useful, let me illustrate how an affective atmosphere of religiosity can sway the otherwise religiously indifferent and make them Just Orthodox. Alena is a middle-aged mathematician from Kharkiv, whom I have known for quite some time.[2] In 2019 she was telling me about a recent trip to France. In the process, she described her areligious religiosity that is largely animated by affect. Along with many other traditional tourist sites, she visited Notre Dame de Paris, as she called it. She explained to me that she went there, much as she did to the Louvre, to see beautiful things. But the experience was different than she imagined. When words failed her, she used a gesture to describe her reaction to the cathedral. With folded arms drawn in close to her chest, she shivered and shuttered as if she were freezing. "It's the spires," her sister later explained to her. Alena realized that her sister was right. The spires prompted a reaction of recoil, of retreat. She went on to explain the extent to which she recognized this was true. "When I returned home," she said, again reverting to gesture, with her arms opening wide and flapping as if they were wings. "I realized those round, golden cupolas make me want to soar. They are uplifting. I realized that I was home, that this was mine."

The reverse sentiment was voiced by Michael Idov, a bilingual Russian-speaking writer who was raised in Latvia and later lived in Moscow and the United States. He said, "I am from Riga, and people from Riga always considered themselves quasi-Europeans. The only thing that tied me to Russia was the language. Otherwise I am a person who grew up among Gothic cathedrals."[3] Idov uses a comfortable familiarity with Gothic architecture to assert his Europeanness, just as his native country asserted a European heritage to gain European Union membership. As a Russian-speaking resident of Ukraine, Alena responds to the same Gothic style with alienation and a clear sense of not belonging. The golden domes of Eastern Christian churches provoke for her a sense of being in flight, of soaring, and she feels at home among them in Ukraine. The architectural and aesthetic elements of religious buildings that dot the urban landscape in both countries have influenced the emotional palettes and feelings of belonging of both Alena and Michael Idov, albeit differently. Only Alena responds to the atmosphere and aesthetics of Eastern Christian churches, which Alexandra Antohin describes as "a feast for the senses, the affective qualities of its rituals and spaces as reaching the impossible standard of materializing 'heaven on earth'" (2019, 1).

Alena might feel a sense of heaven on earth in the form of affective sensations when she is near an Orthodox church, but she rarely enters one. The only time she goes into a church is to light a candle for her parents, both of whom are dead and buried in another former republic-turned-independent-state. It is time-consuming and expensive to travel back to the cemetery. She worries that the neighbors criticize her for disrespecting her parents by not conscientiously tending their graves. In place of the cemetery, she goes to church to light a candle, which makes her feel as if she is with her parents. She says she cries whenever she enters a church, and this is perhaps why. She is not invested in prayer, worship, or any other kind of devotional practice that goes beyond remembering her own parents in her own way. But this feeling of communing with her parents, of feeling their presence despite their absence, happens in a church with tears streaming down her cheeks.

Wanting her son to have these connections and experiences as well, she had him baptized. "It's so that he will feel fully Ukrainian, to feel he belongs," she explained. Her motivation, once again, has little to do with religion per se but is more about creating relationships with others and securing a means to fully actualize them. Alena's attitudes reflect the atmosphere in the USSR in which she was raised. The outer Soviet political world that promoted atheism became part of her inner world, just as the current atmosphere in Ukraine, colored as it is with religiosity, becomes a means to maintain a relationship with her parents and her son and to allow them all to belong in Ukraine although they are not ethnically Ukrainian, and Ukrainian is not their preferred spoken language.

I focus on two sources that feed into the creation of an affective atmosphere of religiosity and the feelings of belonging it makes possible: vernacular religious practices and the built environment, specifically the aesthetics of monuments and architecture. These elements combine to create an affective atmosphere of religiosity in Ukraine that informs self-perceptions, guides behavior, and goes a long way in explaining why some people consider themselves Orthodox when they are not religious. Religiosity mediates the material qualities of the built environment and the sensual experience of circulating-perceiving-feeling-thinking-reacting in those lived spaces. Practices that appeal to otherworldly forces inform the encounters and exchanges that occur in those spaces and therefore play a role in articulating relationships and generating feelings of belonging. In this way, an affective atmosphere of religiosity forms an ecology of experience.

Susanne Langer notes that when it comes to conveying knowledge about the precise character of the affective life, language is almost useless (1957, 91; see also

Anderson 2009). Some experiences elude articulation, but that does not mean that they are unknowable or any less relevant, in a political or any other sense. Such socially organized modes of action contribute to visceral and culturally informed self-perceptions that flow into the formation of identities and political views. In an early and path-breaking essay, Michelle Rosaldo argues that "Emotions are thoughts somehow 'felt' in flushes, pulses, 'movements' of our livers, minds, hearts, stomachs, skin. They are *embodied* thoughts, thoughts seeped with the apprehension that 'I am involved'" (1984, 143). The ethnographic data presented here of vernacular religious practices illustrate how people come to feel involved and connected to others, and specifically how vernacular religious practices performed in an affective atmosphere of religiosity mediate the links between feelings of relatedness and belonging.

## Anthropological Ancestors

My fascination with atmosphere is something I share with some early anthropological thinkers, although they did not label the phenomenon as such. Gregory Bateson's classic, *Steps to an Ecology of Mind*, depicts the analytical and ethnographic dilemmas I have wrestled with in writing this book. The Just Orthodox phenomenon of attachment to a confessional and civilizational tradition is so ethereal that one is discouraged from pursuing it because it is easy to feel but difficult to depict with words. Bateson faced a similar dilemma during his New Guinea fieldwork when he wrote:

> I was especially interested in studying what I called the "feel" of culture, and I was bored with the conventional study of the more formal details. . . . I complained of the hopelessness of putting any sort of salt on the tail of such an imponderable concept as the "feel" of culture. I had been watching a casual group of natives chewing betel, spitting, laughing, joking, etc. and I felt acutely the tantalizing impossibility of what I wanted to do. . . . Equally, I could see each bit as "pragmatic," either as satisfying the needs of individuals or as contributing to the integration of society. Again, I could see each bit ethnologically, as an expression of emotion. (1972, 81, 85)

I have experienced Bateson's frustration of seeing and feeling the pragmatic aspects of an affective atmosphere of religiosity (the sacrality of sites and the spiritualized practices performed there) and how it contributes to the feel of culture. I recognize each bit of the transcendent and transactional as constituent elements of individual religious experience, which contributes to social solidarity even as it satisfies individual needs. When taken together, this yields a sense of shared life-world and belonging. I have experienced this feel most acutely in Ukraine when people mark death with such strong evocations of transcendence that a presence is created from the absence. And yet, there is no clear vocabulary to analyze it. Initially, Bateson referred to an ethos to indicate a constellation of concepts that make up a culture's affective and emotional aspects. (See Nuckolls 1995, 367 for a critique.) An ethos for Ruth Benedict meant the emotional background and distinct cultural configurations that pattern existence and form the backdrop to thoughts and emotions as revealed in forms of behavior and observable rituals, including death rituals and commemorations (1934, 55).

Dale Pesman's ethnography of the "Russian soul" springs from such a tradition. To rise above the cliched meanings of the soul as an enduring trope of national and self-definition, she analyzes the soul as "a deceptive lexical item: not just a notion, image, or entity but an aesthetics, a way of feeling about and being in the world, a shifting focus and repertoire of discourses, rituals, beliefs, and practices more and less available to individuals" (2000, 9). Pesman comes close to the ethereal agentive capacities I seek to depict with atmosphere when she refers to the soul in terms of an "'inner world,' an expansive, authentic 'life force,' and essences of people, places, groups, and other things" (2000, x). I share an interest in essences that inform the lifeworlds of groups, the inner worlds of individuals, and the life forces that motivate them to act. I use everyday religiosity as a lens through which to see the processes of creating these pragmatic bits of the feel of culture in Ukraine today.

It is important to take stock of the larger structural forces, institutions, and power relations that impose themselves on these essences. This is imperative because, as Raymond Williams writes, "The real power of institutions is that they actively teach particular ways of feeling," and in doing so sustain "structures of feelings" (1961, 312). His writings on art and aesthetics analyze how "an affective register," taken in its entirety, contributes to a "worlding" that engages—but also moves beyond—a material analysis. Religious institutions have a particular ability to produce a patterned way of thinking, feeling, and living. They foster structures of feeling by declaring some objects, images, and places sacred and worthy of veneration, whereas they condemn others as blasphemous and therefore to be shunned. These attitudes find expression in vernacular religious practices, especially when sacred images and objects are integrated into the materiality of public space. Figure 2.1 is an example of a sacred image with clear religious connotations set in a mundane public space.

**FIGURE 2.1.**   Icon to St. Tetiana in a Kharkiv metro station in between bank cash machines and metro ticket sales. Such religious iconography in public space is quite common. Photo by the author.

# In Between the Worldly and the Sacred

Matthew Engelke's (2012) concept of "ambient faith" provides insight as to how an atmosphere can facilitate or prevent religion moving from the background to center stage in public life. Engelke analyzes the efforts of the nondenominational Bible Society of England and Wales to produce a Christian ambiance to everyday life, which he calls "ambient faith." This echoes Charles Hirschkind's analysis of how the seemingly omnipresent sounds of individuals listening to cassette sermons inform the soundscape of markets and street life in Cairo. Hirschkind argues that these ever-present sounds create a particular "sensory environment" such that the ubiquity of sermons permeates public and private spheres to such an extent that it forges an Islamic "counterpublic" (2006, 125). In Cairo individuals willingly inject the sounds of religiosity into public space and daily life, whereas the Bible Society of England and Wales must take it upon itself to purposefully and deliberately infuse worldly contexts, such as shopping malls and coffeehouses, with Christian symbolism. The stated goal of the Bible Society is to gently alter the sensorium of the public sphere to change the consciousness of individuals who circulate in that space so as to produce an ambient faith in the doctrines and teachings of Christianity as recorded in the Bible (Engelke 2012, 156). In both of these contexts, the advantages of being a historically and culturally dominant faith group are immediately apparent. It is unlikely that Muslims in England or Coptic Christians in Cairo would attempt to visually and auditorily introduce their religious practices into public space to change the consciousness of city residents to be more in keeping with their religious traditions.

Still, the results of the Bible Society's campaigns have been negligible. Its attempts to publicly display angels during Christmastime on a popular shopping street in England were blocked by government officials, who anticipated their constituents' condemnation. The only figures allowed were such highly abstract renditions of angels that most residents read them in a secular register as decorative symbols or simply ignored them altogether (Engelke 2013, 49–50). Their religious content, and therefore religious affect, was lost. The religious affect of angels was similarly gutted in postwar East Germany when Communist Party officials were faced with remaking the tradition of decorating public space with angels at Christmastime. To render the angels ideologically acceptable, they were renamed "year-end winged figures" (*geflügelte Jahresend-Figuren*) and allowed to remain as a national tradition. Oliphant writes of the "privilege" Catholicism wields in France to be present in public space because of its ability to be "banal" (2021). Banality stems from assumptions that the Catholic Church is nonthreatening, unobtrusive, and often not even consciously recognized as religion per se because it is perceived as enmeshed in French culture. Precisely because religion is also integral to national culture in Ukraine, iconography, such as the shrine to the Virgin Mary seen in Figure 2.2, which is public facing on commercial space, is not only allowed but is also uncontroversial. However, given the volatility of the greater geopolitical context in this borderland region, such strident assertions of public religiosity are not banal.

Thinking comparatively of how religion can and cannot permeate public space can add to our understanding of how an affective atmosphere of religiosity can be fashioned and of conditions of secular modernity across Europe. Many European countries have a single religious tradition that coincides with state borders. Yet state-churches in Europe have exerted varied levels of influence on politics, and this has unevenly shaped the de-privatization of religion across the continent (Henig 2020; Oliphant 2021; Zubrzycki 2006). As religion takes place in the public sphere, it changes the tenor of public life, less in terms of faith per se and moreso in terms of how it can be used to escalate or quell emotions through religious practices mediating the here and now with the transcendent.

**FIGURE 2.2.** A small shrine to the Virgin Mary on the grounds of a television station building in Lviv. Photo by the author.

The philosopher Gernot Böhme (2017) was an early and influential theoretician of the interrelationship between atmospheres and aesthetics and their political potential. He characterized atmosphere as a "tuned space" or a "space with a certain mood" and noted that every place has an atmosphere, an already there ambiance, and that atmosphere is borne of materiality and the human encounters that occur there. Some aesthetics are bland or neutral and not at all affective. The interactions that occur there usually reflect that tenor. An atmosphere becomes affective as a product of the intersection of certain encounters and aesthetic elements that frame the feeling body. Ben Anderson argues that atmospheres "emanate" from the resonance between an assemblage of human bodies and materiality, and that it is the resonance that can become intensified (2009, 80). Most scholars have considered atmospheres in episodic terms. In other words, they have studied how the resonance of an atmosphere has been intensified such that it imposes itself on unfolding events or performances, such as revolutions, concerts, or the Olympic Games (Riedel 2020). Here I consider how an affective atmosphere of religiosity has vacillated during extraordinary events, such as the Maidan protests (Stepnisky 2018), to the everyday, such as passing shrines to dead protesters on the way to work. This allows us to see how an extraordinary event, be it the Maidan protests or a transcendent experience, can remake the ordinary by irretrievably transforming it.

Specific sites and the material objects in them engender practices, including vernacular religious practices, that can turn certain places into spaces of intensity by fostering moods. An affective atmosphere is one where the affects of the materialities in a landscape (built and natural) have the potential to generate a new normativizing power, through what Susanne Langer (1967) calls its "open ambient," as well as shatter norms through "contagions of feeling" (Seigworth and Gregg 2010, 8). Affective experiences provoke change by permeating public and intimate spheres alike through the sensations and bodily practices they generate that make or remake norms of behavior. Affect understood in such a way is a carrier of energy, characterized by "surges of passion that accompany a judgment," that serves to link an individual body to the environment in which it is emplaced (Brennan 2004, 22). Affect mediates emotions and the sensations they generate with an inner awareness of external objects that draws attention into the world and culminates in a flow to judgment. This is the sequence of perceiving-feeling-thinking-acting that affect generates. The enormous mural of children with the Ten Commandments seen in figure 2.3 is not a banal statement of instruction. It is meant to provoke. It reminds the residents of the capital of the timeless ethical and moral guidelines Christianity offers.

The unstructured and fluid nature of affect forms the processual that allows it to transmit so freely and feed into an atmosphere. Affect circulates with contagion through practices and encounters that have physiological effects in the form of sensations with motivational power. Seigworth and Gregg note the "hard and fast materialities, as well as the fleeting and flowing ephemera" that are found in everyday life and color the "persistent, repetitious practices of power [which] can simultaneously provide a body (or, better, collectivized bodies) with predicaments and potentials for realizing a world that subsists within and exceeds the horizons and boundaries of the norm" (2010, 7). In other words, the encounters that occur in spaces with an affective atmosphere can be powerful agents of change. As the next chapter shows, the Maidan protests, as an extraordinary historical event, took an atmosphere pregnant with religiosity and other possibili-

**FIGURE 2.3.** On the side of a residential building in the heart of the capital a mural of the Ten Commandments is superimposed over a map of Kyiv. The Ten Commandments are illuminated at night. For the uninitiated, the bottom of the mural offers ten QR codes to learn more about each commandment. Photo by the author.

ties and intensified them. This facilitated the subsequent insertion of more religiosity into public space and public institutions and, by extension, into the surfaces of exterior lifeworlds and into the inner lifeworlds of individuals as well, thereby infusing ordinary everyday life with the extraordinary.[4] This was made possible by the fact that experiences of everyday life, even mundane routines, unfold in an atmosphere of religiosity, which primed religion to be a formidable

resource during and after the Maidan. Let us now consider how vernacular religious practices, as a set of experiences oriented toward the transcendent, are
present in everyday life and how they become carriers of the political among the
Just Orthodox by informing the relationships that are most meaningful to them.

## Lifeworlds and Experience

The significance of a particular atmosphere is that it colors lifeworlds and informs the experiences of those who live within it. The concept of lifeworld, or
*Lebenswelt* in German, comes from phenomenology. It is meant to distinguish
the world as an object of scientific study from a lifeworld of subjective, everyday
life experiences. For our purposes, a lifeworld consists of social and embodied
experiences that unfold in a particular space and time amid relationships, all of
which are shaped by atmosphere. The word experience is conceptualized more
finely in German than it is in English. *Erfahrung* refers to experience in the sense
of the culmination of daily routines, that is the experience of engaging in vernacular religious practices, my experience as a fieldworker, and your experience
on the job. This is distinct from experience in the sense of *Erlebnis*, which refers
to discrete happenings or events, such as the Maidan protests or participating
in a pilgrimage. An *Erlebnis*, as an experiential event, stands out from the cu-
mulative progression of everyday experiences, or *Erfarhung*. An *Erlebnis*-like experience breaks through the ordinary to create the extraordinary, and in the
process transforms the Erfahrung of everyday experiences that follow (Das 2007;
Henig 2020; Ries 2012; Willen and Seeman 2012, 4).

The third component of experience analyzed here involves the body and its
intersubjective relationship to atmosphere. This is particularly relevant when
studying religion. Sensorial experiences of the felt body, whether the result of
everyday experiences (*Erfahrung*) or extraordinary experiences (*Erlebnis*), become meaningful and an important source of knowledge when sensations in-
scribe themselves on the body (Dejarlais and Throop 2011, 88; Luehrmann 2018).
This is how one knows a particular moment, place, object, or action is important, true, or sacred. You feel it. It is impossible to deny. It is a "prereflexive form
of experience" (Dejarlais and Throop 2011, 88), and this is why moral convictions, and the political attitudes that stem from them, tend to be unwavering.
They draw on intuition, emotion, and prereflexive sensations that feel true and
real. Breaking down experience into these three elements, ongoing everyday life,
extraordinary events, and embodied experience, points to how particular atmospheres shape lifeworlds. The atmospheric qualities of lifeworlds contribute to

the generation of experiences, which then reinforce the affective qualities of atmospheres, carrying the interactive dynamic forward.

I think of an atmosphere as an ecology of experience, informing our capacity to act and to be acted upon in the sense of ongoing daily life as well as extraordinary events, both of which can potentially create embodied experiences. This means that atmosphere, as an ambient space, connects relational structures and the material environment with the interiority of individuals. (Riedel 2020, 269). An atmosphere is already there and different from our "corporeal attunement to it," which is what affect creates (Slaby 2020, 275). Affect tunes a body's relation to the material world or bodies' relation to each other by creating a register of experience that precedes conscious, rational understanding.

Therefore, a tripartite analytical perspective that incorporates everyday religiosity (material culture of place and vernacular practices), extraordinary events or happenings (the Maidan), and the embodied experiences that result from both reveal how lifeworlds come into being and the role an affective atmosphere plays in the process. This makes vernacular religious practices a mediating factor between the material qualities of the built environment and the immaterial qualities of atmosphere, which is what creates sensual experiences. Various everyday practices, such as prayer or meditation, or extraordinary experiences, such as death and burial, are stimulated and colored by atmosphere. In their appeal to otherworldly forces, vernacular religious practices inform the encounters that occur in places with an affective atmosphere of religiosity, thereby making lifeworlds and animating relationships among the living, the dead, and the divine.

# Reading Signs in the Urban Landscape

Reading recognizable semiotic forms in a religious register is fundamental to creating and sustaining an affective atmosphere of religiosity. To give a straightforward illustration, it has become common for some pedestrians on Ukrainian streets to cross themselves when they pass before a church.[5] They do not do this when they walk by other buildings. The architectural and aesthetic elements of the church signal to the pedestrian that they are in the presence of a sacred space, a point of access to otherworldliness. Some people, having read these signs in a religious register, make a gesture of piety to signal their acknowledgment of this social fact.

Illustrating the importance of historical context to this phenomenon, Soviet antireligious campaigns were meant to encourage pedestrians to read the cupolas, crosses, music, and other such signs in a historical or aesthetic register, or ideally, to ignore them. As a result, over time many people in the Soviet period understood churches to be something of a museum, much as Alena still does. They would go there to view beautiful art, architecture, and other objects that might inspire awe, but the political goal during the Soviet period was for these signs, and any experiences they might trigger, to be understood in a decisively worldly way.

Recall that the banner proclaiming "Freedom Is Our Religion" was intended and largely read in a political register, as an assertion of a political principle—freedom—that could be enshrined in religion. The clergy who objected to the message on this banner read it in a religious register. Religion for them is not about freedom. Rather, they countered, religion gives guidance, some would even say firm rules and punishment for their violation, to regulate behavior so as to achieve salvation in the afterlife. An exasperated Orthodox priest lamented to his congregation, "In the twenty-first century we have made a cult of freedom. We think we are free to do what we want, when we want. But this leads to slavery. You think you can drink whenever you want and how much you want? You will be an alcoholic. Our religion is not freedom. Our religion is the laws of God. In order for people in a society to be truly free, they must observe the laws of God." State authorities who mounted the banner counted on a secular reading of President Poroshenko's slogan and on the positive associations religion would deliver to benefit his standing in advance of the election.

Affect-driven processes of feeling-thinking-acting are filtered through a semiotic ideology as people interpret signs. Webb Keane defines a semiotic ideology as people's underlying assumptions about what signs are, the functions they serve, and the consequences they might produce (2018, 65). Semiotic ideologies provide insight into prereflective experiences and the presuppositions that underpin worldviews. Both reveal understandings of agency and form the foundation of a lifeworld. Sign vehicles go well beyond language to include sound, smell, touch, and pain, all in historically contingent ways.

Ideology signals the diverse ethical and political consequences that emerge from different understandings of provenance (divinely inspired, arbitrary, or naturally emergent). Disagreements over provenance are often the root causes of conflicts involving religion that elude compromise. Interpretations of experiences and historical events and the appropriate response to them trade on understandings as to who and what one considers capable of agency and intention. This frames how judgments are made as to who is responsible. In sum, semiotic ideologies center on the intersection of reading signs, engaging sensory modalities, and the ethical and political implications that result from this process.

Keane recalls an example familiar to anthropologists to illustrate the relevance of semiotic ideologies for structuring feelings, reactions, and experiences. E. E.

Evans-Pritchard studied witchcraft among the Azande. He noted that if a termite-ridden granary collapses when a person is sitting under it, for the Azande the cause of the collapse is perfectly clear: termites ate the granary's wooden supports. Why the granary collapsed when that particular person was sitting under it is equally clear: witchcraft caused that person's misfortune (1937, 22–23). A semiotic ideology mediates the connection between a sign vehicle (the collapse of the granary) and its object (suffering) to make meaning. In other contexts, why a particular person suffered because they were under the granary at the exact moment it collapsed would have been explained by bad luck, angry ancestors, or divine punishment for moral transgression, for example.

Once, while giving a lecture in Lviv, I evoked Evans-Pritchard's famous example. 'How would you understand the reason for the granary's collapse?," I asked rhetorically. "The Russians did it," a young man in the first row shot back with deadpan irony. The members of the audience began to shyly laugh, having recognized an only somewhat caricaturized version of their own semiotic ideology. Never mind witchcraft, bad luck, and the like. The Russians make things collapse.

Local, historically specific underlying assumptions govern which signs are meaningful, how they function, and their consequences. This is why the reaction of two Russian speakers raised in the USSR can be so different. One sees Gothic cathedral spires, feels recoil, and realizes she does not belong. Another sees Gothic cathedral spires, feels a sense of familiarity, and this reaffirms his Europeanness and belonging. A semiotic ideology also governs ironic interpretations of signs, including holding Russians responsible for the collapse of a mythical granary. The assumptions and understandings used to make meaning (and humor) are shared. The evolution from a mere presence of religious signs in the urban landscape to an affective atmosphere of religiosity hinges on reading signs in such a way that they prompt a flow of feeling-thinking-acting. For this reason I do not use affect interchangeably with feeling or emotion. A key aspect of affect is its motivational flow into action that generates the experiences that characterize a particular lifeworld.

Some signs can be read in a blended register. Anna Grzymała-Busse (2015) analyzed the multiplex ways national and religious identities fuse for mutual enforcement in several countries. In Ukraine this process of fusion occurs via cultural appropriation. In other words, religious practices, objects, and sites are secularized into culture or cultural heritage. When forms of religiosity are appropriated into a nationalized cultural heritage that belongs to all citizens, these religious objects, symbols, and sites retain meaning collectively and individually (Wanner 2020). At any given moment they can pivot to the sacred. For example, many Just Orthodox have icons in their home and claim the icons serve a decorative function. Yet, they always have the potential to become an object of veneration and revert to their religiously intended use. Similarly, a Just Orthodox could become a pious believer. The potential works in the other direction as well. Icons could become not just decorative objects but decorative objects that are ignored, Someone who is Just Orthodox could become even more alienated from religious institutions. The affective atmosphere of a person's lifeworld makes the difference. The key point is that the icons are already there, to be enchanted or ignored. Someone who is Just Orthodox already feels a connection to Orthodoxy. This duality gives the presence of religiosity in everyday life a certain relevance, even among nonbelievers, doubters, critics, and seekers.

Let us now consider how the signs present in everyday forms of vernacular religiosity are read and acted upon such that they color the lifeworld of those who live among them. We will look at how this process creates meaningful spaces and shared attachments before turning to how this process can be made politically useful.

## Places Animated with Prayer

Place-making is a cultural mechanism by which everyday lived experiences can breed attachments. The concept "place animated with prayer" (*namolene mistse/namolennoe mesto* in Ukrainian and Russian) is widely known although it came into common parlance only after the collapse of the USSR. It is used to note especially sacred places with a historic character from more recently built ones. Developing such concepts involves a "creative process of inventing values and ascribing them to things and places" (Kormina 2010, 277; 2019). *Namolenist'*, or prayerfulness, is a semiotic form that contributes to an affective atmosphere of religiosity and a certain sensory regime that "makes belief" by ascribing certain values of sacredness to particular places (Meyer 2014, 214). I first heard this expression in 2008 at the same time a friend did when she was criticized for the church she chose for her son's baptism. She is not a religious person and simply chose an attractive neighborhood church near her home in Kharkiv. Her friends said this church was not a place animated with prayer; therefore the protective power of the baptism was diminished. The Goldberg Church, she was told, which is part of the UOC-MP, would have been a far better choice for her son because it is the place most animated with prayer in Kharkiv.

I began to inquire what a place animated with prayer is exactly and why a baptism at the Goldberg Church would yield greater protection than at another church. I was told that if people come to a particular place and pour out their heartaches and hopes in prayer, they leave something of themselves behind. This creates a special zone of "positive energy," even "raging energy," which can be felt by subsequent visitors. The powerful sensations such sites produce can burgeon into transformative experiences that result in healing, relief, visions, removal of hardship, fulfillment of requests, and other miraculous feats. The corporality of the experience such energy produces is taken as evidence of its truth. Places animated with prayer, such as the Goldberg Church, are "energized places where a connection to God exists," and this, not the institution or a deity, is what makes for transformative experiences, including an especially protective baptism. In other words, when a place is understood to be animated with prayer, its materiality (aesthetics and objects) discharges affective energies that are transmitted to and among individuals in that place. Experiences involving energy, or *bio-energetika*, with its blend of science and religiosity, involves tangible manifestations of energy as a means to engender change. Stimulating the transformative powers of energy became particularly popular during the religious renaissance, as it was called, that occurred after the fall of the Soviet Union in 1991 (Darieva 2018; Golovneva and Shmidt 2015; Lindquist 2005; Panchenko 2012).

The ritualized discursive act of praying over time is believed to have a sacralizing function. There is no defined sense as to how prayers should be performed or how many believers must pray before a place can be considered *namolene*, which introduces a pronounced element of indeterminacy to a specific status. Such a designation becomes an underlying assumption of a semiotic ideology when enough people recognize, replicate, and interpret their transformative experiences as coming from the power of the energy believed to reside in these places. The designation puts in place an upward spiral as people anticipate and imitate the experience of energy and ascribe a transformative power to it. By doing so, they perpetuate the cycle of validating the energy's power and reaffirming the status of a place as "animated with prayer." Part of the appeal of a place animated with prayer is that it demands little performative competence and no clerical intermediary (Kormina and Luehrmann 2017; Panchenko 2012). There is no prescribed ritual that must be performed there. Anyone can partake by innovating their own ritualized behaviors to appeal to otherworldly forces. Although places animated with prayer are sometimes natural spaces, such as springs or groves, if they are part of the built environment, they are frequently connected to a church or monastery. This is one of the many ways that official religious sites host a variety of worldly inspired, vernacular religious practices.

Once certain places are recognized as carrying this energy, they serve a mediating role, conjuring up the presence of energy that is so sought after for its transformative power. For many, the experience of visceral sensations of an unseen realm, where the presence of specific people is felt, regardless of whether they are dead or alive or known or unknown, can be both calming and invigo-rating. Presence is relational and takes the here and now as a starting point. The problems that prompted a person to visit a place animated with prayer can sud-denly seem surmountable against the vastness of an otherworldly realm. These experiences also introduce expansive dimensions of time. Feeling the energy from the depth of history and one's own ancestral roots in a particular place can deliver comfort and empowerment. The transformative power of this energy stems from the connection it makes to the place and to others who have come before and animated it. When experiences of energy are frequently replicated at a specific place, an informal consensus emerges that declares the place animated by the faith-based practices of prior generations, evoking the original meaning of religion as a binding, connecting force.

The meaning of the designation is specific, but the type of place is open-ended, making for unlimited potential for spatial enchantment. One of the signs associ-ated with a place animated with prayer is a deep mythological vision of a holy past. This is often projected onto a site where a church or monastery now stands with the assumption that pre-Christians worshiped there too, deepening the deposit of devotional energy and marking the site a "place of forces" (*mistse syly*/*mesto sily* in Ukrainian and Russian) (Golovneva and Shmidt 2015; Lesiv 2013, 118).

It is difficult to classify space as either secular or sacred. In Europe empty churches are increasingly converted into exhibit space, concert halls, and con-ference centers. They still retain something of a sacred atmosphere, what Birgit Meyer (2020, 25) calls a "sacred residue," even after being reframed as sites of cultural heritage. These religious buildings might be repurposed to house worldly activities, but the spectrum of appropriate uses is limited in recognition of the building's past. By contrast, many religious buildings during the Soviet period were repurposed for profane uses. The Goldberg Church in Kharkiv, for exam-ple, was turned into a warehouse from 1925 to 1941 before it was reopened dur-ing German occupation of the city. Many churches suffered a harsher fate. They were repurposed as dance clubs and swimming pools to destroy the sacred resi-due left by the devotions of past generations. Declaring the Goldberg Church (and others) animated with prayer in a post-Soviet era is a rhetorical device to purify decades of profane use or neglect. It reestablishes sacrality and reverence for the space by emphasizing the sincere worship of ancestors that occurred spe-cifically in this place and induces forgetting of the decades of desecration.

The Goldberg Church was built from 1907 to 1915 by a Jewish convert to Or-thodoxy when he became the head of the merchant guild. Local lore has it that, in gratitude, he gave the church to the city as a gift. The church's actual name is Three Saints Church, but no one calls it that. Goldberg ran his paint and hard-ware business with two of his brothers, who also converted to Orthodoxy, perhaps explaining the official name. Not only the church's provenance from Jewish converts but also its aesthetic and architectural elements are read in such a way that it has earned the designation "animated with prayer" in the superlative.

As one enters the vestibule, floor-to-ceiling ornamentation of naive folk renditions of sunflowers, cherries, and strawberries greet the visitor and create an unusually playful atmosphere. Painted by a Russian artist brought in expressly from St. Petersburg to create a uniquely Ukrainian folk motif, the vestibule sets the stage for the bright light that streams down from the multitude of windows in the cupola into an open hall. The mysticism of some Orthodox churches is created by the fact that they tend to be shadowy places with minimal natural light, filled with smoke from candles, incense, and human breath. This church breaks with those atmospheric and architectural conventions. In addition to the light, there are no central pillars, which makes for a single open space that was considered quite a feat of construction at the time (see figure 2.4). By local standards, this church is not particularly old, a quality usually attributed to *namolennist'*. However, its choir is famous for medieval Byzantine chants. Music, icons and decorative elements, are sensational forms that mediate practices, patterns of feeling, and contribute to

**FIGURE 2.4.**   Inside the Goldberg Church of the UOC-MP in Kharkiv.
This church is considered the place most animated with prayer in Kharkiv.
Photo by the author.

making religious subjects (Meyer 2014).[6] Such sensational forms, of which there are a plethora in Orthodoxy, govern the engagement of bodies in certain practices that can create experiences, even transformative experiences, of feeling the presence of energy. When such sensational forms are read as religious and are in constant circulation, they promote an affective atmosphere of religiosity by appealing to the senses and by catering to an underlying assumption of lived space as enchanted.

## The Goldberg Church

Natalia is Just Orthodox to the extent that she drops in to this church to light candles but does not attend services. She is aware that the church is associated with the Moscow Patriarchate, but this plays no role in her decision. She describes in Russian the atmosphere of the church as one of peace and comfort that transports her into a state of calmness, and this is what motivates her to come:

> When you arrive in a *namolennoe mesto*, you realize right away that you are where you need to be. You feel a sense of comfort when you approach icons and feel God's grace. Such a sensation. Such calmness (*spokoistvo*). You arrive, you make a request, and you understand that there is an answer. This is why you become calm. . . . That's the kind of atmosphere that exists here . . . you feel some kind of awe and you just start to speak quietly. . . . In that atmosphere of calmness, you suddenly feel warm and you leave with these feelings. You just fall into that aura and you become calm. You feel there is some kind of protection around you and you gain strength from that.

She searches for her grandmother's energy at places animated with prayer because she believes that her grandmother is the source of the protective powers that have positively shaped her life. Although this could be considered a form of ancestor worship, it mirrors official church doctrine that acknowledges the ability of saints to intercede on behalf of the living. At forty-eight, Natalia has been happily married for twenty-six years, as were her sister and mother. Her grandmother was the only person she knew in the Soviet period who admitted to being a believer. She attributes her family's harmony to her grandmother's intervention through prayer when she was alive and the work of her spirit today, and she understands the sensations of energy she experiences at this *namolene miste* as her presence. She comes anticipating and searching for these sensations as part of a process of "inner sense cultivation" so germane to religion and routinely experiences them (Luhrmann and Morgain 2012, 363).

The affective atmosphere of such places, created by light, music, visual stim-
ulation, and other sensational forms, sets in motion a mimetic faculty as people
attempt to imitate the experience of restorative energy that has been described
to them (Gebauer and Wulf 1995, 26). Bodily sensations induced by the affective atmosphere confirm the existence of energies at places animated with prayer.
In this way, the mimetic faculty predictably sets in motion an affective flow in
which sensations lead to thoughts and actions and culminate in experiences.
When there is an informal consensus that experiences of energy at a particular
place fulfill requests and deliver the desired transformation, the place is considered *namolene*. Ultimately, then, becoming a place animated with prayer rests
on the human ability to imitate a sought-after experience. This reflects Michael
Taussig's succinct definition of the mimetic faculty as "the nature that culture
uses to create second nature" (1993: xiii). It becomes second nature for visitors,
such as Natalia, to both anticipate and experience the energy of an affective atmosphere as it circulates around her.[7]

Natalia enters the church with the expectation of experiencing certain sensations that will provide relief and otherwise make her feel calmer than when
she entered. Using icons and candles, she has developed the ability to conjure
up the felt presence of her grandmother. These experiences are increasingly filtered through a semiotic ideology that reaffirms an underlying assumption that
some places are animated with otherworldly powers. These places are situated
within political borders. By repeatedly visiting this place animated with prayer,
Natalia's connection and attachment deepens, not only to the dead who continue
to positively influence her life but also to the Goldberg Church where these encounters occur. Dropping into this church is not a political act for her. It carries
purely personal benefits. Because her visits root her in this place and connect
her to ancestors who were also rooted there, she could be made to care about
the fate of this church, which is situated in a region on the edge of a war zone.
Her improvised and episodic, but nonetheless sincere, forms of religious practice are symbiotic to a religious institution that has become a pawn in geopolitical tensions. This heightens the importance of supporting secular powers that
can deliver continued access to these otherworldly powers.

# An Animated Neighborhood

The first time I visited the Goldberg Church I was with Viktoria, a historian of
the city, and she wanted to introduce me to Yurii, a literary scholar. He has dedicated his professional life to promoting the writings of Yurii Shevelov, a lin-
guist, essayist, and literary critic who lived in Kharkiv until he fled to the United

States during World War II. Yurii's dedication to Shevelov reflects the sacred status of writers as beacons of truth, wisdom, and beauty and the pious devotion with which they are revered among members of the intelligentsia in this part of the world. Yurii's house is filled with handwritten manuscripts and books. It amounts to a shrine to the writer's life.

The Goldberg Church is in a private sector, a neighborhood of small, one-story homes without running water, encircled by wooden fences and connected by a maze of dirt roads. When Yurii asked what brought us to this neighborhood, I explained that I wanted to see the most *namolenoe miste* in Kharkiv. His grandfather had been a priest in the church, and many of the neighboring homes also belonged to clergy and are now inhabited by their descendants. For this reason, Yurii considers the entire neighborhood animated with prayer, and he has no intention of ever leaving it. He recited the church's history in minute detail. When I mentioned that I found his account of great interest, he replied, "To some it is interesting, to others it is sad" (*summno* in Ukrainian). The church and its sordid fate during the Soviet period represented both the zenith of human accomplishment and the nadir of human madness, Yurii insisted.

He is not a believer and voraciously criticizes the Orthodox Church, with special wrath reserved for the Moscow Patriarchate. This does not stop him from being an Orthodox sympathizer and decorating his home with a variety of religious artifacts, including icons, prayer beads, and embroidered cloths. For him, these objects are a sign of his cultural heritage and indicate that he is, as he put it, a "patriot of his country." These religious objects are a material manifestation of a semiotic ideology that Yurii uses to express his political views and his devotion to promoting his cultural heritage, which centers on literature and religion.[8] When a historically dominant religious tradition informs aesthetic sensibilities, it can strengthen attachments to the religious among nonbelievers by allowing them to appropriate and secularize religious objects as art, cultural heritage, or political statements. Yurii's religious artifacts trade on his underlying assumption of the organic integration of national identity and religiosity, giving an ideological meaning to these objects. When a certain faith tradition is a defining pillar of nationality and the institution that claims to be its protector is a political agent, promoting literature and displaying art can become vehicles to articulate political views and feed religiously infused subjectivities.

Illustrating how the political and historical context can change the semiotic ideology through which religious objects are perceived and experienced, the Soviet state vigorously tried to demystify the otherworldly powers of religious objects by claiming that they were mere art objects devoid of sacred residue. Later, in the 1990s, both the Ukrainian and Russian governments, in an effort to silence right-wing extremists, sought to prohibit the use of religious signs and symbols to make political statements. Especially since the war began in 2014, both states encourage a nationalist reading of religious signs and have become more tolerant, and at times even encourage, the use of religion to make political statements. This illustrates the changing underlying assumptions as to what constitutes reverence, critique, and blasphemy.[9]

Although Yurii is an atheist, he uses icons and other religious objects, like his beloved author, to express his ardent pro-Ukrainian political views in this Russified city in close proximity to a contested border. In surveying the decor in his home, I was reminded of Kathleen Stewart's observation, "Politics starts in the animated inhabitation of things, not way downstream in the various dreamboats and horror shows that get moving" (2007, 15–16). These religious objects anchor his small home, with its clerical origins, in the dramatic history of the Soviet Union's promotion of militant atheism. They announce his allegiance to the Goldberg Church, even as he fiercely criticizes the UOC-MP for its subservience to an imperial state and his respect for his grandfather, even as he lambasts the clergy of today. These religious objects are meaningful to him because they express his personal biography and cultural heritage, his political views on national allegiance, and his commitment to dissidence to state powers.

As I went to shake his hand before leaving, Yurii chastised me for standing over the doorway. A long-standing and widely observed custom has it that spirits lurk beneath the threshold and might surface if greetings of arrival or farewell are expressed there. Avoiding the threshold has become second nature for him and he instinctively does it even when the custom trades on the ability of malevolent forces to inflict harm while hiding under a clerical home in a neighborhood animated with prayer. The mimetic practice of not shaking hands over the doorway is common, as are many other such folk customs. They, too, contribute to an affective atmosphere of religiosity because they trade on underlying assumptions of animated places and unseen, otherworldly forces capable of transforming a person's life. They are not carriers of the political the same way as practices connected to institutional settings are. Nonetheless, such semiotic forms of vernacular religiosity are part of a web of practices that draw on a concatenation of otherworldly forces inhabiting the same space as humans. These practices have created second-nature otherworldly instincts in Yurii even as he insists he is an atheist.

## Living among the Saints

Vernacular religious practices move with great ease from public to private spaces. Even the most intimate spaces of home can be the sites of vernacular religiosity.

Yurii might be a member of the intelligentsia, but similar instincts, impulses, and practices of religiosity can be observed among others of different social standing. For example, Raisa lived in many places in the USSR as the wife of a military officer before settling in Kharkiv, her husband's hometown. She keeps icons of saints in her apartment to improve the aura and to extend the benefits of the ritual, practiced across the confessional spectrum, of having a member of the clergy bless a residence or a business to generate the kind of positive energy and protective powers attributed to a *namolene mistse*. This is another way in which institutional religion and vernacular religiosity symbiotically fuse in the home.

A room in Raisa's apartment has a sacred corner with icons, pictures of saints, and an altar with holy water. She does not call her home a place animated by prayer, but she deliberately fills it with many of the same objects Yurii displayed. She does it to create an atmosphere of prayerfulness, whereas he did it to affirm the religiosity of his cultural heritage. Referring to the pictures of saints in her apartment, Raisa says, "They help us and I see the active help that is coming from the saints. Things don't just happen like that. It is a blessing that is coming from them. Because of our sinfulness, we don't see it, but our prayers extinguish the fire. This brings light into this room. This is what is called *namolennost'*," she says.

Just as Natalia searched for her grandmother's energy at the Goldberg Church, Raisa enters this room, with its religious images and objects, to feel the presence of her daughter and son-in-law, who were expecting a child when they were killed in a motorcycle accident four years earlier. Using the saints to imagine them and feel their presence allows her to create a prayerful atmosphere that delivers blessings after this tragedy. The human capacity for imaginative, image-based, sensuous communication, whether from icons of saints or visions of the dead, provides an alternative means of apprehending and acting upon the world and making connections to others through experiences of presence. Individual ritualized behaviors create these experiences in a church, in a neighborhood, and at home, extending the ambient atmosphere of religiosity from official religious buildings to everyday life in public as well as privatized spaces. Prayerful and secular places, and the objects in them, blend into a singular atmosphere of religiosity.

Maria finds *namolene* energy in the home of others. She was born into a nonpracticing Orthodox family but was told that she was christened in secret by her grandmother as a child. In the last few years, following the lead of her mother and father, she began attending a Protestant church in Kharkiv. She has stopped short of being christened again but is otherwise an active participant in her new church's activities. When asked if she had experienced a place animated by prayer, she named two: the Svitohirsk Lavra in Donetsk and the apartment where her weekly prayer group meets. She, like most, is unclear as to what exactly makes a place *namolene*. But for her the apartment qualifies. "You come into this apartment, and you feel right away an atmosphere of kindness, of warmth," she explains. "That's why I think that this phenomenon of places animated by prayer really exists. There is some kind of special energy that exists in this apartment." What the apartment and the monastery have in common for her is that she goes to both places with the goal of getting to know God and of getting to know herself. "These are the two best sacred places I know," she adds. Yet they are judged *namolene* by entirely different criteria. One is prayerful because it is a historically valuable *lavra*, the highest distinction of sacredness for an Orthodox monastery. The apartment is *namolene* because of the tenor of exchanges that occur there and the relationships that form, which give this place its own distinctive aura. In both places, certain energy exists that makes the prayer of others palpable and meaningful to her.

The prevalence of blending of institutional religion with self-designed forms of spirituality is part of a larger global trend (Heelas and Woodhead 2005). The affect a material setting generates can act as a bridge, linking sensations to emotional knowledge to reactions. This prompts those who are in this space to think, act, and feel in particular ways, often with such swift flow that the shift from feeling to thinking barely registers. As such, affect returns us to a holistic perspective that refuses to isolate aspects of lived experiences, whether they occur in public or private spaces, from the thoughts and reactions that both trigger and emerge from them.

Vernacular religious practices create these experiences in private, intimate places, such as homes, and in public places, such as churches and neighborhoods. Making extra-institutional places sacred, or animated by prayer, reflects the "work of the imagination," as Appadurai (1996) terms it, because it engages theodicies and utopian aspirations for kindness, warmth, and hope through the mundane, routine experiences of everyday religiosity.

An atmosphere depends on presence. Presence also matters when considering how a person comes to feel involved and connected to others. Tanya Luhrmann (2020) has made a significant contribution to our understanding of how individuals learn to feel the presence of God and otherworldly forces. The crux of her argument is that people do not worship because they believe. Rather, they believe because they worship. Processes of real-making allow individuals to feel the presence of spirits, energies, and the like and affirms that it is possible to form a relationship with otherworldly forces, and that they are powerful and capable of influencing lives. Spirits are made real through communal experiences in which people hear stories and learn techniques that help them feel and then recognize sensations as the presence of otherworldly forces manifest as God, the dead, and so on. The repeated practice of conjuring up that presence changes the way people experience their own inner worlds, which is why engaging in these practices is often transformative. When communal experiences are interpreted through a faith frame, this allows a person to anticipate, imitate, and eventually habituate spiritual experiences through the use of cognitive strategies to see and feel the presence of invisible others.

The idiosyncratic elements of vernacular religious practice I have observed involve less of a cognitive approach characterized by learned techniques. Rather, they depend more on an imitation of techniques useful to stimulate visceral, sensual experiences through the use of yearnings, memories, dreams, and other sensory registers to generate embodied experiences. Nonetheless, Luhrmann's overall point that "kindling" the presence of otherworldly forces, through vernacular religious practices or some other means, leads to real-making, regardless of whether this is understood as the presence of the dead, the existence of a soul, the purifying experience of bathing in a sacred spring, and so on.

Relationships with higher powers explain why, during the Soviet era, in particular, members of underground religious communities, having had meaningful spiritual experiences that created relationships with otherworldly forces and with other community members, were motivated to participate in communal life even though it frequently meant risking humiliation, sometimes even on a daily basis, and the ever-present threat of imprisonment and death.[10] This also helps to explain why Alena, Natalia, and Raisa use a church, its candles, icons, and incense to maintain an ongoing relationship with dead relatives and keep them present in their lives. The material culture and aesthetics of Orthodoxy are the means they use to provoke embodied experiences that they understand to be the presence of their kin. These experiences color lifeworlds and illustrate how the public sphere of a particular historical moment and a person's most intimate feelings can be mutually constituting. The religious imagination offers the added ability to present a vision of the future and agents in the form of higher forces that are capable of realizing it.

## Pilgrimages to Sacred Places

In addition to visiting places animated with prayer, many Just Orthodox participate in pilgrimages. Given the war, the keen interest in the granting of the tomos, and the support for a local church, I was curious how the connection to the Moscow Patriarchate might affect, if at all, enthusiasm for monastic visits when the monastery was part of the UOC-MP. We saw that allegiances to the Goldberg Church remained steadfast for reasons that had nothing to do with jurisdiction. I visited one of the most coveted properties of the UOC-MP, the

Pochaiv Monastery, as part of a pilgrimage group. In the aftermath of World War II, the Soviet-era practice of forcibly transferring church buildings that were not destroyed to the Russian Orthodox Church had already generated much conflict on the national, and especially local levels, after attempts were made in the final years of the Soviet Union to re-transfer them back (Naumescu 2008). Since that time, fierce disputes have raged over the return, the possibility of return, or denial of the return of churches. Deciding on the fate of a highly coveted UOC-MP monastery located in European-oriented, nationalist-leaning Western Ukraine during armed combat with Russian-backed forces was a formidable task to even consider. Now that there is an Orthodox Church of Ukraine the issue of transfer, like a phantom, haunts those discussions.

Before the war broke out, pilgrimages ignored political borders and transported Russians, Ukrainians, and Belarusians to shared sacred sites all over the former USSR and even around the world. Jeanne Kormina characterizes this widespread form of religious practice as "nomadic religiosity" because it forms "temporary communities of practice" on the move (2018, 144). Orthodox clergy lament that so many prefer such travel to attending a liturgy. A veritable religious tourism industry, sponsored by denominations, parishes, and purely commercial travel agencies, offers a mix of travel catering to pious devotion, self-help, vacationing voyeurism, and spa-like cleansing experiences for the deeply devout and curious alike.

The war has remade this nomadism as travel from Ukraine to Russia has all but halted, and movement in the other direction has significantly fallen off. This has not changed the number of pilgrims to the Pochaiv Monastery. The war has simply changed where the pilgrims come from. Russians and Belarusians might travel to Ukraine in far fewer numbers, but Ukrainians do not leave, so for the monastery it is business as usual.

The hotel at the Pochaiv Monastery has 1,000 beds, and it was booked over capacity on the winter days in February 2017 that I was there. Pilgrimage agencies offer convenient, two-day trips that include visits to three monasteries with miracle-working icons, a cemetery, and a sacred spring. The fee, at the time equivalent to US$20, covers transportation, modest accommodation, and most meals. (Previously, it had been less than one-third this price, so this seems expensive to most Ukrainians.) A text message instructed us to "meet at the tank." An old Soviet war memorial featured wilted World War II-era weaponry, including a tank, and faded images of destroyed hero cities. As I headed toward the tank at 6:45 a.m., I could see in the distance a woman wearing a long black skirt and a scarf covering her head and hair, attire that was expected of women at monasteries. Her name was Valentyna, and she distinguished herself from all the other participants in the pilgrimage group because she observes the fasts, regularly takes communion, and generally has reverence for the institution. This would be her fifth or sixth trip to Pochaiv. She could not remember exactly. She had also been to numerous other monasteries and was planning another pilgrimage for the following week. At sixty-three, she has time to travel. She retired three years earlier from her "man's job," as she called it, as an electrical engineer at a construction firm in Kharkiv. She is highly educated, speaks English, and has traveled extensively throughout Europe.

As we settled into a small van, just barely fitting all the bags, she peered out at me over her gold-rimmed glasses, with several gold teeth glimmering to match, and told me how she prefers to travel by herself. "Why don't you travel alone to Pochaiv then?" I asked. "Because to go alone would be tourism," Valentyna responded. "You would travel about the monastery with people of different faiths for whom the monastery would have other meanings, probably as just a cultural and historic landmark." She assumed, probably correctly, that, excepting myself, the others in the group, even those who had signed up through a travel agency, still wanted and perhaps even yearned to experience the monastery's affective atmosphere. This is why they chose to form a temporary group of shared needs and come to the monastery as pilgrims, not tourists.

The other women participated for various reasons. Tatiana, a forty-one-year-old lawyer who lives in Kharkiv, explained that while she was divorcing her husband, she went through a difficult period and often felt poorly. The place where she found the most comfort was on a bench at the St. Pokrovskyi Monastery in Kharkiv. She explained, "I would just sit on that bench. I didn't even go into the church. I don't know why I did that. I just wanted to sit there. Maybe because there really was some kind of energy there. I felt it but I can't explain it." The habit of going to this bench when experiencing difficulties meant that the monastery was an integral part of her everyday life. A bench became the point of access to the therapeutic qualities of being near saints, angels, and other supernatural forces. This experience of feeling the atmosphere of place by finding comfort and energy on a bench inspired her to travel to other monasteries. After she married for a second time and was feeling better, she first traveled with a friend to Crimea in 2013, before the peninsula was annexed to Russia, to visit a spring at a women's monastery.

Some participants in this pilgrimage were vacationing with a purpose, whereas the others came for redress. We were thirteen women and one man, who was the thirty-four-year-old son of one of the women. He was celebrating his birthday on this journey, and his mother had gifted him the pilgrimage. At one point, his mother offered everyone wine and sweets to celebrate her son. There was also a mother-daughter pair who had registered through a travel agency, and two well-heeled young women who were clearly friends. They wore fur coats, had perfectly manicured fingernails, and designer handbags. Yet they showed up without skirts, scarves to cover their heads, or long shirts for bathing in the sacred spring. The tour guide, prepared for pilgrim-tourists who know little of monastic life, had an extra skirt, which meant that only one of the women was obliged to wrap a scarf around her legs as a makeshift skirt to be in keeping with the monastery's dress prescriptions for women. All six of these pilgrims reserved double rooms in the monastery hotel to enhance their bonding experiences, whereas everyone else slept in open rooms that held upwards of ten beds each. They were vacationing with a purpose; they wanted to take advantage of the blessings that a monastery could deliver and admire the beautiful icons and churches, but they also wanted to enjoy themselves.

The other women had clearly come to find relief from some form of woe that had beset them. Many were in their late twenties or early thirties, an age where two types of difficulties can set in: either they have no partner, or their partner is problematic. Some want children and others want their children to be healthy. These women kept to themselves and were quiet to the point of being somber. Their need to feel the therapeutic, healing energy seemed more urgent. They were shouldering the gendered responsibility of caring for the well-being of their families. One of them, Zhanna, was on her third pilgrimage to Pochaiv. She came to pray for the health of her husband, who for three months prior had visited doctors to heal a hacking cough. She thought he had walking pneumonia, but no medicine seemed to help. One week earlier he left for Israel to receive medical treatment there, and Zhanna left for Pochaiv to put in prayer requests for the monks and nuns to pray, with their learned piety, for his recovery. Each was doing their part to restore his health.

Once we arrived at the monastery, a seminarian gave us a tour. Aware that many people come to the monastery for its affective powers, he warned against expecting the aura or magic of the monastery to heal. He countered with appeals to turn off the television. He wanted us to read, go to adult Sunday school, and study the symbolism of the liturgy. Much like the British Bible Society, he wanted us to learn and for there to be a conscious, informed aspect to our religious experiences. Orthodox church services are sung in Church Slavonic, a liturgical language, which, like a Latin mass, is not readily comprehensible to most. Although a sacred language is meant to be a mystical vehicle to a religious experience, it frequently has the opposite effect, making parishioners passive bystanders. Knowledge, the seminarian countered, is the best insurance against boredom during long services. It would help us, he insisted, to retain a focus on the state of our eternal soul. How do we know we have a soul, he rhetorically asked? Because it hurts, the women answered in unison. Fully prepared for the response, he nodded in agreement. This, I understood, was the purpose of the

**FIGURE 2.5.**  Many pilgrimages include the purifying experience of bathing in a sacred spring. Precisely because this is so widely practiced, a public park in Kharkiv also includes a sacred spring for bathing, replete with Eastern Christian symbolism, in this otherwise public secular space. Photo by the author.

trip: to reduce the pain of an aching soul, the reasons for which were as varied as there were visitors.

A pilgrimage is an efficient means to do so. A monastery offers many possibilities for accessing otherworldly powers through places and things to alleviate suffering. Pilgrims visit the various churches and chapels that dot the monastery grounds on their own and can, if they choose, participate in formal rituals such as confession, communion, and late night and crack of dawn liturgies. One can appeal to God, the saints, elders, monks, and ancestors using sacred spring water, holy water, miracle-working icons, relics, prayer requests, and candles. The shops on the monastery grounds are filled with crosses, books, icons, and a plethora of other religious objects to purchase and take home, as well as bread, honey, tea, and other consumables made by the monks. Each of these material things mediates the religious experience by helping to generate a sense of presence by delivering, in this case, protective or healing energy. Purchasing goods also allows for the recreation of the energy and atmosphere of the monastery elsewhere.

Tetiana was one of the women who brought a fur coat but none of the other requisite clothing. Over the course of the pilgrimage, she purchased books on healing children and put in numerous prayer requests for good health and the dead. A pilgrim can order prayers to be said by the monks. When the monks apply their learned piety in supplications, the belief is that those prayers will be more effective. This brings the UOC-MP monastery and the monks who live there into the networks of care and responsibility for loved ones that women primarily shoulder (Luehrmann and Kormina 2017, 7). It becomes a collective effort between Tetiana, the caring mother, and the erudite monks to help heal her children. The cost of requesting prayers is based on the number of names the monks are asked to pray for. While recording each prayer request, the monk inquired: "Are they all Orthodox? Of the Moscow Patriarchate?" She was the only member of the group who responded that her family members were not believers, which meant she had to pay more. All others automatically responded in the affirmative. "Yes, they are all believers and yes, of course, they are of the Moscow Patriarchate." Privately, however, many spoke differently. Zhanna emphatically told me that she goes to whichever church she wants and that it was none of the monk's business.

Just as the monk seemed to have no difficulty asserting that the Church of the Moscow Patriarchate was the only True Orthodox Church, making the other Ukrainian churches apostate schismatics in spiritual sin and error, the women lied straight to his face with no regret. They told him what he expected to hear so that he would give them what they wanted, reflecting the transactional social nature of religiosity. These women accept the higher authority and greater proximity to the divine that the monks of Pochaiv have. Their willingness to involve them in caring for their families has little to do with the formal affiliation the monastery has to the UOC-MP. They even resent this suggestion.

The duplicitousness of saying one thing and doing another is illustrative of consumerist attitudes toward spiritual consumption and the deep-seated mistrust and cynicism that fuels institutional disaffection and anticlericalism, especially among the Just Orthodox. Such critical attitudes do not diminish the desire for otherworldly help to solve problems in the here and now. They do, however, inspire those in need to make minimal commitments and only agree to participate in temporary communities, such as this pilgrimage, as a forum preferable to membership in a parish. Pilgrimage reflects both the attraction of the monastery as a privileged place and monks as privileged people to access otherworldly energy. It is also a means to live a Just Orthodox commitment to a faith tradition. Pilgrims do not have to choose a parish, and by extension a single denomination. Therefore, there is no risk of receiving condemnation for choosing the wrong church.

## Otherworldly Powers of the Land

This pilgrimage, like many others, culminated with the purifying experience of immersion in a sacred spring. This was the highlight of the trip, and everyone cast aside the possibility of falling ill and participated except for the pious pilgrim Valentyna and myself. The two of us simply could not make that leap of faith. The water in February was a near-freezing 2 degrees Celsius (35.6°F), and the surrounding snow and ice made it seem even colder. There were two options for immersion: a gender-segregated covered area or an open pool (see figure 2.6). Immersion was conducted under the guidance of Marina, the tour guide, who doubled as a lay expert on the ritual. After Tetiana, the woman who admitted that her family members were nonbelievers, immersed herself in the spring, as promised by Marina, she felt a certain "lightness." She said that she suddenly understood why christenings involve water. "At first," she said, "the spirit was so heavy that I could hardly breathe. And then lightness. Marina said to me, 'Do you see how light you feel? It is true! You have taken the bad out of yourself.' I believe it. Maybe because I am the kind of person who believes things. I am not a skeptic. I accept this on faith."

The sensations delivered by immersion in freezing waters at a sacred spring were enough to transform her self-perceptions and validate the trip. She had come on this pilgrimage with a goal in mind. Now that the bad had been removed, she could return to her daily life with that knowledge. On the bus back to Kyiv she was speaking of her next trip to a sacred spring. Discussions focused on which monasteries are accessible given the roadblocks and checkpoints the war has imposed. Valentyna mentioned that when she is unable to go on pilgrimage, a public park in Kharkiv offers the possibility of an immersion experience. An iconostasis-like triad of icon-like images of saints stands before a cross-shaped pool filled with spring water that doctors claim is the purest water in Kharkiv. This vernacular version of a religious ritual practiced in secular public space is uncontroversial. Because such vernacular religious practices are meaningful and common, they are even incorporated into a public park, which contributes to an affective atmosphere of religiosity (see figure 2.5).

## Inbetween Believers and Nonbelievers

The behavior of Just Orthodox reveal several key factors to explain why an atmosphere of religiosity emerges in Ukraine and why it becomes affective, but not in other societies with a historically and culturally dominant faith tradition. The Bible Society of England and Wales, for example, tries to create ambient faith,

**FIGURE 2.6.** Bathing in the Sacred Spring. Some people come on their own and others as part of a pilgrimage group. This is the gender-segregated, covered area for bathing. There is also an open-air area so that families can bathe together in the spring. The spring pool is surrounded by large icon-like images and short citations from the bible. Photo by the author.

which centers on shared beliefs that draw on textual and clerical authority upheld by an institution. The work of learning and applying biblical teachings is difficult. Susan Friend Harding (2001) and Tanya Luhrmann (2012) have analyzed the extensive efforts believers make to feel the presence of God among Baptists and Charismatic Pentecostals, respectively. The same is true for Eastern Christian believers. Naumescu's (2019) study of Syrian Oriental Orthodox in Kerala, India, for example, reveals the taxing nature of learning biblical teachings, mastering the art of prayer, and the elaborate recitation contests that exist to encourage this rigor. Coptic Christians in Egypt expend enormous efforts to teach how to select an appropriate saint to pray to (Heo 2018). Andreas Bandak and Tom Boylston (2014) use their ethnographic research among Greek Catholic and Greek Orthodox in Syria and Orthodox Christians in Ethiopia to argue that Orthodox Christianities form religious worlds that center on correctness (the "ortho" in orthodoxy). When confronted with moral imperfection, they defer to scriptural, oral, and aesthetic practices to form a world "that rests on an authorizing tradition" to rigorously determine correct behavior.

I share the goal of trying to understand the religious world a confession can create and how the presence of invisible others can be made real. Yet, the Just Orthodox offer several important interventions. First, those who self-describe as Just Orthodox actively seek to escape the confines of an authorizing tradition and the obligation of correctness because it carries the vulnerability of incessant judgment. They prefer a greater degree of agency and self-reliance in determining what is correct.

Second, their religiosity exists *in relation to* an authorizing tradition, rather than resting on it. They reject denominational allegiance, but not the authorizing tradition on which it is based. Their emotive, embodied vernacular practices, such as pilgrimages to sacred sites, venerating icons, and immersion in sacred springs, use the authorizing tradition to validate spiritualized practices that respond to individual needs and desires. These forms of vernacular religiosity can be practiced at any time and at a site of one's own choosing. Yet they are symbiotic to institutionalized religion, which helps make the presence of God, spirits, energies, and so on real because the institution and the tradition it embodies provides the "faith frame," or interpretive framework, that primes individuals for an embodied experience to be understood in transcendent terms (Luhrmann 2020, 1–20).

This means that vernacular religious practices exist between institutional sites (churches, monasteries, cemeteries, and the like) and individually chosen sites (at home, in a neighborhood, or on a bench). This allows the Just Orthodox to draw on institutional validation and individual improvisation as needed to "kindle the presence of invisible others," however they might be understood (Luhrmann 2020). These practices thrive because they do not need to form a stable community or make moral judgments, although they often do. Communities of Just Orthodox form bonds that exist as needed on a sliding communal scale from the familial, local, national, to transnational. These communities can be as temporary or as permanent as they need to be. Vernacular religious practices do not require institutional affirmation, although they benefit from it. This gives these practices considerable flexibility, tenacity, and validity, which is why they endure. These are the key differences that distinguish the Just Orthodox from pious, devout Orthodox believers and from others who practice forms of vernacular religiosity that also involve energy and aura and could be called New Age, pagan, or superstition.

Third, although the informality of these practices is born of institutional disaffection and anticlericalism, rather than attempting to roll back secularism, vernacular religiosity integrates worldliness and institutional religion and does not challenge either (Bowen 2008; Engelke 2012; Navaro-Yashin 2002; Özyürek 2006). Secularism can be used to protect and accommodate religious minorities in a religiously plural society and to prevent a confessionalized public sphere from emerging (Asad 2003, 182–83). Here we have a braiding, a symbiotic blending, of individualized religiosity, institutional forms of an Eastern Christian faith tradition, and secular impulses. A form of syncretic secularism results, which simultaneously allows for processes of secularization and sacralization to unfold in public space by meshing seemingly opposed inclinations and desires in novel reconceptualizations of religiosity (Wanner 2014, 435). This obscures the distinctions separating the religious from the secular and the religious from the political, and renders futile efforts to reinforce the barriers that separate them. In this way, religion goes public and becomes a malleable political tool as a form of "ethnodoxy," as Karpov, Lisovskaya, and Barry (2012) call it, meaning a vehicle to closely integrate religion, cultural heritage, and belonging. Integrating religion into a collective and individual sense of self paves the way for religious symbolism to be integrated into public parks, metro decor, corporate headquarters, and residential buildings. Sometimes the state spearheads the process of blending religion into national heritage.[11] Other times it is religious groups themselves.[12] When practices naturalize religion as an organic social fact and normativize the presence of the transcendent, religion is able to hide in plain sight.

Finally, having forgone the insistence on correctness and replaced it with forms of individually tailored, somewhat improvised practices, the ensuing fracturing opens up greater possibilities to instrumentalize Orthodoxy politically. By forgoing the hard work of learning approved techniques to evoke the presence of otherworldly forces in favor of practices that are personalized and more readily available, an engagement in religiosity results that draws on institutionalized religion, however tenuously, and assimilates it into everyday life. Therefore, cultivating the "dangerous passions" of religious zeal are not always the most effective means to deliver the power to politically persuade, as illustrated by Michael Billig's (1995) study of "banal nationalism." Daily experiences of circulating in an affective atmosphere of religiosity can forge attachments that prime people to see themselves as Orthodox, and to act and react in certain ways because they share understandings and moral attitudes regarding relatedness and attachments to certain places. This can render the fates and fortunes of religious institutions of vital importance to the Just Orthodox and even to nonbelievers.


## How the Political Gets into the Person

To analyze how an affective atmosphere of religiosity can become politically useful, let us consider two analogous cases that directly illustrate how atmospheres and reading signs in public space can be connected to the cultivation of political proclivities. In the United States, pressure is mounting to remove Confederate iconography from public space. Growing numbers of people identify Confederate symbols as keeping racial hierarchies alive by allowing continued tolerance, if not endorsement, of the racial inequalities the Confederacy sanctioned.[13] Monuments communicate shared values and serve as sites to gather to reaffirm them.[14] One month after the white supremacist Dylann Roof tried to start a race war by killing nine African American parishioners in a church in Charleston, South Carolina in June 2015, the Confederate flag was removed from the South Carolina State House, the last southern house to fly this flag. In the summer of 2020, following outrage over the murder of George Floyd by a Minneapolis police officer, thirty-eight Confederate monuments were removed, five were relocated, and sixteen public parks and schools were renamed. These actions were taken in response to broad public recognition that ambient iconography in public space functions as a succinct yet powerful statement of values that serve to normativize racial hierarchies and discriminatory behaviors. It often becomes politically untenable to maintain signs that are not read, and therefore not acted upon, in a unified fashion. The accelerating efforts to remove Confederate symbolism from public space, and to question the moral message of certain monuments, suggest that there is growing recognition in the United States that perceiving certain signs leads to an atmosphere of racism, to harboring "unthought thoughts" (Pile 2010,12), and creating prereflexive forms of experience, all of which feed political behaviors.

In a parallel situation, the Ukrainian parliament banned the display of communist and Nazi symbolism in public space in 2015. Decommunization laws mandate the removal of monuments, holidays, and commemorative events that honor communist historical figures and communist ideals. They also bar the naming of streets, towns, cities, and other public sites that could be construed as communist. Law 2558, "On Condemning the Communist and National Socialist Totalitarian Regimes and Prohibiting the Propagation of Their Symbols," was in the making prior to the Maidan protests, but after the war broke out, it was fast-tracked into implementation.

This remake of public space was bundled with other efforts to alter the political values and political behavior of Ukrainian voters. Provisions within the same legislation made punishable the denial of the criminal nature of the "communist totalitarian regime of 1917–1991." Decommunization allowed for the opening of former NKVD-KGB secret police archives and for public recognition of anyone who fought in any capacity for Ukrainian independence. Terminology, such as the Great Patriotic War, was rejected in favor of European conventions of referring to World War II, using European commemorative dates for the war's end (May 8, not May 9), and reframing Victory Day as Day of National Remembrance and Reconciliation. Some historians and public figures objected, arguing that cleansing the public sphere of the Soviet past deceives the citizenry. It suggests change has occurred in the thinking and practices of governing officials and masks the prospect that it has not.[15]

The same government authorities who backed the creation of the OCU offered an ethical argument to justify this purge of public space. They claimed that it provides justice to the victims of communist oppression. Left unsaid was that after weaponizing religion to create distance from the ROC, this purge of communist symbolism is a parallel process of weaponizing history. New signs in public space can potentially remake understandings of historical experience that hinge less on the greatness of Soviet victory during the Great Patriotic War and more on the ongoing Ukrainian national struggle from colonial oppression. Recasting communist signs in the public sphere remakes ethical and political orientations. In sum, in a pragmatic sense, removing or adding iconography shapes the assumptions and presuppositions that inform political inclinations and erases or creates focal points to protest or promote alternatives to the status quo.

When religious signs, weighted with otherworldly presence, circulate with great frequency in the aesthetics of the built environment or in popular vernacular practices, they become one of the factors that makes a nonbelieving, nonpracticing person Just Orthodox. They eviscerate any clear distinction between an individual and the environment and make the impersonal qualities of aesthetic and architectural elements and one's own feelings and practices quite intimate. Brennan asserts, "While its wellsprings are social, the transmission of affect is deeply physical in its effects. It is moreover the key to the social and scientific understanding of what have hitherto been theological mysteries" (2004, 23).

When people circulate in affectively charged places and experience sensations or energy as theological mysteries, it is because they understand these sensations as a form of presence. Feeling the presence of dead children or grandparents can be interpreted as evidence of an otherworldly realm or divine power. The relevance of such experiences depends on the underlying assumptions used to interpret them because this is what guides thought and behavior. When there is widespread belief that particular places generate such experiences, another layer is added. These sites become "moody force fields" as spaces of intensity, such as the Goldberg Church and its surrounding neighborhood and the venerated Pochaiv Monastery and its nearby springs. These places are known to spark embodied experiences in the form of sensations (Stephens 2015, 2). When enough people have the experience, for example, of lighting a candle or submerging themselves in a sacred spring and the intended result materializes, then these practices, along with the sites where they occur, begin to produce an affective atmosphere.

Place-making is a cultural mechanism by which everyday lived experiences can make a place sacred. When this sacrality is recognized as one's own and yet shared with others, it can breed attachments and feelings of belonging, both of which have the potential to escalate into political inclinations and even political attitudes and actions. Orthodoxy is elastic and porous enough to accommodate nonbelievers, doubters, and critics because of its historic conceptualization of an organic assemblage unifying a church with a people in a particular place, usually a nation-state. This forms the basis of religious identity for people who live in that place that is understood to be inherited, eternal, and transcendent. Regardless of whether or how one believes or practices, and how this measures up to an authorizing tradition, any East Slav can claim to be Orthodox and part of its religious world.

Each time someone such as Tetiana, Zhanna, or Valentyna has a transformative experience at a sacred place, they build an attachment to that place and to the imagined others whose faith made it sacred to begin with. That attachment, be it to a UOC-MP monastery or another religiously consecrated site, breeds a will to keep that place accessible. When place-based forms of vernacular practice are politicized by political, cultural, and ecclesiastical leaders, an attachment to place can be understood in terms of state sovereignty. Once place-based sensational forms are perceived and experienced through a semiotic ideology, leading to ethical or political judgments informing behavior, then the affective atmosphere of religiosity can become a political resource capable of mobilizing believers and nonbelievers alike. Given the meaningfulness of the transformative experiences that occur at these places through vernacular religious practices, allegiances turn to the state powers that can secure ongoing access to places with otherworldly powers. When people mobilize to act collectively, as they did during the Maidan protests, an affective atmosphere becomes a facet of politics. It transmits public feelings that sustain a collective and put people "in the mood" to agitate for change. This is vitally important for the success of any political action or social movement. Regardless of how valid a critique of power or feasible the desired change, collective action is simply not possible unless people are in the mood to pursue it, as Jonathan Flatley (2008) asserts.

This is where religiosity is key to shaping the intersubjective relationship between a particular historical context and the sentiments that color it. Numerous theoreticians have alluded to the importance of "mood" in slightly different terms. Clifford Geertz famously characterized religion in terms of the "powerful, pervasive, and long-lasting moods and motivations" it creates (1973, 90). Raymond Williams referred to "structures of feeling" to understand the dynamics of socially shared emotional experiences that contain a measure of "the emergent," of something that has not yet happened (1977). Benedict Anderson notes (2006) the feelings of "deep horizontal comradeship" that characterize the relations among people of a nation. In each of these instances, we are talking about affect that spurs sensorial, emotional experiences and generates knowledge, albeit often unspoken. An atmosphere colors how this process unfolds and the sensations and experiences that emerge, making these experiences pregnant with possibility.

When vernacular religious practices occur at certain sites that are understood as religious because the experiences that occur there connect an individual to an otherworldly realm, then an affective atmosphere of religiosity at these sites begins to take root. The affective qualities of such places provoke "visceral shifts in the background habits and postures of a body" (Anderson 2006, 737) once their otherworldly capacities are recognized. Having considered how vernacular religious practices and iconography in public space contribute to affective atmosphere that has political implications, we now turn to an unexpected historic event, the Maidan protests, that unleashed this potential.

# RADICAL HOPE
## The Maidan as Historic Event

The protests that began on Kyiv's central square on November 21, 2013, became the Revolution of Dignity by the time dead protesters were buried three months later. "The winter that changed us" is how Ukrainians refer to this brief period. Like all revolutionary, extraordinary events, the Maidan imposed change. It was a three-month-long happening that could not be absorbed into existing categories and structures. The cascading events and ruptures that followed prompted a remaking of individual consciousness, collective practices, and social and political institutions. Even years later, the Maidan remains momentous in terms of its transformative potential. An affective atmosphere of religiosity was the backdrop for these events and played into the post-Maidan remake of public space and public institutions under the precarious threat of an ever-present hybrid war.[1]

The Maidan began as a protest *against* something (Russian-oriented, kleptocratic governance) and became a revolution *for* something (a dignified life).[2] Ukrainian president Viktor Yanukovych's unexpected announcement that he would not sign an association agreement with the European Union (EU) sparked the protests on November 21, 2013. They evolved into a fierce demand for a life of dignity and the toppling of government officials and state institutions that impede this goal. The violent deaths of unarmed protesters three months later at the hands of Ukrainian riot police (Berkut) were followed by a series of even more unimaginable events. First, the coveted Crimean Peninsula was occupied by "little green men," meaning soldiers wearing unmarked uniforms but known to be Russian, prior to being officially annexed to Russia via referendum. Then armed aggression flared in the name of separatism in two eastern Ukrainian regions, with weaponry, expertise, and fighters shipped in from Russia. The annexation and war rapidly shifted the priorities away from reform to defending the territorial integrity of Ukraine. Against such pummeling, anxiety and anger morphed into a swirl of intense emotion that was periodically tempered only by shock. This series of events continues to transform Ukrainian society and geopolitics writ large, drive the politicization of religion in the region, and inform the expansion of religiosity into many facets of everyday life. Ukraine's affective atmosphere of religiosity predisposed a turn to a religious idiom and religious practices to express dissent and to generate empowerment and hope. This set the stage for religiosity to be part of the bedrock of the transformation of public space and public institutions in the years following the Maidan.

The protests were born of mounting exasperation with failed, incremental changes as a response to burgeoning expectations and heightened pressures for change. Prior protests were pressure points that escalated from the Revolution on Granite student protests in October 1990 in favor of independence; the Ukraine without Kuchma movement in 2000–2001; the Orange Revolution in 2004; and finally, the Maidan protests in 2013–14. Larysa Ivshyna succinctly characterizes the key differences among the post-independence protests as first, during the Ukraine without Kuchma movement, the country had a president but not a people; five years later, during the Orange Revolution, the people were without a president; and during the Maidan, the people were in search of a worthy president.[3]

The participation of clergy and religious institutions, allied with citizens, mounted with each attempt to indict the state, and ratcheted up demands for political change justified by religiously inspired rhetoric and symbolism. During the Maidan, a religiously infused concept of dignity, drawing on Catholic theological concepts embraced by many clergy and members of the Ukrainian Greek Catholic Church, was used to challenge the kleptocratic means of governing the country and unseat the pro-Russian president. After the war broke out, Ukrainian political leaders set about creating an independent Orthodox Church of Ukraine to deal a blow to the Russian state by diminishing the reach and influence of the Russian Orthodox Church on Ukrainian soil. These moves to weaponize and securitize religion have become widespread in a war of guns, disinformation, and crosses.

The act of not signing the European Union Association Agreement, and deferring to the Eurasian Customs Union, was widely seen as the equivalent of turning the Titanic toward the iceberg. This betrayal shattered the patience and willingness to endure kleptocratic governance any longer and triggered a crisis. Approximately 17 percent of Ukraine's adult population participated in the Maidan in some capacity. (Nikolayenko 2020, 446) The crisis set off a chain of additional ruptures that intensified feelings of indignity and ultimately broke established cultural norms and social practices by weakening the institutions that upheld them. This resulted in a period of tremendous creativity as protesters searched for a way to regain authorship of their own lives and to establish credible forms of authority.

In this sense, the Maidan is a historical event. The protesters knew they were participating in a momentous event, pregnant with possibilities, that would determine their individual and collective fate for quite some time to come. As the protests continued day after day and month after month, the Maidan became a liminal space characterized by emotional intensity that bred feelings of solidarity. The betwixt and between liminal qualities of the Maidan suspended social constraints and hierarchies and produced a profound sense of solidarity among participants. Violence punctured this liminal state. After Yanukovych was ousted and fled to Russia, the annexation of Crimea and the war in Eastern Ukraine unleashed additional ruptures that laid bare the fragility of norms of relatedness and the social, political, and religious structures that upheld them.

When events produce a sequence of ruptures, networks linking structures can be permanently disrupted, which triggers what William Sewell, after studying the French Revolution, has called "dislocations" (1996, 871). When ruptures affect multiple and overlapping structures at the same time, reconstituting those social institutions after dislocations becomes impossible. When preexisting structural networks are interrelated and irretrievably disrupted by dislocations, these ruptures clear the way for new structural configurations to take root, which Sewell calls "rearticulations." New configurations among networks linking social institutions foster rearticulations of qualitatively new cultural norms and social practices (Sewell 1996, 844).

The initial disruptions the protests provoked to interrelated structures, be they political, economic, or religious, altered established cultural understandings and social relations. In those instances when contiguous structures were transformed by these disruptions, they released new causal nexuses for change. This happened, for example, when the economic interests of a businessman, who owns a media outlet, coincided with his political ambitions. Petro Poroshenko had the cameras of his TV company, the Fifth Channel, set squarely on the Maidan 24/7, thereby altering who could participate in the protests and how. Suddenly, anyone anywhere could be on the Maidan as an eyewitness, virtually or on the ground. It also happened when colleagues and family members, whose diverging values led to opposing political viewpoints, strained relationships to the breaking point and severed future collaborative and familial gatherings. This swirl of ruptures prompted cascading breaks in one domain, which triggered others, and led to experimentation with new ideas, forms of social organization, and means of coping, which, in turn, prompted more change, much of which became lasting. This is how the Maidan became a transformative historical event and "the winter that changed us."

## Radical Hope

People characterized the atmosphere on the Maidan and a certain presence they experienced there in different ways. The theologian Hennadiy Tselkovs'kyi commented, "Religion is neither a driving force on the Maidan, nor a mobilizing force, nor a deterrent. It is woven into the landscape of the Maidan as it is in all of Ukrainian society; that is to say, it is present at the institutional level with church representatives and through religious practices, but not as a basic system of values for the majority."[4] Much like the panels over the burnt buildings and gold domed cupolas, he claims religion was unobtrusively, but firmly, "woven into the landscape" of public space. A member of the UGCC clergy called the Maidan a "space of hope." There, he argued, the state of being a slave was destroyed, as were the stereotypes that fed webs of mistrust, skepticism, and disappointment. By becoming a place of struggle, where one searched for "identity, inner desires, and spiritual sensations," the Maidan became a place of hope and faith in a better tomorrow because it inspired people, "not just to exist, but to live" (Ostanniuk 2018, 211, 214). Liudmylla Fylypovych referred to a specific atmosphere of presence. She noted the broad cross-section of people who gathered on the Maidan and asserted that "what united them and what brought them to the Maidan were sensations (*vidchuttia* in Ukrainian) and an awareness of presence (*usvidomlennia prysutnosti*) they felt within themselves that wasn't biological and wasn't even social. Every person has a conscience, a will, strength of spirit, boldness of thoughts of something that is higher than the material, something that is even irrational. For a believer, it's clear that this presence is God, godly forces, and the Holy Spirit" (2014, 149). Others might have experienced this presence in less religious terms but as otherworldly nonetheless. A young man, who described himself as an "ordinary student" described how the Maidan changed him. He began to understand that the future of the country depends on him, that the future of his children (who are not even born yet), and the future of successive generations also depend on him. "I don't want to betray the hope we fought for later with blood," he said. In other words, having accepted his responsibility to improve the future, he acknowledges that should there be insufficient reform, this hope will not vanish. Rather, the tactics to realize it will. Whereas Marx wrote, "The tradition of all dead generations weighs like a nightmare on the brains of the living," here we have a young man whose brain is burdened by the tradition future generations will inherit, which also weighs like a nightmare.

In reflecting on this extraordinary event and the atmosphere experienced, I would say that the Maidan was not just a space of hope but of radical hope. The difference is significant. The philosopher Jonathan Lear defines radical hope as something "directed toward a future goodness that transcends the current ability to understand what it is. Radical hope anticipates a good for which those who have the hope as yet lack the appropriate concepts with which to understand it" (2006,103). In other words, hope gives a person the confidence to strive for a particular outcome. But radical hope inspires the will to strive for an outcome that is longed for but impossible to imagine. The distinction becomes meaningful in situations of extreme despair. If a quorum of people in anguish decide that they do not want to live "like this," as they did on the Maidan, and although it is unclear how to transform what they have and exactly what would be better, they marshal the courage to try, it is thanks to radical hope.

Lear's insight into the difference between hope and radical hope was born after he pondered the reaction of a Native American Crow chieftain to the tribe's forced relocation to a reservation and the near extermination of buffalo. These dual changes decimated their entire way of life. "After that, nothing happened," the chief said (Lear 2006, 2). The set of ruptures that stemmed from forced relocation and the loss of buffalo dealt such decisive blows to the Crow that their cultural schema, social practices, and authority structures shattered. This eviscerated the ability of the Crow to forge meaningful narratives of what happened. An event or experience can have meaning only within a shared interpretive framework that trades on established categories, norms, and understandings. If the cultural schema implodes, it becomes impossible to distinguish extraordinary experiences from everyday experiences. This is why, according to the chief, nothing happened and why it was so difficult to imagine solutions to the multiple, interconnected problems that beset the Crow at that time.[5]

When everyday life becomes unintelligible because so many norms have been obliterated, and what is legible is either frightening or despicable, radical hope nonetheless makes directed action possible by allowing for the expression of unarticulated yearnings to exist in the face of ruptures. Amid despair, communal anxiety, and a period when there seemed to be no future beyond death by fighting an unwinnable war, the Crow chieftain had a dream-vision. Using this "spiritual force," the chief drew on the past to see a "traditional way of going forward."[6] His vision drew on radical hope to lead his people out of desperation by blending traditional cultural schema with new conceptual and moral content to once again make events and experiences happen (2006, 154).

The Maidan protesters, much like the Crow, blended past glories with radical hope to make collective action possible during a historic event even though the goals and consequences of their actions were unclear. Radical hope shifted this post-Soviet borderland country, with its fractures, strains, and challenges, into a similar mode of creative adaptation to the conditions created by the political crisis to instigate change. The protesters were united in rendering a verdict that they did not want "this," which they understood as unrelenting humiliation driven by the greed of government officials that robbed them of their dignity and agency to self-define. Radical hope propelled a vision that there could be a return to dignity and an end to nagging sensations of vulnerability and precarity.

A shared recognition of these common aspirations turned out to be a wellspring of unity in the face of great diversity. Up to one million people at times stood on the streets in subzero temperatures for days at a time to agitate for a future that was only beginning to come into focus. Radical hope transformed the one shared insistence on change into a "deep horizontal comradeship" that even included future generations and harnessed a strategy of self-organization to instigate change (Anderson 1991; Channel-Justice 2016; Marynovych 2018). By not reverting to standard identity politics, such as promoting a common single language or religion, a civic nation was emerging. Rather than asserting a common past and shared memories, the act of choosing a common future became the basis for solidarity. This opened the door for a pluralist and elastic understanding of who belongs, of cultural politics, and of the reciprocal rights and obligations that should exist between a governing elite and its citizenry. The Maidan made the attributes of nationhood and belonging visionary and plural.[7] This was enough to spark and sustain coordinated collective action.

Conceptualizing Ukrainian nationhood in such terms was new.[8] Most political and cultural elites have over time relied on a Stalin-inspired understanding of "historically formed stable communities" based on language, religion, historical memory, or some other seemingly bound trait to craft a nation. In a borderland country such as Ukraine, conceiving of identity politics in singular terms contains the seeds of division and inevitably produces minorities, who could potentially be disadvantaged or excluded. The population is multilingual and multiconfessional. Ukrainian regions were part of the Russian, Austro-Hungarian, and Ottoman Empires. Religion is particularly complex. The Just Orthodox proclaim allegiance to an Eastern Christian faith tradition, but not to a particular jurisdiction. Orthodoxy underlines Ukraine's close historical ties to Russia at the same time that, along with Ukrainian Greek Catholicism, it is seen as distinctly Ukrainian. Growing religious pluralism is compounded by multiple Orthodox churches in Ukraine, each using history and competing memories of the past to distinguish themselves from each other and to justify divisions so as to position themselves as the most authentically Ukrainian (Fert 2020; Yurchuk 2021).

Attempts to interpret certain historical events, usually the Baptism of Kyivan Rus' or World War II, as the basis for independent nationhood—or continued political allegiance with Russia—obfuscates the real fracture in Ukrainian society, which is attitudes toward power and authority. Some people use the shorthand phrase "*sovok* thinking," a derogatory term that refers to submissive attitudes toward power that fosters passivity. *Sovok* thinking is grounded in a circular form of reasoning that stymies agency (Wanner 2016, 214). It trades on the assumption that people with power are good because they have power. It views power as an inherently positive force and as a force external to oneself, which insulates powerful people from criticism and challenge and ultimately reinforces their power. Simultaneously, it cultivates a disinclination to struggle and take responsibility, which perpetuates a "wait-to-receive" disposition.

During the Maidan, critics of Soviet-era *sovok* thinking advocated "self-organization" (*samoorhanizatsiia* in Ukrainian), or initiating action and taking responsibility for those actions, as a way forward in response to passivity as a lingering legacy of Soviet lifeworlds. Moral leaders, such as Mykhailo Dymyd, a UGCC priest and active participant in the Maidan, argued for an "internal Maidan" to encourage personal responsibility for one's actions. Myroslav Marynovych, a Soviet-era dissident and rector of the Ukrainian Catholic University, suggested self-organization as a first meaningful step toward political transformation. As a way forward out of the zero-sum, lose-lose, political strategy of Russian President Vladimir Putin to keep Ukraine in Russia's orbit, Marynovych proposed multiplying the grassroots self-organization, which was on display during the Maidan, in all its forms as a strategy for change that was available to all (2019).

## The Winter That Changed Us

To illustrate the sweep of change that this historical event produced, I contrast how several people I have known for quite some time saw themselves and their life prospects before the Maidan and after. Their altered self-perceptions and changes to everyday life are broadly representative of shifts that many people experienced. I met Luda in 1991, the summer of the year the USSR collapsed, and have kept in touch with her. Her grandfather settled in Kyiv from St. Petersburg in the late nineteenth century. Her extended family had been Russian speaking and Russian in orientation. Her father was a scientist and member of the Communist Party. Following in his footsteps, she and her brothers became engineers and members of the technical intelligentsia. She worked at a closed "box," meaning an institute that developed politically sensitive material for the military. In the post-Soviet period, she worked with her brothers in a small firm they founded, making scientific instrumentation. Before the Maidan, they exclusively exported their products to Russia. Now they export anywhere, but not to Russia. Although she never had any intention of leaving Kyiv, the city of her birth, after the fall of the USSR, she was dubious as to whether Ukraine could make it as an independent state without Russia. Her travels to visit relatives who emigrated to the United States and Europe gave her some perspective as to the long, steep climb Ukraine had before it could be considered a European country. She no longer speaks to these relatives because they fail to understand the relevance of the Maidan and the betrayal annexation and war constitute. Unlike them, she is no longer Russian oriented, and this now strains conversations.

The jarring comparisons of life in the West with her daily difficulties fueled her dedication to following Ukrainian politics. Luda had been a strong supporter of the Orange Revolution and of Viktor Yushchenko and later Yulia Tymoshenko. She was seventy-two years old when on November 21, 2013, her daughter saw a Facebook posting, calling people to the Maidan and urging them to "Dress warmly, bring umbrellas, tea, coffee, good mood and friends." From the first day, Luda and her daughter participated in the protests. Although she continued to work, she came to the Maidan most evenings and weekends to join the protests.

She was impressed to see so many people react the way she did. Empathy is the capacity to place oneself in another's shoes and imagine their frame of reference to co-feel along with them. On the Maidan the dynamic was different. Luda recognized that she was wearing the same shoes as others. There was little need to imagine their perspectives, motivations, and values. Without articulation, she understood that they shared similar frames of reference, which they were all simultaneously using to come to the same conclusion: it is not possible to go on like this. These feelings of connection, of seeing "the other in oneself as a potential 'I,'" were empowering (Akhutin and Berlyand 2016, 251). Luda referred to the protesters as the "crème de la crème of Ukrainian society." Eventually, her whole four-generation family joined her on the Maidan. She was there for the most momentous and some of the most violent episodes of the protests.

We agreed to meet to speak about her experiences on the Maidan in May 2014. When a small car with Ukrainian flags flying out the windows pulled up, I knew it was her. On her balcony and even on the top of her building, as well as that of her relatives in Kyiv, she hung other *zhovto-blakytnyi* (yellow and blue) Ukrainian state flags. Her thinking had evolved from the 1990s when she condemned Ukraine as a *boloto*, or swamp, and the Ukrainian language as useless. Now she self-declares as a "Ukrainian patriot." Although the family language remains Russian, after the Maidan, she wanted her great-grandchildren to be the first generation exclusively educated in Ukrainian and for them to be baptized. The Maidan was pivotal to her change of heart and change of self-perception. She speaks Ukrainian reluctantly but has a perfect understanding of the language. She realized that she had been led to think of herself as Russian by Soviet-era political manipulation that posited Russian as the most prestigious nationality. She is no longer Russian, but she does not see herself as ethnically Ukrainian either. Rather, she has become a Ukrainian patriot, an engaged citizen of Ukraine, and, as a lifetime resident of Kyiv, this is where she belongs.

Anna is another person whose self-perceptions, dreams, and ambitions radically changed as a result of the Maidan. She was born in Western Ukraine and later moved to Eastern Ukraine. Her work brought her into contact with Americans, and this led to several stays in the United States. She grew fed up with life in Ukraine and in 2012 began actively searching for possibilities to immigrate. She and her husband sold their home and moved to Kyiv one year before the war broke out. Later, other family members would all be forced to flee the Donbas. For someone who was so pessimistic about the prospects of life in Ukraine, I was surprised in May 2014 when she no longer had any desire to leave Ukraine. She said with a warm smile, "I love my people. I have just grown to love my people so much. This is where I am from, and I want to stay here among them." These proclamations of love and loyalty replaced earlier pessimistic predictions of Ukraine's bleak future thanks to the genie of corruption, which she had decided was impossible to put back into the bottle. Yet, just when job prospects were bleakest, instability greatest, and when the realities of daily life were very difficult, Anna reaffirmed her commitment to stay in Ukraine and abandoned plans to immigrate.

For others, feelings of solidarity became feelings of attachment that became so strong they had to be formally acknowledged. For example, Ukrainian women, whose last names had been Russified to reflect gender, changed them back to their gender-neutral Ukrainian form (from Bohdana to Bohdan).[9] Others began to use the Ukrainian version of their first name (from Mikhail to Mykhailo). A Russian speaker and resident of Kyiv, who previously saw himself as a "conscious and convinced cosmopolitan," decided to change his citizenship. Realizing that citizenship is based on the capriciousness of birthplace and could be remade by a conscious choice of allegiance, he explains why he acquired Ukrainian citizenship:

> Patriotism for me has always been associated with sayings like "patriotism is a villain's refuge" and the ominous sounding, "we'll teach you to love your country." I never knew how to love a state or even a coun-

try. Although since childhood, and to this day, I have loved Kiev. The city of my childhood was never Ukrainian, Russian, or Soviet for me, but just the city, infinitely loved and best in the world. But the country itself has always seemed abstract and relevant to me only in the sense of formal citizenship. In the winter, however, watching the events on the Maidan, I suddenly saw a nation born, a nation to which I would like to belong! A country is being born that I can love! Not by right of blood, soil, or formal affiliation, but on the basis of a common cause. The fight of the Maidan protesters in the winter and the struggle of Ukraine's battle against Russia in the spring and summer was for me the struggle for human dignity against imperial tyranny. (Akhutin and Berlyand 2016, 245)

Prior to the Maidan, he was a Russian-speaking, Russian citizen, and long-time ethnic Russian resident of Kyiv. Seeing the protests in terms of "dignity" versus "imperial tyranny" prompted feelings of "guilt and shame," and this motivated him to formally renounce his Russian citizenship. Anna reoriented her professional life to Kyiv and renounced plans to immigrate. Luda's experiences on the Maidan prompted her to no longer think of herself as culturally Russian but as a politically engaged Ukrainian patriot. Each was enduringly transformed by their participation on the Maidan.[10] What did they experience that caused them to see themselves, their lifeworlds, and their place in Ukrainian society so differently? Volodymyr Kulyk describes this phenomenon as "bottom up de-Russification" (2018, 121), a process of national reformation that does not stem from a rejection of the Russian language and cultural history per se so much as it does from disdain for the Russian state and its policies. National identity, religious affiliation, and language choice are dependent on the way people perceive them at a given time and place. During a historic event, such as the Maidan, perceptions can change quickly, allowing people to shift inclinations and orientations and move rapidly among the continuum of possibilities. Let us now consider how the Maidan began as an extraordinary event that came to permeate the very ordinary.

## The Spark of Protest

A journalist born in Afghanistan and raised in Ukraine, Mustafa Nayyem, made a Facebook post on November 21, 2013, that set in motion consequences that continue to test global geopolitical alliances even years later as I write. He wrote, "Come on, guys, let's be serious. If you really want to do something, don't just 'like' this post. Write that you are ready, and we can try to start something.'"

An hour later, he posted again: "Let's meet at 10:30 p.m. near the monument to independence in the middle of Maidan."[11] That evening hundreds of Ukrainians assembled on the square, including Luda and her daughter. They were soon joined by thousands more. Although other people also called for demonstrations, the dominant narrative credits Nayyem's post with sparking the Maidan.

The next day, faculty, students, and administrators from the Ukrainian Catholic University in Lviv issued a formal condemnation of the government's decision. Other statements quickly followed from Patriarch Filaret of the Ukrainian Orthodox Church-Kyiv Patriarchate, the Ukrainian Greek Catholic Church, Roman Catholic Church as well as the All-Ukrainian Council of Churches and Religious Organizations. This was the first of numerous condemnatory statements issued by a broad spectrum of religious organizations that essentially spoke in a single voice.[12]

Within three days, there were not only 50,000–60,000 protesters assembled in Kyiv, but other rallies forming in Lviv, Odesa, Dnipro, Kharkiv, and other smaller cities (see figure 3.1).[13] With every passing day, more and more outraged citizens unequivocally condemned Yanukovych's decision to not sign the European Union Association Agreement. The initial slogan was "For a European Ukraine." There were many reasons why the reaction was so sharp and so swift. Most Ukrainians felt widespread disgust for their governing authorities, which garnered approval ratings in the single digits. People accused political leaders of ruling the country according to the principle of "Everything to friends, the law to enemies," which gave government officials free rein to "appropriate" as much as they could while using "administrative resources" to punish or block their competitors from doing the same. The authorities were accused of being "communist tyrants" or "oligarchic kleptocrats," who rule the country in a "raiders' grab of power" and where "underworld laws" and "cruel and cynical anti-rules prevail." One of the sources of discontent was income inequality. To give a sense of the economic imbalance in the country at that time, the fifty richest men in Ukraine had assets equal to almost half the country's GDP. Even Russia compared favorably with the fifty richest men holding only 20 percent of GDP; 10 percent in the United States (Karácsonyi et al. 2014).

The most resented governing practices were the casual disregard for the rule of law, the fee-for-service approach to dispensing justice, and the abuse of police power. This combination prompted businesses to hire thugs (*gopniki* in Russian and Ukrainian) to assure their own security and settle conflicts when agreements were not honored. The reliance on privatized violence only intensified feelings of precarity and the habit of circumventing judicial structures (Dudchenko 2014, 429). Growing numbers, especially in Western Ukraine, felt they had no choice but to migrate to Spain, Portugal, Italy, or Poland to work in health

**FIGURE 3.1.**  One of the earlier religious themed shrines on the Maidan.
Photo by Tania Mychajlyshyn-D'Avignon.

care, construction, or cleaning. Estimates of the number of migrant workers fluctuate between one and seven million because so many are illegal. The acute need to leave the country to earn a living was so widespread that Ivashchenko called the Maidan a "movement of dispossessed workers" (2014).

On the other end of the economic spectrum, some oligarchs were also primed to protest. Poroshenko, the so-called chocolate king, in recognition of his successful confectionary business, was shrewd in forging alliances and articulating his political preferences in a flexible, nonabrasive way. He served in the administrations of two former presidents who were (and remain) archenemies, Viktor Yushchenko and Viktor Yanukovych. Poroshenko was a member of Yushchenko's national security council, and later served in Yanukovych's cabinet as minister of trade. In addition to his sprawling candy company, among other things, Poroshenko owns a television station. During the Maidan protests, he suspended all programming and placed cameras around the Maidan and simply transmitted the happenings there 24/7. This Foucauldian panopticon not only protected the protesters; it allowed Ukrainian citizens and interested parties around the world, including me, to "be there" morning, noon, and night.[14]

## The Night the Doors Opened

The protests began as a civic initiative to advance an essentially neoliberal, nationalist agenda centered on European integration and opposition to Yanukovych. This was all to change. A student strike had been called on November 26, 2013. Some, having traveled to the capital from the provinces, were living on Independence Square in a tent encampment. The atmosphere at first was carnivalesque, even jubilant, with music, song, and spontaneous performances of all kinds. Television crews labeled it a "protestival." The early protests were decentralized, nonhierarchical, steadfastly nonviolent, and heavily reliant on social media to create a counter-discourse to what was reported on Russian television.

The machines of several political parties soon joined in: Batkivshchyna (Fatherland), led by jailed oligarch and former "gas princess" Yulia Tymoshenko; the Ukrainian Democratic Alliance for Reform (UDAR), led by the world heavyweight boxing champion Vitalii Klitschko; and the ultranationalist Svoboda (Freedom) party. The viability of the first two parties was heavily dependent on their charismatic leaders, who exemplify the personalization of authority and patronage networks that so ably feed insider corruption. Svoboda is the only one of the three with defined policy initiatives, many of which were nationalist, xenophobic, and anti-Semitic. Some media outlets, notably those in Russia, spun the narrative so that the ultra-nationalism of Svoboda was emblematic of the Maidan and its leaders, who were called Banderivtsi, or Banderites.[15]

Most Western observers anticipated the protests would go the way of the Occupy Wall Street movement in the United States. After Occupy protesters encountered bureaucratic inertia, over time they ran out of steam and petered out. The authorities' job morphed from stalling protester demands to simply removing unsightly demonstrators from public space. Indeed, the protests in Kyiv might not have evolved into a historical event had it not been for the state's resort to blunt legal and violent intimidation. Each coercive action only exacerbated tensions and propelled the radical hope that motivated more and more protesters to insist on durable change.

The first pivotal moment began in the early morning hours of November 30 when the Berkut attempted to forcibly remove the 300–400 activists on the Maidan with batons, stun grenades, and tear gas. The official explanation for the brutal eviction was that, given the impending holidays, the government needed to erect a Christmas tree on the Maidan. (It became known as the *yolka* carcass.) The use of violence against young people in the dead of night during a peaceful protest provoked outrage. Anger magnified when word spread that many members of the Berkut were shipped in from Eastern Ukraine, and even from Russia, a point that is difficult to confirm. Violent dispersal shifted the object of protest from Yanukovych's rebuke of European integration to dissatisfaction with his government.

Caught unaware, the protesters scrambled in the dark to escape the baton blows of the Berkut. Some appealed to the monks at nearby St. Michael's Monastery for shelter and protection. The newly reconstructed monastery was at that time under the jurisdiction of the Ukrainian Orthodox Church-Kyiv Patriarchate (UOC-KP). Faced with protesters pleading for safety, the monks opened the monastery doors and let them in. This act of protecting protesters against state forces amounted to complicity. By opening the door, after November 30 the UOC-KP, and religious institutions more broadly, were no longer neutral in this standoff. They had broken the historic pattern of church-state allegiance. This was the first of many instances in which this particular monastery would play a critical role in assisting the protesters. Myroslav Marynovych, a Soviet-era dissident, commented that, "One had the impression that a tremendous jolt had passed through society, which had shaken off yet another deceptive chain from the communist era. . . . even if just for a moment—[the church] found its true and legitimate place" (2015, 55). Marynovych characterizes this legitimate place as a "protector, a safe haven and a sanctuary, in short, what the church was meant to be for its people." The status of organized religion and the attitudes of believers and nonbelievers alike began to shift that very night.

The Ukrainian Deputy Prosecutor General Anatoliy Pryshko confirmed that seventy-nine people were injured during the raid, including some who required hospitalization. The protesters responded by taking over several government buildings on December 1, including the House of Unions and the City Hall, located near the epicenter of the protests, right on Khreshchatyk, the main artery of the city. The Presidential Administration Building was also attacked on

December 1. Members of the far-right Pravyi Sektor (Right Sector) were visible during these actions and were initially held responsible by Western and Russian media for the attack on the Presidential Administration Building. While not numerically significant, Pravyi Sektor is a disciplined, organized, ideologically unified group. They succeeded in mainstreaming their slogans, a call-and-response "*Slava Ukraini!*" (Glory to Ukraine!) followed by "*Herom Slava!*" (Glory to the Heroes!) by divorcing them from their association with Stepan Bandera's World War II-era controversial Organization of Ukrainian Nationalists. They became a signature rallying cry of the Maidan, and later of the war.

General strikes were called in Lviv, Ternopil, and Ivano-Frankivsk, and protests broke out in cities across Ukraine on December 1. From now on, Sundays were recast as a day of collective protest. A nascent social movement was beginning to take root that was searching for political registers to exploit and connections and alliances to cultivate. They found a willing and capable partner in religious organizations. From the moment the monks opened the door to the monastery, religious organizations crossed a threshold and entered into the fray.

Consider some of the widely held disparaging assessments of organized religion at the time to appreciate how momentous this change was. Anatolii Kaliuzhnii claimed that pharisaism, or the sheer arrogance and contempt with which some people treat others, is a serious problem in Ukraine. He charged that the church has taken on this pharisaism through its dependence on a corrupt and self-serving state and therefore had become one of the biggest stumbling blocks to reform (2014, 37). The author and journalist Ekaterina Shchetkina is even harsher in her characterization of the church as a "vinaigrette" made of "scorn and reverence, mysticism and superstition, business and faith, politics and again superstition."[16] She protested against the reconstruction of the St. Michael's Monastery before it was rebuilt in 1999 and all but rolled her eyes in derision when the "mystical and superstitious" among the protesters emphasized that the Maidan began on the Patron Saint Day of Kyiv's Archangel Michael. But within one week of the opening of the monastery doors, she said the church had become, what up until recently existed only as a possibility theoretically and rhetorically, namely, part of the society. "We are beginning to understand why, in fact, we trust them," she wrote on December 6, 2013. The clergy during the Orange Revolution, she asserted, often engaged in grandstanding. Now they are simply present and demonstrate "consistency" in their views on Euro-integration. In short, the opening of the monastery doors on November 30, 2013, was the first significant moment during the Maidan that softened the highly critical and dismissive attitudes toward organized religion held by these two and many other Just Orthodox.

# Pray for Ukraine!

Just as protesters walked through the open monastery doors, clergy began to walk out onto to square and condemn the use of force in biblical and religious terms. The Archbishop of the UGCC was one of the first to respond. He said, "We condemn the actions directed toward limiting civil rights, including the freedom of expression and the peaceful expression of the will of the citizens of Ukraine. We pray to the Almighty for unity, peace, justice and a victory of truth for our people" (Gordeev 2015, 79). Patriarch Filaret of the Ukrainian Orthodox Church made pleas for dialogue between the protesters and state officials on the same day. Viktor Tantsiura of the Union of Evangelical-Christians underlined the ruling elite's systematic violation of many of the Ten Commandments against killing, stealing, and perjury, and asserted the protesters exhibited "essentially biblical values" (Gordeev 2015, 89). Statements of support also came from religious leaders in the United States, Canada, Poland, as well as the Ecumenical Patriarch in Constantinople.

A stage with jumbotron screens on either side became a nave used for liturgies as easily as it was for a rock concert. It also became a pulpit from which politicians, clergy, and protesters alike expounded on the ills befalling Ukraine. Theologians from multiple confessions claimed that "the Church became part of the Maidan and the Maidan became part of the Church" (Dymyd 2014; see also Cherenkov 2014). On December 4, 2013, two weeks into the protests, Iroh Onyshkevych, a Greek Catholic priest, suggested that an interconfessional prayer tent be erected on the Maidan as a place to experience "calmness in the soul."[17] A *khram*, or small chapel, in the form of a tent with a cross on top was set up, replete with an altar, icons, and candles. The *khram* became an ecumenical site of prayer and services and was held up as a symbol of interfaith unity (Cherenkov 2014). A series of scheduled liturgies was held there along with scheduled times where clergy from different confessions would accept prayer requests. The UOC-MP was the only denomination that declined to sponsor services in the *khram*. Their clergy, however, participated in myriad ways, albeit without openly signaling their affiliation.

This initial *khram* inspired Oleh Mahdych, a pastor from the Protestant New Life Church, to organize an open-air prayer every evening in the center of the Maidan by the monument to Ukrainian independence, the archangel Berehynia.[18] These prayer sessions mirrored a traditional Eastern Christian response to a fall from grace by encouraging prayer and fasting, meaning abstaining from meat and dairy, as means to engender transformation. Such civic engagement on the part of Protestants ushered in two key developments. First, it moved Protestant groups far beyond their principle of "rendering unto Caesar what is Caesar's," which had long been used as a biblical justification to avoid confrontation with state authorities. Second, this began to change popular opinion of them.[19] Previously, Baptists and Pentecostals had been derided as "totalitarian sects" and criticized for "fanaticism" and betrayal of their national faith, views that would later be heard in the separatist regions of Eastern Ukraine, which have traditionally been a stronghold of Protestant communities in Ukraine. The ecumenical use of prayer came to symbolize the emergence of "one Ukrainian Church" that suddenly now included minority confessional groups and would later feed into such expressions as "Muslims of the Kyiv Patriarchate." An orientation of "unity through plurality" began to take root and redefine minority status by asserting that neither a single denomination, single language, nor a single historical narrative defines what it means to be Ukrainian (Portnov 2016, 216).

Vasyl Rudeyko reflects: "There were instances when Greek Catholics and Orthodox prayed together during the liturgy in a prayer tent. It seems to me that when our Churches hear about this now, they ignore it. . . . During Maidan people showed the absolute insignificance of church divisions and that such splits do not exist for them in reality. When Ukrainians stood up and started to fight evil, it was Christianity that became clearly visible. There were no Roman Catholics, Greek Catholics or Orthodox of different confessions. There were only Christians. This was clearly apparent and needs to be understood" (2016, 676–77). In fact, there were not only Christians but Jews, Muslims, and a wide variety of New Religious Movements as well. The emerging narrative of unity in plurality drew on the idea that Ukrainians were ecumenically inclined pious Christians. A Just Orthodox orientation began to go mainstream. Two weeks after the protests started, the extensive use of multiconfessional prayer, first in these ecumenical prayer tents, open prayer sessions, and in collective religious worship from the Maidan stage, is how the slogan "Pray for Ukraine!" took root.

# Looking Back to the Future, Looking Ahead to the Past

An archivist told me that she went every day during the Maidan to her workplace because she was afraid raiders would either pillage her collections or destroy documents. On December 8, 2013, while traveling as usual in the metro, she suddenly realized that everyone was going to the same place. She vividly described the sensations she experienced when she realized that everyone, in silence, with resolve, was going to the Maidan. Seeing everyone exit a packed metro car, all at the same station, all with the same purpose, is seared in her memory. On this day, in an effort to move forward, the past was made not only usable but even inspirational. The Narodne Viche, or People's Assembly, is a town hall-like tradition to discuss the people's business that dates to Kyivan Rus'. It came to life again on December 8, 2013. Such huge crowds turned out for the first Narodne Viche that this particular Sunday was proclaimed a "March of a Million."

This day also marked the beginning of the "Leninfalls" (*Leninopad*), a movement to topple Lenin statues, which would later inspire the 2015 official policy of decommunization to remove official Soviet symbolism from public space (Gaidai 2021). The Leninfalls began near the Bessarabian Market. With television cameras rolling, the police stood by as protesters chiseled away at one of the last Lenin monuments left in the heart of Kyiv until it unceremoniously fell to the ground. Although the political party Svoboda took credit for the spectacle, others chalked up this, and the other popularly initiated Leninfalls that followed across the country, to Pravyi Sektor. Ukraine had the greatest density of Lenin monuments of all republics in the USSR, numbering over 5,500. Numerically, there were only more Lenin monuments in Soviet Russia. Even the massive Lenin monument on Kharkiv's central Freedom Square came down on September 28, 2014. By 2017, there was not a single Lenin monument left standing in Ukraine. The greatest number were toppled right after the violence on the Maidan, from February 21–23, 2014, before legislation was even passed, which means that they were illegally dismantled.

Although city authorities closed the metro stations in the center of the city to stem the flow of people to the Maidan, it was to no avail. Taxi drivers and ordinary citizens formed the Auto-Maidan and ferried people to the protests. Increasingly desperate, the government cut power to the buildings held by protesters. The anxiety of government officials was not matched on the ground. Julia Orlova described the atmosphere on December 10, 2013, as "summer sunshine." That day she had gone to the pharmacy to buy some medicine, and the saleswoman asked, "Are you going there?" Upon hearing yes, the saleswoman gave her additional medicine and bandages. The same thing happened at the bakery. She received two extra loaves of bread to bring to the protesters (2014, 26–27). The next day, as Orlova was walking to the Maidan along Mykhailovskii Street near the monastery, the crowd in the street stood still and sang the national anthem "in one breath with their hands on their heart." She wrote in her journal that day, "Isn't this a united nation? Today we were one family in spite of all the differences in age, religion and social status . . . We are one nation, we are one family" (2014, 29). A series of such moments and the sensations of solidarity they triggered were key to reconfiguring the understandings of who was Ukrainian. It was becoming possible for anyone who cares about Ukraine and the people who live in it, even if they had previously declared themselves to be ethnic Russians, Russian citizens, or were planning to leave forever, to feel as if they belonged. These sensations of solidarity not only linked people to each other, but they formed the bedrock of attachments to the country. The Maidan—let alone the eventual violent crackdown against it and subsequent war—did more to advance nation-building than any politically engineered programs could have ever hoped to accomplish.

## Stand Up Kyiv!

The UGCC and the UOC-KP offered unqualified support for the protests, which they saw as an opportunity to create civil society based on religious and biblical values. During morning prayer on the Maidan on December 11, the US-born Borys Gudziak, at that time the bishop of the Ukrainian Greek Catholic Church for France, Switzerland, and the Benelux countries and former rector of the Ukrainian Catholic University in Lviv, reaffirmed the protesters' actions as an exercise of civil rights and directly addressed the Berkut riot police. "Guys, listen to me, don't bring sin to your soul. Think about what you will tell your children and grandchildren. There is nothing worse than a brother killing a brother, nothing worse than Cain's sin," he said.[20] The Biblical reference reflected the very real possibility of civil strife erupting among "brothers," despite Yanukovych's assurances that he would only use nonviolent means, such as roundtable discussions with former presidents and clergy, to end the protests.

Kyiv Patriarch Filaret (Denysenko) of the Ukrainian Orthodox Church also attempted to stem the escalating tensions by saying, "The use of force to restrict the constitutional rights of citizens to exercise their right to freedom of peaceful assembly and expression is unacceptable and this is why the entire world has become our witness to the events of these nights. The existing political and social crisis cannot be solved by force. It will only lead to increased tensions. The consequences of violent actions will only lead to a radicalization of the protests and the slipping of our state into a full-scale civil conflict."[21]

As temperatures fell to minus 13 degrees Celsius the night of December 11, 2013, the police were ordered to remove barricades around the tent city, but not the tents themselves. Barricades, made of loose wood, park benches, trash, and other found objects, protected the self-defense units, as the protesters living in the tent encampment were now called, who, in turn, guarded City Hall, which the protesters held. At the time, protesters numbered around 15,000. Once again, St. Michael's Monastery played a key role. As the Berkut was moving in, for the first time in 800 years, the Cathedral bells rang out in alarm and continued to ring all night long. The last time this happened was during a Mongol invasion in 1240. Almost all confessional groups issued formal statements of condemnation. The spectrum of religious organizations that now reliably participated in protest widened to include various Jewish, Muslim, and Roman Catholic groups. Although each represents less than 1 percent of the population, they all have extensive networks of coreligionists abroad, including Israel and Poland, where large numbers of former Ukrainian citizens and Ukrainian migrants live. Such public, anti-state, clerical civic engagement on the part of religious minorities was new.

The Ukrainian Orthodox Church-Moscow Patriarchate was in an increasingly difficult situation after the latest round of violence on December 11. Yanukovych's government and the ROC pressured the UOC-MP to exhibit restraint. Some UOC-MP clergy were protesting on the Maidan, but they had to do so as private individuals, without any clerical insignia. Russian media and the Russian Orthodox Church labeled the protesters fascists, *zapadentsi* (a pejorative term for Western Ukrainians), and *Banderovtsi* (Banderites, after Stepan Bandera). Although Metropolitan Onufryi, the head of the UOC-MP, publicly called for the ROC to refrain from using such language, some UOC-MP clergy were quite vocal in their condemnation of the growing political disorder (*smuta* in Russian). For example, on December 12, 2013, during a sermon Metropolitan Agafangel (Savvin) of the UOC-MP Odesa eparchy claimed that on the Maidan, "the forces of hell are gathering with the goal of changing our system by creating angry mobs, hate and separation of our peoples."[22] His statement reflects a growing recognition that the Slavic brotherhood united under the ROC, including the UOC-MP, was under strain.

# Promoting the Allure of the Russian World

As tensions mounted, the Russian Orthodox Church encouraged its spokesmen in Ukraine to discuss the Russian World (*russkii mir* in Russian) doctrine. In 2007 Putin created the Russian World Foundation to promote Russian culture and heritage abroad. Initially, it sought to unify Russian speakers as "compatriots abroad" (*sootechestvenniki za rubezhom* in Russian) into a self-identifying cultural group. The political concept recalls Iosip Brodsky's famous assertion, "*Moia rodina russkii iazyk*" (My homeland is the Russian language). The Russian World was meant to capitalize on the emotional attachment a person might have to their native language and by extension to the ability of language to inform identities and political loyalties. The goal was to parlay a sense of Russianness that the Russian World would create or reaffirm into pro-Russian political influence abroad. As a project of linguistic-cultural promotion, the Russian World offered ominous

assurances of protection by the Russian state should a host country discrimi-
nate against Russian speakers.[23] Mikhail Suslov argues that the Russian World
concept is ultimately a means for the Russian state to justify the right to an ex-
clusive sphere of influence and privileged interests in the territories of the former Soviet Union as a means to "make sense of post-imperial debris and to
contemplate an alternative Russia" (2018, 333, 335). For a variety of reasons, the
allure of linguistic loyalty proved fickle (Suslov 2016; Laruelle 2015). Rapidly
evolving circumstances and the fluidity of loyalties forced the Russian World
Foundation over time to shift its priorities and strategies.

After the enthronement of Patriarch Kirill (Gundiaev) in 2009 and Putin's
return to the presidency in 2012, the Russian World evolved into a civilizational
justification for Slavic unity that drew on historical legacies. It became an instrument to advance geopolitical ambitions in the near abroad by positing that
the Russian Orthodox Church was the embodiment of the True Christian values of Holy Rus'. The mission to defend God-given attributes (gender, national,
confessional) against the encroachment of Western liberal values that allow for
choice in violation of God's will became the calling card of the Russian World.
The Russian World concept increasingly traded on anti-Western, conservative,
even militarized values that rested on the assumption that religious values could
equate to political values. I have argued that the support for the Maidan drew
on a shared vision of a better future. The Russian World ceased to imply a
forward-looking project of reform and began to mythologize different periods
of Russian history (Suslov 2018, 344).[24]

Some UOC-MP clergy decried the "Eurosodomites" and the pro-homosexual
"Gay-ropa" agenda that comes with the European Union and its wealth (Stoekl
2020). Others blessed the Berkut and encouraged them to fight to the death
against the "obscurantists" (*mrakobesy* in Russian), meaning the Maidan protesters. Yet, when asked to endorse an appeal for European integration, only two
leaders of the eparchies of UOC-MP refused to sign. Many rank-and-file UOC-
MP clergy supported a "rapprochement with Christian Europe" and genuinely
objected to the Yanukovych regime's casual disregard for the law and the extent
of corruption.[25]

The primary concern of the UOC-MP was expressed by Metropolitan Ant-
onyi (Pakanych), who cautioned on December 5 that the splintering of the Ukrainian state is to be avoided at all costs (2014, 244–46). He asserted that the
church should be a site where people of all political views can find a place for
themselves and should not be an actor in political agitation and struggle. Individuals should express their political views outside the church, not within its
walls. If an individual wants to see political change in the country and turns to
the church for counsel, as it always has, the church will encourage believers to

fast and pray to deliver inner purification and contemplative self-awareness. The Metropolitan stressed that positive change in the world starts with individuals working on their soul as a means of moral self-fashioning (*rabotat' nad svoei dushoi* in Russian). Transformation begins on the individual level and is achieved in quiet, contemplative acts, with the church as an intermediary and facilitator of dialogue between an individual and God. This advocacy of the continued privatization of religion and turning away from a fallen world and praying for redemption with the church as intermediary placed the church in a derivative position, as serving the needs of individuals or the state, but not as an independent actor in civil society. Such a position was increasingly in stark contrast to the vigorous and visible engagement of other religious organizations to solve social and political problems.

## Simulacrum

Amid such debate on the social and political role of religious institutions and the turmoil of the moment, Archimandrite Cyril (Hovorun), a UOC-MP theologian and fellow at Yale University when the Maidan began, penned a statement in Ukrainian on December 12, 2013. He translated it himself into English and had it translated into Russian.[26] I remember receiving this trilingual treatise via email from an unknown sender and being riveted by it. The insight and urgency with which Hovorun offered his interpretation of the meaning of the Maidan—when it was just three weeks old—instantly struck me as honest and spot on. He made the stunning assertion that it was "already clear that the Maidan, regardless of its future, has changed the country, the society, as well as the relations between the Ukrainian churches and the Ukrainian society."

Although it was high time, he noted, that this sea change in church-state relations came about, the church was finally severing the servile and appeasing posture it has historically had toward state authorities in favor of serving the community (*spil'nota* in Ukrainian). This recalls the submissive-to-power "*sovok* thinking" I referred to earlier. Hovorun saw the Maidan as an opportunity for the church to remake its relationship with the state and with its own believers by exchanging its bilateral relationship with the state with one that foregrounds the church's commitment to serving the community. To move forward, he reached back to the past and recalled the examples of Eastern Christian saints, such as Fr. John Chrysostom and the Archbishop of Constantinople, who criticized the abuse of power within the church and within the Roman Empire. Hovorun asserted that the example of these Orthodox leaders should caution against calls for biblically justified allegiances to state power. The Soviet state kept the church contained in a "ghetto," beholden and dependent on the state to legitimate and facilitate its existence. Disengaging from the state is especially imperative now, Hovorun argued, because "the present Ukrainian regime is not Christian." Its Christianity is a mere "simulacrum . . . (with) no Christian morality in it," he flatly stated. The charge of simulacrum was particularly poignant.

After this indictment, Hovorun made a second point with galvanizing implications: the people have taken on the mission of the church by demonstrating that dignity can be restored. Hovorun saw this moment as an opportunity for the church to recover its original, God-given mission of serving humanity. In his view, the church should follow the lead of the protesters and "reach for the moral heights of the Maidan" by forging an alliance with the people, over the state, to promote the Christian values that unite them. These values include "dignity, honesty, non-violence, solidarity and readiness for self-sacrifice." In sum, his harsh assessment of the regime and the church's blind allegiance to it was as fierce as his appreciation was heartfelt for the Maidan protesters' quest for change. Perhaps most important of all, like the Crow chieftain, just as violence was looming, Hovorun offered a path out of the growing impasse. The way forward, he said, is a Maidan every day. If radical hope for a better life had ignited the Maidan protests, whose end point was unknown, acting on shared values to bear witness every day that a human being deserves to live in dignity is the way forward.

Hovorun's statement was highly influential. Over time, some clergy began to allude to their participation in the Maidan as culminating in "Maidan theology," or a new kind of "political theology," in recognition of the new public role for religion that was emerging. No longer the "handmaiden of the state," religious institutions were becoming actors who took the pursuit of social justice seriously by standing with those in need against the powerful (Cherenkov 2014; Dymyd 2014; Hovorun 2017, 2018; Krawchuk and Bremer 2016). The momentum had started for this extraordinary event to begin remaking ordinary, everyday life.

## Dignity as a Theo-Political Concept

Dignity became the primary orienting concept for the sweeping initiatives to self-organize an internal Maidan and a Maidan on the main square every day. Dignity figures prominently in Orthodox and Catholic confessional traditions and provided a framework for nonviolent opposition. Dignity is neither a purely theological nor an exclusively secular, legal concept, but it is foundational in both ecclesiastical and legal domains.[27] Dignity evolved over the course of the modern period as understandings of virtue shifted from feudal notions of honor to citizen dignity (Taylor 1994, 27). Whereas honor involves safeguarding one's honor by prescribing certain actions and reactions to do so (such as honor killings), dignity manifests itself by respecting the dignity of others. As a political principle, dignity draws on Kantian ideas of the human capacity for moral action, which is what gives humans their intrinsic worth. Kant argued that every human being was worthy of "world citizenship," which would deliver respect and recourse for justice whenever basic rights were violated (Kant [1795] 1983). Hierarchies of rank that previously generated automatic power and deference gave way in some places to a recognition of universal equality among citizens of a particular state, making dignity an achieved status, albeit a fragile one.

A theory of human rights developed from Kant's understanding of dignity (*würde*) as a metaphysical property and moral value (Barilan 2012, 82–83). This stimulated a reimagining of the moral order and the secular, sovereign, and scientific institutional dimensions to protect dignity. The abolition of slavery in the French Empire in 1848 was justified by assertions that slavery was an affront to the dignity of the slave as well as the to the slaveholder.[28] Pierre-Joseph Proudhon, the French philosopher and socialist, insisted that the capacity to feel the dignity of others motivates behavior and underpins the realization of justice. The International Labour Organization, created in 1919, sought dignified working conditions to advance socioeconomic justice. Coal miners in Donbas protested for better working conditions in the 1990s by insisting on the "dignity of labor" (Siegelbaum 1997). On a political level, four states in the first half of the twentieth century, Mexico, Cuba, Finland, and Ireland, included in the preamble of their constitutions the state's responsibility to ensure the dignity of their citizens.

World War II provided a formidable catalyst for rethinking the ethics of power. The ravages of the war, and especially the Holocaust, prompted a reconsideration of the means and modes of intervention to ensure human dignity. The will to establish internationally recognized political mechanisms to protect the universality of human rights culminated in the UN Declaration of Human Rights in 1948.[29] The resulting commission included a self-referential assertion of the existence of human dignity and a mandate to protect it, which has since been used to inspire political interventions in a number of domains, such as global public health issues, correctives to the excesses of global capitalism, and to legitimize or condemn military action. The impetus in Ukraine in 2013–14 was similar: to harness the power of multinational organizations, such as the EU, as was done in the postwar period with the UN, to ensure the protection of individual rights, human dignity, and the rule of law.[30]

The Roman Catholic Church has long had a voice in debates over the relationship of dignity to moral law and has great influence in the UGCC as most of its priests, when possible, study in Rome. Pope Paul VI's address to the United

Nations on October 4, 1965, *Dignitatis Humanae*, stressed the consonance and overlapping interests of the Roman Catholic Church and the United Nations concerning responsibilities for human dignity by asserting a certain division of labor. The church upholds the dignity of the souls of the faithful, and the UN does the same for member states, with both maintaining dignity as an absolute feature of human life (Bennett 2015 280–81). In addition to encouraging political modes of intervention to achieve dignity, the Catholic Church asserted the ethical and moral obligation of believers to actively do the same. Most important, the church reframed the commitment to freedom of conscience to be a matter of human dignity. It proclaims not just the right of Catholics but of all persons to follow their faith or to have no faith at all. In addition to encouraging political modes of intervention to achieve dignity, the Catholic Church asserted the ethical and moral obligation of individual believers to actively do the same.[31]

These measures only increased the Soviet state's antipathy to the Roman Catholic Church. In 1946 Stalin outlawed the UGCC over fears of Vatican meddling in Catholic communities in the newly annexed territories to Soviet Ukraine (Bociurkiw 1996; Plokhii 2010). This made the UGCC with its five million believers the largest confession to have been outlawed throughout the Cold War period. Caught between the Austro-Hungarian and Russian empires, the UGCC never had a collaborative, cooperative relationship with state authorities. Much like the Roman Catholic Church in Poland, it remained a formidable foe of state power in the postwar period. The UGCC became a key proponent of Catholic interpretations of dignity in Ukraine.

Since the collapse of the USSR, the Orthodox Church has also made significant pronouncements regarding human dignity based on the principle of *Lik Bozhii* (*Imago Dei*), or the belief that humans were created in the image of God. Orthodox theology draws on the idea that the church is a salvific institution whose mission is to restore a fallen world. The 2008 *Russian Orthodox Church's Basic Teaching on Human Dignity, Freedom and Rights* acknowledged that "human rights theory is based on human dignity as its fundamental notion," and concludes by stressing "personal dignity implies the assertion of personal responsibility."[32] The Orthodox idea of dignity, rooted in moral purity and virtue, is spelled out in no uncertain terms,

> Clearly, the idea of responsibility is integral to the very notion of dignity. Therefore, in the Eastern Christian tradition the notion of 'dignity' has first of all a moral meaning, while the ideas of what is dignified and what is not are bound up with the moral or amoral actions of a person and with the inner state of his soul. Considering the state of

human nature darkened by sin, it is important that things dignified and
undignified should be clearly distinguished in the life of a person. . . .
God-given dignity is confirmed by a moral principle present in every
person and discerned in the voice of conscience.[33]

The section on dignity concludes by flatly stating in bold, "Thus there is a direct
link between human dignity and morality. Moreover, the acknowledgment of
personal dignity implies the assertion of personal responsibility." Other key Orthodox pronouncements from this document implore that "citizens of the
heavenly homeland, should not forget about their earthly homeland" and that
"Religious institutions have provided the support to keep a struggle for a dignified life alive."[34]

The decisions of the monks of St. Michael's Monastery of the UOC-KP to provide a safe haven for students after they were attacked by police, and later to allow
the monastery to become a hospital for the wounded and shelter for protesters,
were in keeping with Orthodox pronouncements on dignity. Still, when such
teachings are enacted quite literally, as the monks of the UOC-KP did, this placed
that church squarely on the side of the *narod*, or people, against the state. The
concept of dignity, with its theological, moral, and legal nuances, was reframed
on the Maidan as church and society engaged in common endeavors. The moral
community emerging on the Maidan, using dignity as a guiding principle for a
common vision of an ideal society, became an element in a collective identity in-
extricably linked with faith that was capable of overriding divisions based on socioeconomic backgrounds, political leanings, and confessional allegiances
(Horkusha 2014, 61–75; Nikolayenko 2020, 454; Yelensky 2014, 53–55).

The Maidan was not the only mass action where protesters responded to calls
to restore dignity. During the Arab Spring, which began in 2010, dignity was
also evoked, along with economic equity and the rule of law, during mass up-
risings in Egypt, Tunisia, Libya, and Turkey. In Tunisia the slogan of the protesters was "Dignity, Bread and Freedom!" reflecting a "collective feeling of a loss
of dignity" (Eyadat 2012, 14). The call to dignity proved to be a powerful moti-
vator of action in Egypt in 2011 as well as during the 1956 Suez Canal Crisis before it (El Bernoussi 2015). Nawara Najem, an Egyptian journalist who followed
the protests on Tahrir Square, said, "Why did the people not fear death? No one
knows. It was not only religion. It was not only poverty. It was not only despair.
Perhaps the answer is human dignity. No force, however tyrannical, is able to
deprive human beings of this."[35] Although the concept of dignity has religious
and legal underpinnings, it also has a certain universality. Repeated humiliation, deception, and betrayal offends an individual's sense of their own dignity,

leaving them with little to lose. When this combines with a certain type of atmosphere, as was the case on the Maidan, the fear dissipated rapidly and was replaced by radical hope, as the protests accelerated.

## Day of Dignity

It is difficult to pinpoint who used the concept of dignity in such a way that it came to characterize the Maidan as a Revolution of Dignity. However, on December 15, 2013, in addressing the crowd, Arseniy Yatsenyuk, one of the negotiators for the opposition, proclaimed this day a Day of Dignity (*Den' Hidnosti*). With crowds estimated at around 150,000, representatives of six confessional groups, the Ukrainian Orthodox Church-Moscow Patriarchate, Ukrainian Orthodox Church-Kyiv Patriarchate, Ukrainian Greek-Catholic Church, Ukrainian Autocephalous Orthodox Church, Roman Catholic Church, and the Protestant Union of Evangelical Christians, all prayed together on the Maidan for a peaceful solution to the problem of injustice and pledged to use ecumenism as a bulwark against authoritarianism and violence. This moment firmly established two things: the moral authority of the clergy as critics of state power and the growing alliance between the citizenry and religious institutions against the state (Shotkina 2014, 49). Many have argued that this day was definitive in shifting the goals of the protests from simply rejecting Yanukovych's political and economic agreements with the Russian Federation to a general resistance to the injustice committed by his regime (Gordeev 2015, 93–94).

Theo-political concepts, such as dignity, combined with historical mythology to inform how daily events were conceptualized. The tent camp on the Maidan became known as the *Sich* after the Cossack military encampments and brigades were called *sotni*. At a certain point, each *sotni* had a member of the clergy attached to it, who were called "Maidan chaplains." Many would go on to become military chaplains in the war effort later. Sundays became the *Narodne Viche*, or the day of People's Assembly, after the medieval Slavic tradition of public gatherings. On the third *Viche*, December 15, 2013, Okean Elzy, a popular band from Lviv, Western Ukraine, performed in a concert that opened with clergy reciting prayers. This concert was among the many moments that assured religion a powerful afterlife when the protests ended. Founded in 1994, Okean Elzy is led by singer Svyatoslav Vakarchuk, who would become a presidential candidate in 2019 against Petro Poroshenko. Vakarchuk introduced the performance by condemning the beating of innocent protesters and proclaiming, "from east to west of the country we are united around European integration . . . politics does not unite us but this one shared conviction does." Most poignantly, he offered, "Each Ukrainian answers for the country, for its constitution, which says quite clearly that all power belongs to the people." He then launched into the well-known song, "*Vstavai, moya myla*" (Rise, my dear!).[36] The audience, with cell phones illuminated in the night like candles, swayed to the music and began to sing back to him every other line in a coperformance of the well-known song. The band ended with reference to the Orange Revolution: "Together we are many" (*Razom nas bahato* in Ukrainian).

The atmosphere of the Day of Dignity concert was notable in several respects. There was a remarkable lack of fear among the spectators given the teeming crowds crammed into a concentrated urban space (Kaliuzhnii 2014, 34–37). Emile Durkheim coined the term "collective effervescence" to describe the energy and emotion unleashed during ritual (1995, 208–20). Ritual effervescence provides the "propulsion" to construct moral orders by sparking individual transformation via sensations experienced in a particular atmosphere, which can result in the creation of social cohesion as easily as "bloody barbarism."

Taking inspiration from Durkheim, Joel Robbins suggests that the experiences of collective effervescence reveal ideals, but it is effervescent performance that realizes them (Durkheim 1912 [1995], 215–16, [1924] 1974, 92; Robbins 2015, 222). Robbins asserts that "values produce collective effervescence as much as collective effervescence produces values." He justifies such a position by arguing that "subjects sometimes find themselves experiencing moments of happiness when they act in terms of a shared value, and they sometimes discover they are in the presence of a shared value when they feel such happiness" (Robbins 2015, 222). An atmosphere of effervescent energy and transcendence on the Maidan, and particularly during this concert, reaffirmed the radical hope that fostered a collective sense of possibility and promise. The affective atmosphere was such that people felt connected to one another, to the singers, and to a cause far larger themselves. This affective energy was generated by sensual stimuli that lifted people out of the concerns of their everyday lives and into an exceptional experience that connected them to something greater than themselves. A moment of sensing a presence and experiencing feelings of oneness and relatedness in the form of affective energy is central to those experiences being understood as religious, as we saw in the last chapter among those who visit places animated by prayer.

The significance of this concert is that it generated an atmosphere of "emotional energy," which Randall Collins describes as "a boldness in taking initiative . . . a morally suffused energy; it makes the individual feel not good, but exalted, with the sense of doing what is most important and most valuable" (2004, 39). Much like affect, this emotional energy is agentive and bundles feeling, thought, and action into a seamless flow (Collins 2004, 26). Individuals crave experiences of "emotional energy" and actively seek them out, which is why Collins speaks of "chains" of interactions (2004, 44; Robbins 2015, 225). Social media and YouTube gave this concert and its transcendent atmosphere eternal life. Postings and forwarded postings mean that people around the world vicariously experienced the atmosphere of this concert.

# From Mass Protest to Mass Uprising

Rankled by Greek-Catholic priests conducting open-air services, confessions, and collective prayer, Yanukovych began the New Year by threatening legal prosecution and possible repression of the UGCC. A recourse to Soviet-era tactics only invigorated the protests. There was so little confidence in the government that few feared the UGCC would be forcibly disbanded, as it had been in 1946 under Stalin. Rather, the reliance on discredited Soviet repressive methods to silence dissent was taken as a sign of just how desperate and unresourceful government leaders had become. Nonetheless, this was the prelude to a package of laws designed to curb civil liberties passed by parliament in less than one hour by a show of hands on January 16, 2014. This legislation paved the way for the establishment of a dictatorship by including new provisions restricting freedom of speech and assembly, a new law on extremism, and a law requiring Western-funded NGOs to register as foreign agents, as they are required to do in Russia. The new laws also banned wearing masks and prohibited the formation of a column of more than five cars, which specifically targeted the Auto-Maidan as a form of protest that crippled movement within and around the city. In response, the crowds swelled and demanded the restitution of the 2004 Constitution.

January 19 became another turning point. According to the Orthodox calendar, this is Epiphany, or "water baptism" (*Vodokhreshcha*), which along with Easter and Christmas constitute the three most important annual celebrations. Although Western Christianity celebrates Epiphany as the arrival of the *magi* (wise men) in Bethlehem to venerate Jesus twelve days after his birth, Eastern Christianity celebrates Epiphany as Christ's baptism in the River Jordan by John the Baptist. "Ice swimming," or breaking a hole in the ice and plunging three times into freezing waters in a simulation of baptism, has become a popular means of noting this important Orthodox holiday. Those inclined to interpret events in a religious idiom noted that as the confrontation on the Maidan grew ever-more tense, the protesters began to burn tires in self-defense. The opaque, billowing smoke from burning tires formed something of a shield protecting the protesters in addition to the barricades (see figures 3.2 and 3.3). This new tactic prompted the renaming of this day to "Baptism by Fire" (*Vohnekhreshcha* in

**FIGURE 3.2.** Barricades on the Maidan in late January 2014. Photo by Oksana Yurkova.

Ukrainian). Government forces used water cannons to drench the clothes of protesters in sub-zero temperatures to get them to move on. Epiphany in 2014 was marked by one side using baptism by fire and the other water baptism as weapons in a mounting political standoff.

Three days later, snipers killed the first causalities of the Maidan. The first victim was Sergii Nigoian, a twenty-year-old of Armenian origin from the Dnipro region, whose parents came to Ukraine from Azerbaijan after armed conflict broke out in the Nagorno-Karabakh region. The second was Mikhail Zhiznevskii, a Belarussian citizen who fled to Ukraine after he was persecuted for participation in anti-Lukashenka protests a decade earlier in Belarus. Yurii Verbytskyi, a geographer and seismologist from Lviv, was the third person to die on January 22, 2014. Twenty-four protests erupted in other cities. After these initial deaths, meetings on the Maidan were punctuated by violent skirmishes with the Berkut, primarily on Hrushevskyi Street. Clergy, clad in long black robes, wearing clerical headgear, and carrying large crosses to distinctly mark their status, began to form human shields to separate the protesters from the Berkut. By late January several of the protesters' demands were met. Prime minister Mykola Azarov resigned, and parliament repealed the antiprotest laws. An

**FIGURE 3.3.**    Protesters burned tires on the Maidan as protection from the Berkut Special Forces. Photo by Tania Mychajlyshyn-D'Avignon.

agreement was reached on February 14–16, whereby all 234 protesters arrested since December were released in exchange for no longer occupying the Kyiv City Hall, which protesters had held since December 1, 2013.

# Violence and the Beginning of the End

By February 18 it was becoming clear that government control was significantly slipping beyond Kyiv. In Lviv, Ternopil, and Ivano-Frankivsk in Western Ukraine and Poltava in Eastern Ukraine, people began to attack police stations, raid their arsenals, and occupy administrative buildings. Local police offered little resistance, not just because they thought challenging the protesters was futile, but because there was genuinely little support for the Yanukovych regime, which built its loyalty on networks of corruption and favoritism from which rank and file law enforcement officers were largely excluded. Beyond that, there were no ideological loyalties that the regime could use to encourage or coerce compliance. As government buildings fell under the control of protesters, members of Yanukovych's Party of Regions defected to opposition parties that threatened to reinstate the 2004 Constitution and give Parliament the power to call for Yanukovych's resignation.

On February 18 snipers were ordered to shoot to kill. St. Michael's Monastery went from a shelter to a morgue and hospital. Twenty-five people died that day, and the dead bodies were brought to the monastery. Over 800 were injured. At this point, not just St. Michael's Monastery but also the main Roman Catholic and Lutheran churches of Kyiv, both of which were near the Maidan, were also actively serving as hospitals, feeding centers, and shelters from the cold. A statement issued by the Council of Churches the next day criticized the use of force which took another eight lives. The prayer tent, IT tent, and other temporary structures the protesters had built were set on fire and destroyed. The corridor separating protesters and the Berkut was growing thinner by the hour, and the barricade was no higher than one meter. Opposition leaders tried to convince the crowds that compromise was necessary and preferable to, as the Crow chieftain said, fighting an unwinnable war. Although the government offered elections in December, the reinstatement of the 2004 constitution immediately, and police withdrawal, the crowd would not have it. Yanukovych responded to the stalemate by ordering the square cleared in the early morning hours of February 20, 2014. Snipers opened fire from surrounding rooftops, killing eighty-eight people within forty-eight hours (Fylypovych 2014, 19).

Worldwide condemnation was swift, but the anger of Ukrainians was harsher still. Surrounded by coffins under piles of flower bouquets, candles, and thousands of highly emotional mourners, on the evening of February 21, Volodymyr Parasiuk, a twenty-six-year-old from Lviv took the microphone and demanded Yanukovych's resignation by the next morning. If not, he threatened the protesters would overtake more government buildings, a demand that was met with bellowing cheers from the crowd. Footage at Mezhyhirya, Yanukovych's private residence, shows him packing his bags as early as February 19. He left during the night of February 22 for the safety of Russia.

From this moment, events surged at lightning speed. Tymoshenko, a former prime minister and oligarch, was freed from prison, where she had been since October 2011. She traveled directly to the Maidan and, from her wheelchair, made an emotional appearance, further stirring the crowds. Even though Yanukovych later declared his departure a coup d'état, which would still make him the legitimate president of Ukraine, a parliamentary vote of 317 out of 331 declared him removed from office. A new election was set for May 25, 2014. An interim government formed, headed by a former member of parliament, Arseniy Yatsenyuk, a Baptist who preached lively sermons in his local Kyiv congregation. The new government had four members from Svoboda in its cabinet, including Tetiana Chornovil, an investigative journalist and leading Maidan activist, who led the National Corruption Committee.

The protesters seized Yanukovych's personal residence and opened it to the public as a "Museum of Corruption." Even for people accustomed to the lavish lifestyle and decadent, narcissistic consumption of their leaders, the tours of Yanukovych's residence were eye-opening. Exuberant materialism in the form of a petting zoo, a collection of foreign cars, a restaurant within a ship docked along his riverfront property, and other such indulgences left no doubt about the level of pathological, excessive consumption. Unrestrained accumulation and garish display of tsarist-like aristocratic decor illustrate the extent to which oligarchs like Yanukovych were removed from the impoverished daily lives of average citizens.

## "We have no time even to be astonished"

When socialist regimes began to collapse in Eastern Europe in 1989, Vaclav Havel, the Czech playwright and leader in the Velvet Revolution that brought down the Czechoslovakian communist regime, memorably proclaimed, "We have no time even to be astonished." The same was true in the aftermath of the Maidan. The waves of change crashed onshore with the force of tsunamis. Amid the shock over the shooting on February 20, 2014, the UOC-KP called on the UOC-MP and UAOC to unite as part of a prolonged campaign to "securitize" religion.[37] Serious discussions to form an independent Ukrainian church as a bulwark against the Russian World and other forms of Russian presence and influence in Ukraine had barely begun in earnest, when on February 27 a Russian flag was hoisted on the parliament building of Crimea and "little green men" arrived. That is how Ukrainians referred to the military men in unmarked uniforms who became a formidable presence on the streets of the Crimean Peninsula.[38]

From there, events escalated dramatically. Putin asserted his moral obligation to defend compatriots (*sootechestvenniki* in Russian) against suffering in Novorossiia, a region in southeastern Ukraine seized from the Ottoman Empire in the late eighteenth century and incorporated into the Russian Empire. Putin cited Article 61 of the Russian Constitution, which states that "the Russian Federation shall guarantee its citizens protection and patronage abroad," and the internationally recognized "Responsibility to Protect" norm as the legal justifications for doing so.

In short order, Crimea was annexed to Russia via a referendum in March 2014, and a new border was established to prove it. The transfer of the peninsula back to Russia was justified by the fact that Crimea became part of Ukraine only in 1954, an argument that held little sway with Ukrainians. Several regions in Western Ukraine were also only incorporated into Soviet Ukraine some years prior

(Volyn 1939; Bukovyna 1940; and Transcarpathia in 1945). Moreover, after 1954, many Ukrainians from Central Ukraine relocated to Crimea to work in sovkhozy, or Soviet collective farms. Although the loss of Crimea was not to be the last blow, it was the first that altered the focus of governmental and public attention away from pragmatic tasks, such as how to get roads built, to how to protect the territorial integrity of the Ukrainian state. Establishing a formal border between Russia and Ukraine had never been a priority for either country. A Russo-Ukrainian border demarcation agreement was only signed in 2010. Until the beginning of 2014, only 222 kilometers of the border had even been marked.[39]

# Armed Conflict

The Donbas had been a relatively unimportant region until the second half of the nineteenth century when coal was discovered there, and railway lines were built to transport it. Workers came from all over the Russian Empire, and later the USSR, to work in the Donbas, especially as part of Stalin's industrialization drives. The Donbas developed into a vibrant industrial region, known as the "cradle of the proletariat," and became emblematic of Soviet progress. At the time of the Maidan, the Donbas was the most industrialized, urban, and populous region of Ukraine. Six million people lived there, or 14 percent of Ukraine's total population, and the region produced 13 percent of its GNP, including 25 percent of its exports (Portnov 2015, 726). The engine of the local economy was based on old Soviet industries, mostly coal and metallurgy, which had been sold off at bargain prices in the 1990s. This gave the Donbas a significant number of oligarchs, including the richest of them all, Rinat Akhmetov. Many of the enterprises in the Donbas traded with Russia. Neither the oligarchic owners nor the workers wanted any kind of armed conflict with Russia. They supported the Eurasian Customs Union because it held out the promise of a measure of security and stability at the local level, much as the EU association agreement would have done for other Ukrainians working legally and illegally in Europe. The industries in the Donbas, particularly coal mines, were very dependent on state subsidies and the faltering of the coal industry portended trouble. The Donbas has long represented the potential for geographically concentrated poverty in a region characterized by reliance on a dying industry.

It was in this context that pro-Russian Ukrainian separatists, Russian volunteers, and other mercenaries came under the command of Igor Strelkov (Girkin), a former Russian military officer who participated in the annexation of Crimea. He was a key architect of the Donetsk People's Republic militia groups and would play a key role in the fighting in Mariupol and Amvrosiivka as early as June 2014. The constitution of the self-proclaimed Donetsk People's Republic asserts that the new state recognizes itself "to be an integral part of the Russian World as well as of Russian civilization confessing to the Orthodox faith." To prove the point, minority faith groups, primarily Baptists, were harassed.

The Russian Minister of Foreign Affairs Sergei Lavrov claimed that "Novorossia is returning to its traditional values, to its roots in Orthodoxy, and, as a result, is becoming even less understood [by the West]" (Interfax 2014). The aftermath of the Maidan, with its annexation of Crimea and the festering of civil strife in the Donbas, illustrated the ongoing relevance of a colonial past. The Russian Empire might have indeed ended, but lingering imperial formations were easily reanimated. Rather than fixating on denying sovereignty, the option of, what Stoler calls "graduated forms of sovereignty and what has long marked the technologies of imperial rule" became a strategy for reconstituting colonial relations through the destabilization of regions turned newly independent countries (2007, 193). Resurrecting a sliding scale of differential rights for different places and faiths became a means by which to insert imperial forms of authority in the near abroad.

# The Atmosphere of the Maidan

In a moment of extreme despair the Maidan was born. It was always a place, but on November 21, 2013, the Maidan also became an ideal that symbolized the aspirations of Ukrainians for a dignified life because that is where they congregated to assert this very powerful social fact. The experiential transcendence on the Maidan became manifest in social bonds that connected diverse individuals to each other in common purpose, forming something of a civic nation. Emotions are the great shaper of human actions. These experiences of transcendent bonding and the sensations, new self-perceptions, and actions they generated are key factors that recast the first months of 2014 as "the winter that changed us."

The Maidan triggered certain cultural formations that threw into sharp relief attitudes toward power and a rejection of the "soft knife of everyday oppression" that destroys any sense of agency and certainty (Das 2007, 218). Dignity, as a form of global cognitive mapping, became a means to orient the country out of the chaotic *tupik*, or cul de sac, into which the Yanukovych government had driven the country.[40] Dignity, human rights, and the law of the European Union gave radical hope a direction. An extraordinary crisis produces a historic event when multiple interlocking social institutions, cultural values, and governing practices break down under the strain of rupture. Das and Kleinman assert, "The social space occupied by scarred populations may enable stories to break through routine cultural codes to express counter-discourse that assaults and even perhaps undermines the taken-for-granted meanings of things as they are. Out of such desperate and defeated experiences stories may emerge that call for and at times may bring about change that alters utterly the commonplace— both at the level of collective experience and at the level of individual subjectivity" (2001, 21).

During this unforeseen watershed moment, an affective atmosphere of religiosity intensified emotional reactions that changed how individuals saw themselves, their relation to the place where they live, and to the people with whom they live. This produced new understandings of what it means to be Ukrainian and who belongs. Sensorial and affective emotional experiences acted as a spark, as a motivating force, that influenced the political by producing new allegiances. The affective bodily experiences yield feelings of having experienced something extraordinary. The significance of the Maidan, as an extraordinary event, is that it "attaches itself with its tentacles into everyday life and folds itself into the recesses of the ordinary" (Das 2007, 1). The extraordinary irreversibly changed the ordinary. Everyday life, and specifically everyday religiosity, was to be transformed after the Maidan with the enhanced integration of vernacular religious practices, clergy, and religious institutions into public space and public institutions thereby intensifying an atmosphere of religiosity that was already there.

4

# THE AESTHETICS OF RELATEDNESS
Commemorative Spirits in Public Space

After snipers opened fire on protesters in the middle of the night on February 20, 2014, and killed over one hundred people, shrines were immediately erected to the slain as part of the emotional work of grieving. Sacrifice, loss, and redemption are reflected in these commemorative shrines, as well as in the monuments, exhibits, museums, and other sites of memory-making that are in various stages of development across Ukraine to commemorate what was the Maidan and its aftermath. As a historic event, the Maidan changed the aesthetics of public space and expanded the sites of everyday religiosity and the devotional practices they inspire. Public expressions of shared grief over the loss of life on the Maidan were quickly overtaken by shock, more grief, and rage over the annexation of the Crimean Peninsula and the outbreak of armed conflict on the Ukrainian-Russian border, which ushered in over 13,000 more deaths.

Public commemorations of these deaths in shrines, monuments, murals, and other affective urban forms amount to a political, aesthetic project of sacral framing of sacrifice. By crafting public spaces where death can be mourned and victims can become venerated martyrs, these extraordinary events enter ordinary, everyday life and remain present. They illustrate the appeal and efficacy, both political and popular, of using religiosity to link people in new ways. Commemoration in public space contributes to remaking understandings of relatedness, including their moral obligations of reciprocity, among "brotherly nations" and between "mother" and "daughter" churches.

This chapter analyzes how the deaths of those who died during the Maidan protests and as defenders in the Anti-Terrorist Operation (ATO) in Eastern

Ukraine, are curated into well-known, kin-like patriots. The aesthetics of the initial memorial shrines (*sviatynia* in Ukrainian) were replicated in subsequent contexts, media, and cities. These commemorative practices connect sacrifice and death with the quest for dignity and threats to Ukrainian sovereignty via acts of everyday religiosity that reaffirm belonging and express new understandings of relatedness. To the extent that religious institutions can persuade people to accept certain interpretations of the past, they influence understandings of who is a victim, who sacrificed for whom, and why. This is among the reasons why religious institutions are so invested in promoting particular visions of a shared past. As the presence and practice of religiosity go increasingly public, and religious institutions become ever more engaged in managing death and fostering spiritualized practices of recall and mourning, a religious idiom in the aesthetics of public space expresses relatedness and obligation that alters the emotionalized tenor of the atmosphere of public space.

## Mourning and Immortality

On February 21, 2014, throngs of mourners carried scores of red roses and, when they sold out, red carnations tied with black ribbons to the Maidan and to St. Michael's Monastery, which had served as a first aid station. Red symbolizes blood and black evokes the black Ukrainian soil (*chornozem* in Ukrainian). Mourners steadily moved down city streets in the days following the shootings to pay their respects to the dead. They laid flowers, forming huge piles, before grave-like shrines that were spontaneously built to mark the exact site of a protester's death. The elements included in shrines became part of a personalized, religiously laden, commemorative aesthetic of patriotic sacrifice.

These flower-strewn shrines were embellished with icons, rosaries, candles, and other religious objects, as illustrated in figure 4.1. They created a focal point for the sincere outpouring of grief over the crushing of radical hope and the loss of life. The dead protesters were mourned as victims, heroes, and martyrs in quick succession because of the broad social recognition of the *podvyh*, or heroic feat, they had performed. As objects were added and debris was cleared, the shrines evolved. Along with a nearby chapel, the shrines were initially built without authorization. Once they became highly frequented sites of ritualized mourning and remembrance, it was obvious that it would be impossible to remove them.

By April 2014, the dead became known as the "Heavenly Hundred" (*Nebesna Sotnya*). The term *sotnya* refers to late-medieval Cossack military divisions, which numbered one hundred. The protesters had organized themselves into

**FIGURE 4.1.**   Photos, flowers, icons with rosaries, and candles mark where protesters died. Photo by Tania Mychajlyshyn-D'Avignon.

*sotnya*: the Self-Defense Sotnya (*Samooborona Maidana* in Ukrainian), Art *Sotnya*, Women's *Sotnya*, and so on. Over time, the state coopted the shrines, embraced them as emblematic of the heroism of the Maidan, and institutionalized them as official commemorative markers. The shrines became standardized and were professionally produced. The handwritten notes, poems, photographs, and mementos were systematized into memorial material that could be easily reproduced in other contexts. However, the initial personalization of the victims in the form of close-up facial portraits became a signature element in the aesthetic style of commemorating the slew of deaths that were to follow. As days turned to months and years, the faces and biographies of protesters were emplaced in a plethora of ceremonies, commemorative art, and public spaces across Ukraine, as seen in figure 4.2. After a while, the dead became not just recognizable but even familiar.

Objects that illustrated their engagement in combat, such as makeshift helmets, paving stones, tires, and found objects cobbled together to make defense barricades, formed the outer perimeter of the shrines when they were initially built and left no doubt as to how these fellow citizens died. Why they died was expressed through the multitude of Ukrainian flags, the coat of arms *tryzub* national symbol, the red and black flag of the Ukrainian Insurgent Army, and

**FIGURE 4.2.**  An early shrine to the first person who died on the Maidan. These shrines were part of an early aesthetic that personalized victims of state violence as the Heavenly Hundred. It took months to clear away the cobblestones, tires, and rubbish that was used to build and defend barricades around the protesters. Photo by Tania Mychajlyshyn-D'Avignon.

Cossack imagery.[1] The addition of professionally produced gold-engraved black granite plaques made the memorial markers seem grave-like. The challenge became commemorating death and burial without killing and burying the will to resist injustice as well. The solution was to make the Maidan, as the site of mortality where the protesters were shot, symbolically the reverse, namely the site of immortality. The vernacular religious practices that occur at these shrines as part of everyday religiosity include mourning, recall, and prayer. They provide a means to overcome physical death by assuring the protesters a social afterlife.

## Commemorative Spirits

The initial response of most to these shrines was grief. Although grief is an emotion and mourning is a social practice, grief and mourning mutually constitute one another. Mourning results from grief and produces more grief, which often perpetuates mourning. This is why death is so disruptive to communal stability.

Grief, and the emotion it impels, can be intensified by an atmosphere laden with words grounded in theologies, songs with liturgical overtones, and religious objects integrated into memorial shrines. The portraits, candles, icons, and prayer beads that adorn the shrines invoke the veneration of saints. These, and other objects with clear religious meaning, were placed around the portraits and tributes to the slain. Crosses and crucifixes unite the sacrificial death of Christ with the sacrifice and death of protesters (see figure 4.3). The mimetic sympathy that is created from the objects and the eventual designation Heavenly Hundred conjure up sensations of the dead as martyrs. Ritualized behaviors set these sites apart and tautologically reaffirm the sacred qualities of mundane objects that were placed around the shrines, such as gas masks, lumber, tires, and other things relating to the righteous violent fight.

The etymological root of sacrifice makes clear its origins in religious experience, "sacer" and "facere," or "making holy." Although comparatively few people might make sacrificial offerings to God or gods these days, sacrifices in everyday life abound. Sacrifice has acquired new heterodox meanings through devotional practices and sacrificial forms of exchange that extend into everyday life for the purposes of acquiring certain benefits. The constitution of community and social life itself depend on the sacrifices members are willing to make. If no one is willing, then the community ceases to exist. Benedict Anderson's (2006) landmark study decades ago drew our attention to the emblematic nature of Tombs of the Unknown Soldier, not only for imagining a national community into existence, but one that was grounded in sacrifice and veneration of that sacrifice. Today visiting dignitaries are now frequently brought to these shrines to pay homage to the protesters, much as other countries would escort visitors to a Tomb of the Unknown Soldier, as seen in figure 4.4. When a sacrifice inspires awe, it garners the potential of enhancing communal allegiance or fidelity to certain moral and political principles that define it. In its most extreme form, self-sacrifice motivates suicide bombing, self-immolation, and other means of ending one's life in exchange for the life of the group or its principles.

These shrines make the Maidan a politicized site of place-making and self-making. They contain both an absence and a presence. The protesters are dead and obviously absent. However, as heroic compatriots who sacrificed themselves for the pursuit of the common good of the nation, they are very much present. In other words, people might have died, and the protests might have ceased but the momentum and values that fueled the protests can live on when the sacrifice, undying glory, and immortality of participants is extolled in these shrines, in other sacred spaces, and in the transcendent practices they engender.

Noninstitutional forms of public religiosity do a great deal of cultural work. They communicate specific meanings through the sensations and forms of ex-

**FIGURE 4.3.**   A large wooden cross stands before a small wooden chapel built in honor of the Maidan. Numerous photos and black granite engraved plates now mark who died and where. This remains a site to which people bring flowers and national memorabilia. Photo by Tania Mychajlyshyn-D'Avignon.

perience they generate. Rituals, such as the post-Maidan mass funeral rite held in public space, are episodic and constitute an experience in the sense of an extraordinary event. Mourning, by contrast, often occurs outside a formal ritual context and is connected with the experience of ongoing, emotional work of grieving. Both become part of the lifeworld of people who circulate in these

**FIGURE 4.4.**   The shrines to the Heavenly Hundred have become the equivalent of a Tomb of an Unknown Soldier. Visiting dignitaries frequently lay flowers at this site. The key difference is that that here the person who died for the country becomes well known through a personalized commemorative aesthetic. Photo by the author.

spaces. Just as religion is inescapably social, the process of remaking moral impulses correlated with relatedness happens collectively within communal ritual experiences.[2]

Mourning, veneration, and contemplation are not a response to the sacred, rather they are what make a site sacred. These practices propel forward the official state-directed commemorations of the Maidan as the Revolution of Dignity. Mourning builds solidarity by collectively assuring the protesters the dignity in death that eluded them in life. This is part of the affect these commemorative shrines convey in the form of politicized, morally laden grief. When experiences of mourning are understood in transcendent terms, they link practitioners not only to the dead but also to previous generations, yielding deep vertical solidarity, much as the reenactment of Cossack Sichs did during the Maidan.

Whereas the moral significance of what is being commemorated is forged through the sensations generated at a particular place, the meaning of that space is also articulated by the ritual and ritualized behaviors that are conducted there (Smith 1987, 18, 104). The capacity of these shrines to repeatedly generate emotional sensations that lead to ritualized behaviors can be used politically to link a person to a specific place and, by extension, to the people living there. These attachments, plus the recall of common experiences and the sensations of sorrow and rage they prompt, are politically useful, and therein lies the significance of the forms of religiosity that are practiced at these memorial shrines. They generate an affective atmosphere of grief, mourning, and loss that now characterizes part of the city and serves as a lasting commentary to the legacy of the Maidan and all it stood for. This is why, although they were initially spontaneously created, the state coopted them for its own purposes.

Affective markers in the built environment, such as these shrines, are surfaces where solidarity and belonging can be inscribed. They articulate a relational sense of self to nation and self to compatriots to form a template for understanding history. Actively sacralizing public space and stimulating emotions of grief during ritualized behaviors of mourning heightens a sense of the past in the present and is a key means of sacralizing history. The fixation on the past and the vast scholarly and popular interest in memory studies can in part be explained by a tacit acknowledgment that the dead can be made present.

Oft repeated spiritualized practices of recall strengthen the attachments between the living and the dead. Vernacular religious practices to the dead constitute a form of offering that perpetuates communal relationships and the reciprocal obligations embedded in them. The dead are remembered and honored in gratitude for past acts and with the hope that their spirits will offer protection in the future. Everyday religiosity finds a place in commemorative sites in the public sphere of a pluralist society with a secular state. Vernacular practices that draw on generalized, nonconfessional Eastern Christian sentiments, signs, and theologies maintain horizontal relationships of solidarity among the living and as well as vertical relationships of connection that link the living with past and future generations.

# State Encouragement of Vernacular Practices

Commemorative space is a product rather than a blank slate that is simply filled in. It is consciously produced to have a certain atmosphere that will prompt feelings, practices, and messages. Because these shrines have evolved into permanent fixtures of the urban landscape thanks to state intervention, they have lost some of their luster and magnetism. The standardization of a commemorative aesthetic, however, creates a reference point in terms of form, content, and tone that has been replicated in subsequent commemorations of the death, linking death on the Maidan to death in war.

All societies engage in acts of collective remembrance aimed at providing comfort to the living. Although it might seem surprising that memorial shrines in the form of graves to political protesters sprang up in the heart of the capital, perhaps it should not. Most cities began as ceremonial complexes, as sites of ritual display, and certainly Kyiv did. Until the end of the eighteenth century in Europe, cemeteries were located in the heart of the city, next to the main cathedral. Spatially separating the deceased from everyday life in cemeteries served to underline that the dead are no longer part of the community. The use of coffins coincided with the relocation of cemeteries to the outskirts of the city. Michel Foucault makes the interesting argument that as doubt arose as to whether a person really has a soul and if a body resurrects after death, care for the bodies of the dead increased and continues to be a veritable industry (Foucault and Miskowiec 1986, 25).

Forcing a separation between the living and the dead was specifically rejected in these memorial shrines. The shrines were consciously erected as near as possible to the sites of death. Emplacement is key to sacrality. The shrines are squarely located in lived public space, near the city's single largest metro station. Streams of city residents pass by them every day. Incorporating commemorative space into highly trafficked areas is a growing trend in memorial commemoration. One need only think of the 9/11 Memorial in New York in the center of the financial district or the enormous Memorial to the Murdered Jews of Europe in Berlin, which is situated along busy thoroughfares. Both memorials were specifically built to erase separation from daily life. They trade the set apart qualities that make space sacred for immediate and unavoidable encounters within everyday life. These memorials are considered successful because they retain emotive qualities that create an atmosphere that provokes recall of past events and sets in motion the affective flow of sensations, thoughts, and actions.

Recall is not the bringing forth of an image stored in the mind or sensations stored in the body. Rather, recall triggers feelings, thoughts, and sensations that newly emerge each time. This makes the Maidan, dotted as it with shrines, "pregnant with the past" (Ingold 2011, 153). The same can be said of other commemorative sites in Ukraine that recall sacrifice, immortality, and the afterlife of the dead. Material representations of the dead affect our thoughts and emotions via "regimes of invisibility" that have iconic power, recalling Bruno Latour's assertion that some of the most powerful actors are invisible (2010). Their sources of agency are not merely social constructions, nor are they autonomous realities. Rather, their agency and presence are both made and made real. The materiality of commemorative sites, the objects within them, and the practices they inspire engage the bodies that circulate there. In doing so, they make an affective atmosphere pregnant with possibility.

When the sensational forms that trigger an affective reaction of feeling-thinking-acting are linked to an otherworldly realm and located in otherwise mundane public spaces, such as a city street or square, these experiences mediate the twin processes of producing the materiality of urban space and constructing the meanings of that space (Wanner 2016). Experiencing the sensations of grief generated by reading the signs of death and loss in a religious register makes for an atmosphere where an otherworldly realm can feel palpable, and those who inhabit it knowable. By drawing on the legitimating authority of a confessional tradition to ritualize grieving and mourning and forge shared meaning into these feelings, the transcendent can be kindled and experienced.

Roy Rappaport (1999, 387) noted that for a work of art or a shrine to be effective, "It need not stimulate the same emotional response in all who experience it. Indeed, if emotion is in its nature not fully describable, how can anyone know if another feels as he or she does? It is likely that everyone responds emotionally to a particular object or event rather differently, for each person brings a uniquely conditioned emotional and rational constitution to it. What is important is that the work elicit a response of some sort." Commemorating the protesters killed on the Maidan so lavishly and sincerely recognizes the exceptional nature of their death. The multiplicity of the shrines' symbolic forms produces a variety of reactions among those who were present, those who were virtually present, and those who imagine themselves to have been present (Kertzer 1988, 69–75). The past speaks directly through the contagion of the objects, and specifically the aesthetics and religious iconography. The important point is that public expressions of grief and indebtedness call for a reciprocal response, which often comes in the form of a commitment to a place and its people, which contributes to feelings of belonging.

## *Panakhyda* Funeral Service for the Dead

Religious institutions make pronouncements as to how one should properly re-late to the dead, to their soul, and to burial. When death occurs, burial prac-tices are ritualized into two phases: first, to transfer the living to the dead and second, to make the transition from the realm of the dead to the world of ances-tors. Each transition is separated by a liminal phase. Cremation is not practiced in the Eastern Christian tradition. Although in 2016 the Vatican decided to al-low cremation, but not the sprinkling of ashes, Ukrainian Greek Catholics rarely cremate the dead. The belief is that cremation would burn the soul along with the body and until the third day after death, the soul remains close by. Funerals and burials are a means to separate from the body, to mark the deceased as no longer among the living. At the grave, it is common to burn incense, light a candle, pour water or wine, and later bring food and other valued items for the deceased. The fortieth day after death is another important commemorative moment because the soul is believed to be nearby until that day. Thereafter, the soul finally leaves the world of the living. Sometimes the three-, six-, and nine-month anniversaries of the death are commemorated as well as the one-year and subsequent annual anniversaries.

On February 21, 2014, a publicly televised open-air funeral was held on the Maidan. Priests led the crowd, along with politicians, in an all-night memorial service for the dead. The Maidan became a liturgical space once again. A *panakhyda* funeral rite took place with teeming crowds in attendance and more virtually watching. This transformed the Maidan from a place to assert the as-piration for dignity to a site of commemorating death with dignity. Mortuary rituals frame death as rebirth (Bloch and Parry 1982). By hauntingly commem-orating the Heavenly Hundred, a form of life springs from these deaths, draw-ing on the Christian idea that the death of Christ is the source of eternal life. Revolutionary heroes in other situations, most notably the Soviet Union, were treated in a similar fashion. One need only think of the grandiose burial sites of Communist Party leaders and their elaborate funeral ceremonies.[3]

Music during the funeral rite played a pivotal role in creating an atmosphere of transcendence that conferred an otherworldly martyred status to the sacri-ficed protesters. Jeffers Engelhardt notes the prominence of music as a spiritual and ethical endeavor that links Orthodox liturgy and theology to Orthodox per-sonhood (2015, 217). The highly emotive, hauntingly beautiful, mournful song *Plyve Kacha po Tysyni* (A Duck Floats on the Tysyn River) emerged as the signa-ture "gesture of accompaniment" for the dead in funeral services (Ricoeur 2009, 17–20). The song was performed during the public funeral for "national heroes" by *Pikkardiis'ka Tertsiia*, a six-man acapella group whose harmonies draw on liturgical chants and Ukrainian folk music. The emotive power of the song's grieving lament over sacrificing a son to war later prompted the families of soldiers who died in Eastern Ukraine to make it a custom to come to the Maidan and play this performance on loudspeakers for all to hear as part of their mourning on the fortieth day after death. This song, and the sensations it generates, captures the ability to attune listeners to each other by creating an atmosphere of "being and being together" (Slaby 2020, 275). Like so many other folk melodies and folk healing practices, the song evokes the protective powers of a mother. The refrain is a soldier speaking to his mother before he goes off to war:

| | |
|---|---|
| Сам не знаю де погину | I don't know where I will die |
| Гей, погину я в чужім краю | Oh, I'll die in a foreign land |
| Хто ж ми буде прати яму? | Who will bury me? |
| | |
| Гей, виберут ми чужі люди | Well, you will be buried by strangers |
| Ци не жаль ти, мамко, буде? | Won't you regret this, dear mother? |
| Гей, якби ж мені, синку, не жаль? | Oh, how could I not regret this, dear son |
| Ти ж на моїм серцю лежав | You have rested on my heart |
| Гей, плине кача по Тисині | Oh, a duck floats on the Tysyn [a river in Ukraine] |

During the public funeral, a procession carried the corpses in coffins through the crowd in close proximity to the mourners in a deliberate effort to erase any separation between the living and the dead. Some of the coffins were open, and all were draped in flags. At one point, the crowd erupted in a repeated rhythmic chant, "Heroes do not die" [*Heroi ne vmiraiut'* in Ukrainian].[4] Immortality, as an illusion or aspiration, contributes to feelings of transcendence. A body might die, but a spirit can live on when individual undying glory is extolled. The dead are counted among the immortal ancestors, and specifically those who, in their sacrifice, were willing to act morally for others. Thanks to personalized depictions of each sacrificed protester in the shrines and the unearned intimacy of televised close-ups of family members and other mourners during this funeral, the dead were no longer strangers. Feelings of comfort arise from the recognition that what is performed for the dead today will be performed for those who die tomorrow. As the coffins were carried away through the crowds, the funeral service concluded with the crowd chanting in unified, almost trance-like repetition, "Glory to the Heroes!" This is meant to overcome individual transience and reaffirm the righteousness of ongoing political struggle despite the real tragic deaths that occurred.

Anthropologists have long debated the significance of funeral rites, and specifically whether they enhance or quell the threat death poses to community stability. Robert Hertz (1960) placed great emphasis on mortuary practices as a means to resolve the disruptiveness of death. Mourners need to be purified because of their polluting contact with a corpse, he argued.[5] Especially in instances of "bad death," meaning murder, suicide, or accident, contact with the corpse is usually minimal.[6] What is striking about this public funeral service is that it goes against the established pattern of avoiding contact with corpses, much like the shrines also refuse a separation from the dead. Moreover, Jean Baudrillard argues the purpose of funeral rites is to control the expression of grief so as to "beg and bribe the dead to stay away," which is why, he argues, burial grounds became "the first ghettos," segregating the dead from the living in restricted spaces (1976, 195ff.). A long-standing fear exists in this part of the world, often referred to as "the bloodlands" (Snyder 2010) that, given the theological view of bodily resurrection, the spirit of the "unquiet dead" could return in the afterlife to torment the living. Prolonged ritualized mourning serves to restore the social fabric by casting death as a manageable threat. It suggests that the disruptive loss due to death can be overcome and that the spirits of the dead can be appeased.

By contrast, O'Rourke (2007) argues that mourners need to be purged of grief, for it is grief, and specifically the public expression of grief, that poses a far greater threat to social stability than death. Although the deliberate, repeated conjuring up of grief has the potential to remake relationships based on compassion and solidarity, in other instances grief inflames rage and recasts relationships in terms of antipathy. Death can be instrumentalized for political ends when a curatorial emphasis on sacrifice, martyrdom, and veneration of slain patriots draws on grief to amplify primordial visions of the nation and revive national glories in the name of defense against the aggressor. Therefore, provoking grief through ritualized mourning at commemorative sites and public funerals can generate compassion and solidarity with those who sacrificed as easily as it can generate rage toward the other who created the unrelenting grief in the first place. The unspoken solution to grief is the elimination of its source.

## From Grief to Rage

Not only did the material form of makeshift shrines change over time as the state became involved, the larger political context in which they were experienced also changed to include war and the loss of territory. Many young people with whom I have spoken resent what they see as a glorification of victimhood achieved through the commemoration of tragedy. Although an incessant confrontation with a painful past is meant to yield allegiance to the dead and produce solidarity, for Mykola, who studies architecture at Kyiv Mohyla Academy, it has the opposite effect. He asked me in an exasperated, rhetorical tone, "Don't you think it's terrible that these memorials are all sad? They focus only on the past and what is bad about the Maidan." He really wanted me to condemn the grave-like shrines, but I said that I thought it fit a country whose national anthem is titled, "Ukraine has not yet died." Death has always played a central role in Ukrainian self-presentation, and especially death due to violent, tragic infractions on the innocent. "But that's the problem," Mykola shot back, "who wants to be part of a nation that is constantly getting beaten down?" He has a point. The galvanizing power of imagining a shared future, which propelled solidarity on the Maidan, is giving way to established tendencies, often led by religious institutions, to emphasize the shared burden of a tragic past. Although the need to redeem the suffering and sacrifice of others does not motivate Mykola as intended, others react to perceptions of unfair onslaught by banding together for the purposes of protection or revenge.

Matvei Veisberg, a celebrated Kyiv artist who actively participated in the Maidan protests, called the Maidan "one of the most beautiful things I have seen in my life." He was inspired to paint a series of twenty-eight paintings, all hung in four rows of seven across, which he called "Stena," or Wall. He made the paintings over forty days, ending on March 8. When I asked why he depicted the Maidan in almost monochromatic black tones punctuated by a piercing red and billowing grays, he said, "It was because of the ever present fire and smoke. I'm not a religious person, or a believer, or even a mystical person. But the wind always took the smoke to them." He meant the Berkut Special Forces charged with controlling, disbanding, and finally shooting the protesters. He saw the smoke drifting into their eyes as evidence that even the elements were on the protesters' side. He sought to illustrate the majesty of "ash, burnt tires, and smoke" as almost a celebration of the weapons the powerless have against the powerful.

As meaningful as the Maidan is to him, he does not like the way it has been commemorated. Before explaining why, this articulate man begins by saying "I don't know" several times in fits of starts and stops as he searches for words. "That kind of atmosphere corresponds to the new mood. It is even helpful to some because it validates those who think, "What have you done! It has only gotten worse!" He continues on, "When they say, you didn't accomplish anything, that's ridiculous. It seemed as if each of us couldn't influence anything, but then we succeeded in not letting them turn our home into a prison."

Commemorative space that began with graves as shrines now serves as a reminder of war and a cautionary tale that could discourage further protests. The possibility of more mass discontent lingers because grief, like the shrines themselves, can morph into something else. The use of an affective atmosphere to generate grief, sometimes inadvertently and other times directly, can also demonize other places and peoples and lead to rage. By channeling grief into rage or rage into grief, these sites of mourning can spark moral obligations of an entirely different kind, often involving revenge, retribution, and the glory of honor killings.

Renato Rosaldo wrote an article that has since become a classic after his wife tragically died while conducting research among the Ilongot, a headhunting people in the Philippines (1984). She slipped on a mountain path and fell sixty-five feet to her death. One minute here, the next gone. In the depths of Rosaldo's grieving and what he called the "heaving sobs with no tears," he had insight as to why the Ilongots headhunt. Long before, he had asked them why they cut off people's heads. They told him, "We need someplace to carry our anger." The rage from bereavement when grieving the loss of a loved one impelled them to headhunt, he was told. It took the death of his wife and his feelings of rage amid grief to understand the Ilongot. Rage, born of grief, impels violence, he finally understood. Unexpected reminders of painful loss unleash that rage.

For a long time afterward, Veisberg did not want to go to the Maidan. "It's a cemetery," he said, "Many people were killed there. Only after many months could I cross that line, the line where the barricades were." He crossed it after several friends approached the National Museum to arrange an exhibit of his Wall painting series. The museum is located near where some of the worst standoffs took place and next to buildings that doubled as a hospital and shelters, which hardly makes it a neutral space to exhibit paintings depicting the Maidan.

The museum staff began to hesitate and complain that the works were not in a museum format. They are unframed, and Veisberg proposed hanging them in a straight line like a wall. He described himself and his friends at this time as "short-tempered" and "cut to the bone." He grew furious and exploded at their hesitation and trite concerns. As he stormed out, he yelled to the staff, "You don't exist for me anymore!" Returning to that space by crossing those lines with those paintings and encountering that reaction prompted both grief and rage. But it was rage that dominated his feelings, thoughts, and actions that day. He noted sarcastically that reservations about formatting did not preclude the museum from exhibiting Yanukovych's famous paperweight, a two-kilo loaf of bread made of pure gold. The golden loaf was a gift to Yanukovych on his birthday in 2013 from Vladimir Lukyanenko, a Russian oligarch with investments in the oil and gas industry.[7] "That was interesting to them," Veisberg said despondently with equal measures of grief and lament.

All interpretations, especially of someone's emotional inner life, are made by anthropologists who are positioned subjects, able to grasp certain innuendos, gestures, and tones, but not others. I cannot say to what degree Veisberg or visitors to the Maidan feel grief or rage at the shrines and during encounters that involve memories of the Maidan. I can only tell of the fury of an otherwise calm and thoughtful man. I can attest to the fact that every time I visit the Maidan, and I have done so many times over the course of years and always with camera in hand, I observe people captivatedly staring at these chapel-like shrines. They seem to study the photographs and objects for clues as to who each was and what motivated them to risk their lives on that day in February 2014. Are the faces in these gravestone portraits victims, martyrs, heroes, or just dead bodies? The only thing that is not disputed is that the heart of the city is now a site of mourning and that the project the Maidan launched, the pursuit of dignity, has been sidelined by a war in a country that has been truncated and divided once again.

## Never Will We Be Brothers

Veisberg used painting as a medium to express his emotions in response to the Maidan. Anastasia Dmytruk, a twenty-three-year-old student in Kyiv at the time, decided to stand outside on a dark wintery night in 2014 and recite a rhymed poem she penned while a friend recorded it with a cell phone.[8] She wrote the poem in Russian for Russians after the annexation of Crimea in 2014 and released it soon after Vladimir Putin delivered a speech to the Russian Duma on March 18, 2014. Much as he did later during his 2021 historical essay, Putin refers to Russia's "special calling," a phrase the Russian Orthodox Church uses, to assert its leadership over the organic unity of Eastern Slavs as one people under a common Orthodox tradition. "Everything in Crimea speaks of our shared history and pride," Putin says, "This is the location of ancient Khersones, where Prince Vladimir was baptized. His spiritual feat of adopting Orthodoxy predetermined the overall basis of the culture, civilization and human values that unite the peoples of Russia, Ukraine and Belarus. The graves of Russian soldiers whose bravery brought Crimea into the Russian empire are also in Crimea. . . . Each one of these places is dear to our hearts, symbolizing Russian military glory and outstanding valor."[9] In other words, the graves of Russian soldiers in Crimea justify the territory as Russian.

Dmytruk sought to give voice to the sting of betrayal that annexation of Crimea brought. The poem went viral and within two months, it had already been viewed over one million times, and over three million times a year later (Stahl 2015, 450). The poem sparked extensive discussion in Ukraine and revealed fissures in attitudes, experiences, and political views toward Russia and the Soviet past more broadly among neighbors, kin, and across generations within families. Some found the poem unnecessarily combative, even Russophobic, and others found it refreshingly honest. Titled "Never will we be brothers," the poem draws on the familiar trope of Ukraine and Russia as "fraternal nations" (*bratskie narody* in Russian). Socialist and Soviet propaganda, as well as Russian Orthodox theology, posits that there is an "unbreakable unity" among peoples who share "fraternal ties" and that this natural, almost Herderian, form of solidarity is eternal and can never be destroyed (Rakowska-Harmstone 1977, 75). The poem takes issue with such claims of relatedness and the unequal hierarchical relationship on which they are based, and the obligations of loyalty and reciprocity they imply.

| | |
|---|---|
| Никогда мы не будем братьями ни по родине, ни по матери. | Never will we be brothers, not by motherland, not by mothers. |
| Духа нет у вас быть свободными— нам не стать с вами даже сводными. | You have no spirit to be free— not even step-siblings can we be. |
| Вы себя окрестили "старшими"— нам бы младшими, да не вашими. Вас так много, а, жаль, безликие. Вы огромные, мы—великие. | You are "older" than us, you say, younger perhaps, we hold you at bay. You are so many, but, sadly, without face. You are enormous, but we are great. |
| А вы жмете . . . вы всё маетесь | You wear yourselves out, mad and zealous, |
| своей завистью вы подавитесь | you will choke from being so jealous. |
| Воля - слово вам незнакомое, вы все с детства в цепи закованы. | Freedom for you is unattained, since childhood you've all been chained. |
| У вас дома "молчанье—золото", | In your house "silence is golden," |
| а у нас жгут коктейли Молотова, | but we throw Molotov cocktails emboldened. |
| да, у нас в сердце кровь горячая, | Yes, our heart is seething with blood, |
| что ж вы нам за "родня" незрячая? | you blind ones are no kin to us! |

| | |
|---|---|
| А у нас всех глаза бесстрашные, | Our eyes are calm and unalarmed, |
| без оружия мы опасные. | We are dangerous even unarmed. |
| Повзрослели и стали смелыми | We've grown up and become fighters |
| все у снайперов под прицелами. | while being shot at by snipers. |
| Нас каты на колени ставили— | The henchmen forced us to the ground, |
| мы восстали и всё исправили. | but we stood up and turned things around. |
| И зря прячутся крысы, молятся— | The rats are hiding, in vain they pray, |
| они кровью своей умоются. | with their own blood they'll be washed away. |
| Вам шлют новые указания— | They are sending you new orders, |
| а у нас тут огни восстания. | but our uprising burns and smolders. |
| У вас Царь, у нас - Демократия. | You have a Tsar, we have Democracy, |
| Никогда мы не будем братьями. | and never will we brothers be. |

A Lithuanian vocal group, Klaipeda, instantly set the poem to music. The group had significant commercial success with the song. Singing in solidarity in accented Russian, they claimed the song was a protest to the annexation of Crimea. As a small neighboring country, Lithuanians also see themselves as vulnerable to Russian aggression (Klumbyte 2019: Ozolina 2019). In the music video, with the final line, "Never will we brothers be," the five-member group arm-in-arm turns their backs to the camera in a gesture of finality and stares out to the open sea.

Rather than endorsing an impending permanent fracturing of Slavic brotherhood, others countered with their own rhymed responses. Over one hundred performed, filmed responses to the poem were posted on YouTube within a year (Stahl 2015, 450). Some Russians picked up a guitar and sang a response from their living room and condemned the impulse to dismiss them all as *Moskali*, a derogatory label for Russians. Others, through implication or direct reference, asserted that Russians and Ukrainians were both victims and instigators of the tragic events that have defined their shared history. The poems of still others insisted on the irreversibility of a shared fate. Like it or not, shared Slavic blood means that they have always been and will always be "brothers." The trope of the glory of the Soviet period, particularly with regard to the Soviet victory during the Great Patriotic War over fascism, was already present in some poetic responses, although it would take on even greater meaning in the years to come. These poems noted that such victories were achieved thanks to cooperation among fraternal nations, and this inspired them to endorse the Russo-Ukrainian relationship. And, finally, some capitalized on the patriarchy and male privilege inherent in the notion of brotherly nations to agree that the two countries will never be brothers because Ukraine is a sister.

President Almazbek Atambayev of Kyrgyzstan delivered a speech at a summit of the Collective Security Treaty Organization in Moscow in May 2014. The event was attended by presidents of Armenia, Tajikistan, Belarus, and Russia, the main participants in the Eurasian Customs Union. His remarks reveal understandings of the organic solidarity inherent within "fraternal" nations. He said,

> It is a grave misfortune when fraternal nations, who fought together for victory in World War II begin to split. . . . Sovereignty is good, but we should make all efforts to make our borders as borders of friendship and fraternity. We see how fraternal nations, who used to fight together, begin to split. We know well what will happen if ethnic split exacerbates. It would be very hard to stop it then. It hurts a lot to see this split now. I wish conflicts and misunderstandings between fraternal nations, who stopped plague and fascism together once, would leave. We should put friendship and fraternity forefront.[10]

"Fraternal nations," as Kolstø and Rusetskii remind us, is a concept that normativizes and naturalizes power differentials among groups. It creates a seemingly unchanging perception of one's own country vis-à-vis a stronger, larger, more powerful, neighboring country so as to fix an expectation, and even a realization, of inequality (2012, 140–41). This is captured in the Soviet-era anecdote of two men discussing how to share a single apple. The Russian says, "Let's share it in a brotherly way" (*po-bratskii* in Russian). "No, let's share it 50–50," the Ukrainian replies. The concept of fraternal nations also finds echoes in the Russian World, which posits that a Slavic brotherhood enshrined and morally validated by Orthodoxy and led by the Russian Patriarch, who sits at the helm of this theo-political space, will safeguard traditional values against corrupting, foreign encroachment.

# From Maidan to Monastery

Many members of the Maidan Self-Defense units, the impromptu groups that formed to protect the protesters from Ukrainian special forces, subsequently joined the volunteer Territorial Defense Battalions to fight in Eastern Ukraine. It has become a tradition for volunteer fighters, soldiers, and others actively engaged in the war effort to come to the Maidan to light a candle near the portraits of the slain as a form of blessing before they head to the front. Deaths that result from fighting in the war are commemorated with the same aesthetics of portraiture, the same mournful song that celebrates a mother's protection, and religious motifs. Those who see the Maidan protests as an event independent of the Russian annexation of Crimea and the war object to the conflation of their commemoration.

Originally, there were even shrines to slain soldiers alongside those to protesters. However, when the number of soldiers killed in the East continued to mount, those shrines had to be relocated. Tributes to soldiers killed in Eastern Ukraine were relocated in 2017 to the exterior wall of St. Michael's Monastery, which was where protesters took refuge during the Maidan protests. The monastery was then affiliated with the UOC-KP and now is the seat of the OCU and residence of the Metropolitan of Kyiv and All Ukraine. The same aesthetic practice of using close-up portraits and biographical details to create a sense of familiarity was maintained to commemorate dead soldiers. Rows of photos of "defenders," as the soldiers became known, were mounted on the exterior wall of the monastery facing the main artery that leads to the Maidan. The site is called the "Wall of Remembrance for those Fallen for Ukraine."

The use of personalization here is much like the Vietnam Memorial in Washington, DC, which was so controversial when it was built and yet is considered successful now. Early objections were that the monument was a "black gash of shame and sorrow," "a tombstone," and a "wailing wall." Now the Vietnam Memorial is considered an accomplishment because it emotionalizes memorial space and affects viewers by making them feel the loss. The endless listing of names humanizes the soldiers and gives a stark sense of the magnitude of deaths. At both memorials, people leave photographs, texts, and other objects for the dead as if they were there and as if it were possible to communicate with them. Yet, the Vietnam memorial is also considered controversial because the over 58,000 American casualities pale in comparison to the three million Vietnamese who lost their lives during this conflict, a fact that remains unacknowledged.

As of late 2020, the official pronouncements of Ukrainian Army casualties numbered approximately 5,000, with another 5,000 on the separatist side. If civilian casualties are added, the total tops 13,000 in the first seven years. Aesthetic styles that link the death of protesters on the Maidan with the death of soldiers become ensnared in growing dissatisfaction with the slow pace of reform and a persistent lack of trust in state institutions. This resentment combines with anxiety over the state's ability to defend Ukrainians in this hybrid war as the fighting grinds on, leaving ever more corpses and refugees in its wake. As the frontiers of war become hardened and even normalized in this increasingly frozen conflict, religion and the history of the recent past are weaponized to fortify the cultural boundaries and securitized to strengthen the political borders separating Russia from Ukraine. Be they protesters-turned-victims of Ukrainian state aggression or slain soldiers from a war in separatist regions, the impulse to mourn the dead brings the frontiers of war into the everyday lives of Ukrainians and generates grief that can easily morph into rage.

## Memory Lane

Given the tremendous importance of monuments for marking urban space and structuring interactions and encounters, I have always been curious as to the process of deciding what gets commemorated and how. I was invited to join a commission in 2016 to discuss how to commemorate the Maidan. At first a raucous group of nearly fifty urban activists, artists, leaders of NGOs, government and city officials, architects, urban planners, and others met in a downtown building on the fifth floor for hours at a time to discuss what was needed. During these meetings, I was struck by the willingness to hear the thoughts of young people and to cater to what they articulated as their preferences.

As the actual planning of the competition took shape, the group whittled down to about two dozen urban planners who met at the Presidential Administration Building in plush surroundings. There was agreement that the process had to be transparent, and that this monument needed to reflect the extraordinary character of the Maidan by being an un-monument monument. An open competition generated proposals that were publicly displayed on the Maidan. A small group of commission members selected an official design in February 2018, exactly four years after the events. To underline the swiftness of the commemorative process in Kyiv, for the sake of comparison, consider that discussions to commemorate 9/11 began five years after the event, and a monument opened nearly a decade after that in 2014.

The winning design was submitted by two Ukrainian women, one who lives in Lviv and the other in Rotterdam. Their design featured a "Memory Lane," a quiet garden-like allée, with almost a monastery-like atmosphere of peace and contemplation.[11] The design formalized the atmosphere and patterns of movement already established. Key portions of where the shrines are located had already become pedestrian zones and created a firm separation between the noise and life from the harried vehicular traffic of Khreshchatyk Street below and the quiet, contemplative shrines up on the hill. For many reasons, including the swiftness of the decisions involved, the monument has still not been constructed and the shrines remain the commemorative focus of the Maidan.

However, this aesthetic has been replicated in the first official monument built to commemorate the Heavenly Hundred in Lviv, a city in Western Ukraine. It features a similar sense of sacrality, created by emplacement in a quiet, set-apart space, using the same contemplative aesthetic as in Kyiv. Numerous ideas were proposed to commemorate the Heavenly Hundred, including making a formal hymn from the signature song of accompaniment, A Duck Floats on the Tysyn River; commissioning a symphony; building a pedestrian bridge over a gap linking two hillsides, as was done in Kyiv; and creating a pedagogical program for school children about the Maidan. A competition in 2017 resulted in a jury selection and a formal monument opening in 2019. The monument was built up on a hill, above the historic part of the city, in a park-like setting. It is preceded by a long walkway with panoramic terraces from which, as plaques note, ten churches are visible. The terraces are integrated into a long path that snakes around the monument and down to the street below. Following the pattern established by shrines and the Wall of Remembrance to soldiers in Kyiv, the Lviv monument features an extended wall of portraits of those killed during the Maidan with biographical details. The portraits are etched on metal plates that are mounted on a deep rust-colored wall in the shape of a wide-open V that is meant to be an allegory for barricades. There are three rows of such portraits with an inscription above that reads, "Do not let your heart harden—for then the person in you shall die" (*Ne dai zacherstvity sertsiu—bo todi pomre u tobi liudyniu* in Ukrainian). In other words, keeping grief alive is a means to retaining humanity. The atmosphere of both these commemorative zones in Lviv and Kyiv is awe, sorrow, and perhaps sometimes rage as these sacred, set apart spaces recall collective attempts to pursue dignity in life and dignity in death. At the same time, by establishing a single aesthetic, an atmosphere of homage to sacrifice using religious and national symbolism, and replicating it in multiple urban locations, an integration of public space across the country grows.

# Enshrining Memories

In this war of information, crosses, and arms, the first causality to prevent is the ability to write one's own narrative of what happened and why. The Ukrainian

Institute of National Remembrance, with support from city and state authorities, created a commemorative memorial of the Maidan protests to instruct the public on the succession of events and their consequences in advance of an official monument. The exhibit attempts to build consensus as to what, how, and why events unfolded as they did. Social media played a pivotal role in sparking and sustaining the protests. Therefore, panels in the open-air exhibit feature some of the most poignant and revealing posts of the time, including the one by Mustafa Nayyem, which is credited with starting the Maidan in the first place. One in particular resonated with me because I had heard so many versions of the same sentiment. The exhibit on the Maidan drew heavily from an article published in 2015, in which a Facebook post made by Olena Babakova was reproduced. Although she gave permission for the post to be included in the article, she only learned that her post had been mounted and incorporated in an exhibit on the Maidan when several acquaintances visited the Maidan, saw it, and contacted her in mid-2019. I spoke with Olena Babakova on New Year's Eve in 2019, almost six years after she penned the original post and several months after she learned it had been included in an exhibit on the Maidan.

She is a journalist who has lived in Warsaw since 2008. In the post she wrote that her reaction to a multitude of violent episodes during the Maidan was stoicism. She did not cry, not even when she witnessed police brutality, saw dead bodies, and heard the mounting number of causalities. She simply continued to report on the uprising. However, one day in the Warsaw metro, three people stopped her. They had seen an interview she gave on Polish television and wanted to know how they could donate money to the protesters. At that moment, the chance expression of empathetic concern by strangers in Warsaw contrasted so sharply with the loud silence and stinging lack of empathy from her own family, friends, and colleagues in Russia that she was overcome by sorrow. She realized that, although her phone, email, and Facebook page were filled with expressions of concern and words of support from strangers and friends, near and far, none were from her family, friends, or colleagues in Russia. How should she understand this silence? Is it indifference? A fear-induced inertia?

She posted in Russian: "NOBODY from Russia, wrote to me saying that they felt sorry for the families of the dead or that they wanted to somehow help the people who were grieving. I read only angry comments about what nationalistic beasts do with peaceful law enforcement agents and unfortunate regional officials. I will not try to explain what is happening in Ukraine now—anyone who has ears has already heard everything." With a profound sense of sincere disappointment, she ended her post by writing, "I will only say that we measure our humanity by how much we are able to feel compassion." Her indictment included some of her own family members living in Russia, who, much to Olena's

THE AESTHETICS OF RELATEDNESS     141

chagrin, condemned the Maidan protests and endorsed the annexation of Crimea.

When I interviewed her in 2019, she noted, "most of the people I know in Russia are from Moscow and St. Petersburg; they spend their vacations in France or Italy; they speak foreign languages; they have money; and many have sent their kids abroad to become educated. But still they think that Putin is right about Ukraine and Crimea. It is not a good decision for Ukraine to be part of the EU because European civilization is not as spiritual as Russian civilization is." In other words, the superior religiosity that Orthodox civilization offers needs formal recognition through political and ecclesiastical unity. To this end, although these Russians can compare Europe and Russia, they still insist on keeping Ukraine in Russia's orbit as a brotherly nation in the name of maintaining this spiritual civilization. This made her realize that the problem is not an inability to understand but rather a lack of willingness, which forecloses the possibility of empathy arising. If there are no longer shared values and aspirations, then familial, friendship, and professional bonds become devoid of compassion and are permanently lost.[12]

"If we are talking about history as a narrative, it is the context that gives that narrative its meaning," she explained. "This exhibition on Maidan is really nice from a human point of view. But is it good from a professional historical viewpoint? I'm not so sure. The context has changed." Her perspective on empathy and antipathy has changed in tandem with earthquake-like changes in the circumstances. "I don't want to say that when I was writing these words in 2014, I wasn't sincere. I was sincere. That was what I felt at that moment. I felt the support of Polish civil society and felt abandoned by the Russian one. This reflects the picture I saw from my angle at that time. Reactions in 2013–14 were very emotional. But it is high time to no longer be emotional. That would be my message today."

She, too, condemns the rush to embrace suffering at the hands of others and calls this phenomenon the "Central European Victimicity Festival." She refers to the penchant for seeing geographic proximity as automatically leading to solidarity among the "especially offended" (*osoblivo obrazhenyi* in Ukrainian). It is understood that these nations are offended by Russians. Topping the list are Poles, Lithuanians, Latvians, Georgians, and others. They are expected to feel solidarity and have empathy for Ukrainians for the suffering they have endured, as evidenced by the commercial success of the poem set to music in Lithuania. Shared victimhood creates forms of relatedness and an empathy-induced reimagining of geopolitical alliances. Characterizing historical experience in terms of victimhood serves two purposes, she argues. Such a perspective does not oblige the victim to consider the experiences and perspectives of others in a conflict situation, which means any grievances separatists in Eastern Ukraine might have are illegitimate and therefore dismissed. Further, the focus on victimization exonerates the victim from responsibility for any miscarriage of justice he or she might have perpetrated and allows for a sense of moral purity and purpose even as it perpetuates grief. In other words, expressions of a shared past based on victimization and suffering articulate new boundaries that validate separation of the victimizer from the victimized.

## Religious Engagement

The Greek Catholic Church was particularly active, visible, and vocal in its calls for political reform on the Maidan and later in its efforts to address the conflict in the east. Continuing the tradition of formal portraits of army servicemen killed in combat on the outer walls of St. Michael's Monastery, the Garrison Church in Lviv doubles as an exhibition site. The church houses the Center of Military Chaplaincy for the Ukrainian Greek Catholic Church. In 2019, those who attended mass in this church were surrounded by material evidence of an ongoing war and the death and destruction it continues to bring to Ukraine.

Much like the shrines on the Maidan incorporated helmets, tires, and other materials used in defense, both outer aisles of the church were lined with spent rockets, grenades, and other discarded military weaponry, as well as national symbolism exemplified by uniforms, banners, and flags, as illustrated in figures 4.5 and 4.6. As has become common, the personalization of fighters was achieved through large close-up facial photos and biographical details. Even more poignant was a display of the remains of weapons designed to kill presented side-by-side with intimate, close-up portraits of children from the Donbas who have been forced to flee. The implication is that soldiers are protecting the next generation of Ukrainians. Such emotive renderings of war victims have led to the practice of people lining the streets on their knees when a dead soldier returns home for burial.

As I studied the serious expressions of parishioners who viewed the exhibit, I was haunted by the degree to which the integration of war debris in a church, side by side with the assertion of innocent children suffering, sanctified violence. Whereas an exhibit underlining the sinful and tragic nature of war might generate grief, at what point does grief turn to rage over the injustice of it all? When do otherwise compassionate people move beyond songs, paintings, poems, and grieving to express their sorrow? What might be the consequences of repeatedly seeing victims of violence in such familiar visual and biographical terms in a multitude of settings affectively communicating sacrifice, martyrdom, and loss?

**FIGURE 4.5.** War in Eastern Ukraine exhibit in the Garrison Church in Lviv, replete with religious and national symbolism that stand above spent military hardware and weaponry. Photo by the author.

The greater historical and political context is likely to suggest which way a viewer will interpret the material evidence of death and destruction. Acknowledging the offenses that led to woundedness is, as Gabodo-Madikizela writes, "a sign of ethical responsibility toward the other. It invites reflection on the historical circumstances that divide, and continue to divide, individuals and groups who are trying to heal from a violent and hateful past" (2008, 344; see also Kirmayer 2008). When a sense of a violated patrimony is framed by religiosity and mediated by the sacred, religious configurations suggest divine exaltation of sacrifice culminating in martyrdom as easily as they evoke the existence of evil forces and the demonization of others (Bakker 2013, 324).

The Ukrainian state, now together with the active participation of several denominations, commemorates the war in Eastern Ukraine in multiple ways. These actions also imply who is to blame: Yanukovych and his ruling clan, and increasingly all of Russia. Such demonization is potentially useful. Widespread popular disappointment with the slow pace of meaningful reform and deep concerns over the war fuel suspicions that commemorative efforts are simply governing authorities trying to coopt the righteousness of the struggle as their

**FIGURE 4.6.**   Continuing the personalized commemorative aesthetic developed after the Maidan of honoring victims as recognizable heroes, the war exhibit features portraits of slain soldiers. Photo by the author.

own, even as they mine the legal gray zone for continued self-enrichment through corrupt governing practices. Nonetheless, this leaves the Ukrainian Orthodox Church of the Moscow Patriarchate in an increasingly precarious position because of its connection to the Russian Orthodox Church and inclusion of prayers for the Russian leadership during services.

The commemoration of World War II is shaping up to be a litmus test of allegiance, a defining moment and, therefore, a highly divisive issue. Victory Day commemorations of the end of World War II have held heartfelt meaning over generations, whether as tragedy, as triumph in the face of adversity, victorious grandeur, or some other interpretation. Moreover, for believers and Just Orthodox alike, clerical involvement in death rituals, be they funeral rites or commemorative ceremonies, remains an expectation. When combined, we have the makings of a polarizing moment.

The confrontation was on full view during a special session of the Verkhovna Rada, Ukraine's parliament, on May 9, 2015, when a commemorative ceremony to mark the end of World War II was staged one year after the Maidan. Along with acknowledging the sacrifice of World War II veterans, President Petro Poroshenko decided to include a reading of the names of soldiers who died fighting in Eastern Ukraine and would be posthumously awarded the "Hero of Ukraine" designation for their service to the country. When the lawmakers stood to honor the dead veterans of the Ukrainian Army, Metropolitan Onufrii, leader of the UOC-MP, and his delegation refused to stand. They were the only ones in the chamber who remained seated. Harsh criticism ensued. Metropolitan Onufrii later explained his seated posture as an indication of his opposition to war in general, and not the inclusion of war dead from the current armed conflict, an excuse that was widely discarded. Still, this moment signaled a sea change in attitudes among the different Orthodox churches toward death, sacrifice, burial, and salvation.

Within one year, the UOC-MP's position on burial radically changed. They placed restrictions on conducting burial services for soldiers who died fighting in Eastern Ukraine and would no longer perform a funeral rite for anyone baptized in another Orthodox denomination. The issue became shrill when a two-year-old child in Zaporizhzhia was tragically killed by falling scaffolding. The child was baptized in the UGCC, but the UOC-MP predominates in Eastern Ukraine. The parents went public with their desperation over their inability to find a priest who would perform a funeral rite for their child. Feelings morphed into rage, first among the parents and then more broadly across the country, when baptism in another denomination was used as a justification to exclude a child from receiving a proper burial. Still, the incident illustrated the effectiveness of using burial as a means for the various Orthodox churches to distinguish themselves from each other, to advance the political orientations and allegiances they advocate, and to force the Just Orthodox to choose an affiliation with a particular denomination.

If the UGCC and other pro-Ukrainian denominations across the confessional spectrum would play a leading role in commemorating the tragic deaths from the war in Eastern Ukraine, the UOC-MP would claim the commemoration of death—and victory—resulting from the Great Patriotic War. The UOC-MP now hosts a *mobelen*, or special prayer, to commemorate Victory Day on May 9 as the Soviet Union always did, and not on May 8 as is done in Europe and now in Ukraine too in a newly renamed Day of National Remembrance and Reconciliation. For the UOC-MP, the Great Patriotic War is positioned as a battle with evil forces in which Orthodox warriors fought and triumphed. The UOC-MP commemorations of Victory Day feature processions of the cross in public space, the performance of Soviet war songs, priests in camouflage, and references to patriotism in the form of love for one's land and love for God. Most notably, the UOC-MP increasingly asserts Victory Day as a second Easter, and as such, a family holiday that centers on resurrection. It becomes a religious obligation to honor the fallen because they are kin. Participants in processions carry not only icons and religious banners but also photos and portraits of family and friends who perished in the war, replicating the aesthetic used to commemorate those who died on the Maidan and in the East. The UOC-MP, like the other denominations, displays its ability to forge transcendent bonds through ritualized behaviors that connect those who sacrificed in victory with the UOC-MP today. The church, as a mnemonic agent, promotes the idea of the Great Patriotic War as a holy war, a true victory over evil, in which our forefathers participated. It is a battleground and moral victory from which women are excluded. Military men performed it and clerical men commemorate it, which contributes to the militarized masculinity on the rise in both Ukraine and Russia (Martsenyuk and Grytsenko 2017; Mayerchyk 2014; Fomina 2017).

Commemorating World War II serves other purposes for the OCU, UOC-KP, and other religious organizations. Their commemorations of World War II position the war as an anti-Soviet struggle that involved occupation and national suffering. The Organization of Ukrainian Nationalists and the Ukrainian Insurgent Army, long demonized in the USSR for their collaboration with Nazi forces against the Soviet Red Army, become defenders of Ukraine. They are also forefathers, but of an earlier generation of warriors for Ukrainian independence against Soviet forces that sought to denationalize Ukrainians and promote godless atheism. By linking their commemorations to *Pomynal'nyi Den'*, or the day after Easter when according to the Orthodox calendar the departed are remembered (also called *Provody* in Ukrainian; *Radonitsa* in Russian), a secular commemoration of veterans takes on religious overtones.

In sum, all sides find a usable past when they seek to sacralize history and even weaponize it to advance—or destroy—the legitimacy of institutional religious connections. As mnemonic agents that shape recall and understandings of the past, religious institutions use performative rituals in public space to link certain people together and exclude others. By blending the love of God into the love of country with the willingness to sacrifice and defend them both against evil, religious institutions not only weaponize religion but history too for the advancement of their preferred politics of belonging. The past as a holy battleground between good and evil lends itself to the depiction of two camps of religious organizations and a bifurcated choice of a political future or a political past, Constantinople or Moscow, a patriarch in Kyiv or Moscow, the EU or the Eurasian Customs Union, and so on. It also bespeaks the unresolved trauma of a war fought over seven decades ago even as armed combat continues to deliver new dead bodies in need of burial, commemoration, and resolution.

# Affect and the Power of Persuasion

Violence leaves traces, not just in the bodies and minds of those who experience it, but also in lived spaces. The mediating space of the city is a site where affect is generated in particularly concentrated and palpable ways inspiring bodily sensations, emotions, and recollections of an agentive nature. Such affective spaces shape the encounters that occur there and the meanings imparted to those experiences. The materiality of these commemorative spaces communicates the sacrality of the events, the spiritualized practices of recall, and the ritualized commemorations of the martyred dead in these set apart spaces and contribute to a certain atmosphere. Because of the sensations these experiences create, this atmosphere potentially has the power to persuade.

In taking such an analytical perspective, I acknowledge a form of agency, and even a certain power, in the built environment and the material things that adorn it over those who circulate in its affective spaces. Navaro-Yashin's (2012) study of a divided Cyprus urges us to recognize the "codependence and codetermination" between the outer environment and the interiority of subjects and how this can serve to replicate divisions. The affective charge of the atmosphere, first from the Maidan and now from the war, creates experiences of grief and ritualized mourning with a common aesthetic. This shapes lifeworlds, including a shared sense of place and one's place in the world. Once such emotive understandings are predictably fixed as signs that are part of a semiotic ideology, they can be made politically productive and carry ethical and moral connotations validating relatedness or a severing of relatedness.

This adds a certain fluidity, even volatility, to the forms of consciousness that might arise from an affective atmosphere. Affective spaces around shrines, monuments, exhibits, and commemorations are often intentionally designed to provoke certain sensations, only to see that the results produced are entirely different (Bennett 2001; Latour 1993; Navaro-Yashin 2012). These commemorative markers of death can prompt grief as easily as they can rage. Grief over sacrifice of life can yield rage that craves more violence. Mourning loss can evolve into venerating martyrs. As a mediating force between the ongoing processes of producing places and giving meaning to shared experiences that occur there, infrastructures of feeling link the living to the dead in new ways as easily as they can sever relationships among family members, friends, and colleagues who fail to understand grief and rage in the same way.

Revenge is all about recouping honor, which the embrace of dignity is meant to overturn in favor of developing a form of conscience and integrity (Sherman 2009, 76). Yet the alloy of grief and rage can linger for years when the loss is refreshed by an affective atmosphere that refuels the obligation to seek vengeance or to right a wrong. This is the burden of dreams that has long colored the life-worlds of Ukrainians, which I wrote about decades ago (Wanner 1998). By keeping victimizations of the past alive, does healing become elusive? Do the shrines and the spectrum of commemorative ceremonies draw out Paul Klee's Angelus Novus? The angel is blown into the future while remaining fixated on the past, staring in wide-eyed horror, like those at the shrines, as the pile of wreckage and dead bodies from snipers and war grows.

Dmytruk's poem asserts that an era has ended, an era that was characterized by "brotherhood," the widespread use of Russian language, a warm embrace of aspects of Russian culture, and most important of all, expansive networks—familial, personal, and professional—connecting people in both countries in myriad ways. I think she is correct. The post-Soviet era has ended. We are now in a new period that is characterized by different norms of relatedness that find expression in political policies and the creation of new religious institutions. For many, the grief is tremendous over the collapse of social and familial relationships that spanned political borders that have dissolved in the face of mutual miscomprehension. Inevitably, commemorations recall these losses too and evoke even more grief. However, the lines separating grief from rage and the urge to mourn from the impulse to seek revenge can be precariously thin.

Is it surprising that rage is not far behind sorrow? These emotions are the ends of the spectrum that an affective atmosphere produces. The sacred shrouding of these shrines, monuments, and exhibits to exalt dead heroes and martyrs makes them either part of processes of healing from violence or glorifying and perpetuating violence. By magnetically drawing people into their sacred orbit, the shrines and monuments—through spiritualized practices of recall and mourning—shape political and religious subjectivities through the sacral framing of sacrifice, which informs the obligations of the living to the dead. Those who are moved by these deaths belong to this place and to these people.

# SERVING ON THE FRONT AND THE HOME FRONT

## Military Chaplains in Public Institutions

The Russian parliament signed off on Vladimir Putin's request to send military forces to Crimea on March 1, 2014, making official what had already begun. Troops wearing unmarked uniforms occupied the peninsula and staged a referendum two weeks later that affirmed the people's will to transfer the territory from Ukraine to Russia.[1] Not even one month after the Russian annexation of the Crimean Peninsula, separatists in the Donetsk and Luhansk regions, with support from Russia, declared independence from Ukraine after staging referendums of their own. By mid-April 2014, the provisional Ukrainian government launched formal military strikes against two of its own eastern provinces. Since then, Eastern Ukraine has become the site of the bloodiest conflict the European continent has seen since the Yugoslav wars of the 1990s.

Some initially called this a civil war. However, after a Malaysian commercial airliner flying from Amsterdam to Kuala Lumpur was shot down on July 17, 2014, killing all 298 on board using sophisticated weaponry based in territories held by pro-Russian rebels in Eastern Ukraine, it became obvious that the separatists were not acting alone. As the conflict progressed, unclaimed corpses began to pile up in local morgues and were eventually buried in mass cemeteries as "temporarily unidentified soldiers." This underlined that many of the fighters were not local, and some were even mercenaries. As the fighting escalated, a surge of post-Maidan patriotism produced a plethora of volunteer fighters, who were untrained and fought alongside an unprepared and undersupplied Ukrainian force. Some clergy, who were active on the Maidan, became military chaplains attached to combat units. To date, this conflict has resulted in over 13,000 casualties, nearly two million people displaced, and airports, schools, hospitals, and roads bombed to rubble throughout a region once known as the "cradle of the proletariat."

The confrontation between Russian-backed separatists and Ukrainian armed forces continues to simmer and shows no signs of resolution despite international mediation, a series of ceasefires, and sanctions brought against Russia. The concern is that Donbas will join the growing list of "frozen conflicts" in the region that already includes Transnistria in Moldova, on Ukraine's western border, and Abkhazia and South Ossetia in Georgia, to the south. Such internationally-unrecognized sub-state structures can be used to uphold a limbo-land of organized lawlessness. Transnistria, which shares a border with Ukraine to the west, in particular, became a site of unfettered trafficking in people, drugs, and arms. Donbas could become a similar "black hole" of illegal trade in the east.

Although an international border between Russia and Ukraine has only existed since 1991, after the armed conflict began in 2014, a new iron curtain of a border has been built to separate—depending on one's perspective—the "aggressor" or the forces of a "fascist junta." Although it is clear that Putin's regime enables this combat and even sent Russian special forces from the beginning and regular army units as of July 2014, it is difficult to say who is fighting who exactly. Unquestionably, some Ukrainians from the Donbas are fighting for succession from Ukraine over grievances with what they see as discriminatory and otherwise ill-advised policies of an anti-Russian Ukrainian state. Other Ukrainians fight with the Ukrainian army against these separatist forces, giving this conflict a prominent civil dimension. Postwar reconciliation will have to be among Ukrainians every bit as much as it will have to be between Russians and Ukrainians.

For other ethnic and national groups, this is a proxy war, which is why mercenaries played such a significant role, especially in the beginning. To cite just two examples, Georgians are still smarting from the Russian invasion and annexation of their territory in 2008. They team up with Chechen fighters, who have fought two excruciatingly brutal wars since the collapse of the USSR that produced mass destruction and staggering civilian casualties. Some members of both groups have joined Ukrainian forces in an attempt to strike a blow at Russia, whereas others from exactly the same regions express their pro-Russian allegiance in conflicts at home by fighting on the pro-Russian separatist side in Donbas. Mercenaries from Brazil, Serbia, Canada, the United States, and elsewhere have also been found among the corpses and combatants captured alive.

The task of confronting the horrors of war, the human toll it has taken as well as the challenge of advancing reconciliation increasingly falls to military chaplains, a newly formalized profession.[2] Military chaplains bring the extraordinariness of war into everyday life with the express purpose of creating change. In addition to providing liturgical and counseling services to soldiers in combat situations, the stated goal of the military chaplaincy is to "be close by" (*buty poruch* in Ukrainian), on the front as well as on the home front, according to the head of the Ukrainian Greek Catholic Church.[3] Chaplains give guidance on understanding the vexed relationship between forgiveness, responsibility, and moral justice (*moral'na spravedlivist'* in Ukrainian), given the contentiousness of the conflict and the shrill tone of political debate. Much of the broader ongoing work chaplains do addresses healing the wounds that arise, not just from combat but from a lack of empathy that manifests itself as indifference. Cultural norms and the particulars of a specific historic period shape how empathy is expressed and how forgiveness and the unforgivable are understood. In myriad ways, military chaplains have become arbiters of these important issues. Andriy Zelins'kyi, a military chaplain from the UGCC, who was the first chaplain to serve in a combat situation in Eastern Ukraine, succinctly said, "If the task of the military is to win the war, the task of a military chaplain is to triumph over the war by achieving victory over the consequences of war in the human heart."[4] How can this be done?

As we saw in the last chapter, the post-Maidan period saw an expansion of vernacular religious practice in public space that involve mourning loss and commemorating sacrifice. As the number of casualties mounted, so did the number of public sites where they are mourned and remembered. Here I consider how in the face of war everyday religiosity slips into public institutions with great speed and little resistance. These developments are fed by the nature of the work military chaplains perform when they rotate from the front to the home front, which is changing the tenor of public social institutions and, by extension, the cultural values and dispositions they shape. Drawing on military and religious credentials, military chaplains provide counsel and care to the families of wounded or slain soldiers; humanitarian assistance by collecting material goods and money to help Anti-Terrorist Operation (ATO) forces, the displaced, and needy; and work to develop the next generation of patriotic leaders. Above all, these chaplains remind the larger population that the war is not somewhere out there, but it, too, like the chaplains, is always close by. Their perceived success is thanks to the therapeutic religiosity, or healing and empowerment techniques they offer that are grounded in religious worldviews.

## From the Maidan to the Battlefield

In recent armed conflicts, it is not the war but winning the peace that is the true challenge, whether we speak of hybrid wars, as in Eastern Ukraine, or more conventional wars, as in Afghanistan and Iraq. In North and South Korea, Israel and the West Bank and the Gaza Strip, and the disputes over Kashmir, for example, violence was only quelled after the erection of physical barriers that severed connections and contact but delivered no peace. Random violence and palpable tensions keep alive a credible threat of renewed armed combat at any given moment. No one doubts that winning the peace in Eastern Ukraine will be any different. This hybrid war produces neither the single casualty that is a tragedy nor a torrent of deaths that become statistics. By generating a handful of dead and wounded combatants each week and having destroyed the infrastructure of the region, the stinging need to "win over hearts and minds" to achieve peace has not been lost on Ukrainians. Military chaplains are shaping up to be providers of this soft skill in a hard war.

Clergy who offered calming, motivational support to Maidan protesters were called "chaplains of the Maidan." Once the war began, military chaplains provided the same to protesters, many of whom enlisted as soldiers. The war sparked the remaking of the almost freelance status the military chaplaincy previously had and the ad hoc way in which it functioned.[5] Before the war, commanders were allowed to use "discretion" as to whether to "invite" priests or provide "prayer space" or not (Volk 2020, 35). Clergy simply volunteered to provide spiritual counseling and other forms of service to men in uniform (at that time they were all men). Once the war began, church-state initiatives multiplied to create a more formal and strategic role for clergy and their religious organizations as part of the war effort. The first priority was to prepare chaplains for ATO servicemen in the East.

As of early 2020, about 400 military chaplains worked in an official capacity as employees of the Ministry of Defense.[6] The service of at least double that number is financed, as it was before, by individual denominations or parishes. These chaplains are called volunteers because they do not receive the medical, pension, and legal protections that military chaplains do who are employed by the Department of Moral-Psychological Services of the Armed Forces of Ukraine (*Upravlinnia Moral'no-Psykhologichnoho Zabezpechennia Zbroynykh Syl Ukrainy*). In short order, the military chaplaincy expanded beyond the Armed Services to include chaplains in the National Guard and the State Border Service in July 2014; in prisons as of the summer of 2015; in government transportation services (railways and airports) in December 2016; and thanks to Covid, legislation was fast tracked to establish medical chaplains in healthcare facilities, such as hospitals and rehabilitation centers, in 2021. The chaplaincy is now divided into military and nonmilitary branches. Beyond, the prison and medical chaplaincies, the other nonmilitary chaplaincies in development are aimed at the next generation and include an "orphan chaplaincy," as service in state-run boarding schools is called, and student chaplaincies, where clergy serve youth in educational institutions.

# Factors Shaping the Chaplaincy

Developing the chaplaincy in Ukraine became an important litmus test for issues of tolerance in an increasingly pluralist society. The process of formalizing military chaplains as employees of the Ukrainian Ministry of Defense triggered tensions, intense legislative debate, and broad popular discussion. Two factors were particularly influential in remaking the chaplaincy after the Maidan. First, legislation governing the military chaplaincy forced an answer to the question of just how independent the Ukrainian Orthodox Church-Moscow Patriarchate is from the Russian Orthodox Church, and by extension the Russian government. Should tolerance include allowing religious representatives of an "aggressor state" to counsel soldiers during times of war? The verdict rendered by the Verkhovna Rada was no. This made the military chaplaincy an instrument to publicly chastise the UOC-MP as a Russian institution, limit its presence and influence, and simultaneously expand the activity and visibility of other confessional groups.

This generated an international outcry among human rights activists (Volk 2020: 35–36). There are over 12,000 religious communities registered with the UOC-MP, which makes it the largest denomination in Ukraine. Law 2662, which passed in 2018, does not allow priests from the UOC-MP to serve in an official capacity as military chaplains, meaning as employees of the Ukrainian Ministry of Defense. They can, however, serve as volunteers. Nonetheless, this legislation established Orthodox jurisdictions as politically pro-Ukrainian (the OCU) and politically pro-Russian (UOC-MP), which may or may not accurately reflect the political views of each institution's clergy and parishioners.

For example, on the local level, many I spoke with understand a parish to be "theirs" because of a family history of participation. Perhaps family members helped renovate the church, were baptized there, or that is where they go to light a candle. This is the basis for their attachment, far more so than a statement of political allegiance. The administrative affiliation a particular church building has to a faraway patriarchate in Moscow or Constantinople, while usually known, has not been the driving force in selecting a church, except when it comes to life cycle rituals, such as weddings, funerals, and the like, when a deliberate choice is made. The commitment, especially among the Just Orthodox, is to a particular church building and usually hinges on an appreciation of the aesthetic experience the church offers through its icons, choir, or decor. Sometimes the appeal of a particular church is simply its convenient location. The understanding that Orthodoxy forms a national community that includes the Just Orthodox, sympathizers and agnostics, who are welcome in any Orthodox church, diminishes the appeal of fixating on a particular face-to-face community that meets regularly. Therefore, choosing a church has not necessarily reflected the political implications of a parish's placement in a greater religious institutional structure, although most people are aware of it. Many loyal to a particular UOC-MP parish did not see their church as the arm of the Russian state in their city, town, or village. These are among the factors that explain why legislation to block UOC-MP clergy from serving as military chaplains in an official capacity was so hotly debated and why most individual parishioners did not seek to reaffiliate away from the UOC-MP to the OCU after the *tomos* of autocephaly was granted.

The Ukrainian Parliament passed additional legislation on December 20, 2018 (Law 5309) regarding the name of religious organizations. According to this law, which was specifically crafted for this historical moment, religious organizations whose centers are located in an "aggressor state" should reflect the name of the aggressor country in their name. The goal was to oblige the Ukrainian Orthodox Church-Moscow Patriarchate to acknowledge in its name that it was really the Russian Orthodox Church. The chaplaincy became an available means to announce the UOC-MP as an inherently anti-Ukrainian force in Ukrainian society. This was controversial, especially beyond Ukraine. It instantly made the chaplaincy a lightning rod to measure issues of religious tolerance. Naturally, the UOC-MP objected vigorously to all restrictive legislation and to being positioned as a Moscow-based organization. To prove its patriotic credentials, it insisted that it too blessed the Ukrainian army in its defense of the Ukrainian state and asserted that military duty is the fulfillment of the Savior's commandment to love one's neighbor. However, it was unable or unwilling to rein in the inflammatory rhetoric coming from Moscow, the effects this had on their own clergy and parishioners, their use of their churches to stockpile weapons in the East, and their repression of non-Orthodox faith groups in the Donbas.

In addition to using the chaplaincy, at least bureaucratically and in name, to disempower the UOC-MP, a second factor shaping the chaplaincy is that it is a portal for a variety of foreign-based religious groups with well-established chaplaincies to exert influence on the development of the chaplaincy in Ukraine. Chaplaincy training is primarily guided by Catholic social doctrine that comes to Ukraine via the Roman Catholic Church's influence on the Ukrainian Greek Catholic Church and through Ukrainian Protestant clergy, who have extensive contacts with American Protestant communities.[7] These two minority faith groups, and their ever-expanding programs of military and nonmilitary chaplaincy, outreach, and humanitarian assistance, put pressure on the Orthodox churches to be more socially engaged. There is little in the way of a parallel process underway in Russia. Foreign religious organizations do not exert anywhere near the same influence or degree of support in Russia on the chaplaincy.

By enhancing a multidenominational chaplaincy, and especially by integrating military and nonmilitary chaplains into the workings of secular, public institutions, ever more differences are being created between the social and cultural landscapes of Ukraine and Russia. The military chaplaincy in Ukraine moves clergy far beyond the front lines and the parish and places them in state-run social institutions, often where people experiencing pain, vulnerability, grief, and rage congregate.[8] The infrastructure that religious institutions offer, not just hierarchical authority structures and meeting places, but also in terms of rituals, traditions, and symbols as a means of nonverbal, performative communication, is a base chaplains use to cultivate empathic dialogue as a first step to addressing social problems in a spiritual, therapeutic, and tangibly material way.

The trust that clergy and ATO volunteers currently enjoy among a large sector of the population is key to unlocking these processes through interfaith, ecumenical work in an increasingly militarized society. A 2019 Gallup poll found only 9 percent of Ukrainians have confidence in their government. For the second year in a row Ukrainians expressed the lowest level of confidence in elected officials in the world, far below the 2018 median average for the governments of former Soviet states (48%) and the global average (56%).[9] The little trust there is goes, as it has in the past, to the armed forces (69%) and to the church (62.5%).[10] This makes military chaplains are the ultimate beneficiaries of public trust. They embody access to military and divine power, hold positions within two institutional hierarchies that demand obedience and accountability, and they do a job that provides little, if any, financial incentives and yet imposes hardships that potentially include loss of life. Against the backdrop of the Donbas war, the loss of territory, and a heightened sense of vulnerability, military chaplains address the fears and concerns of the population at large by providing therapeutic techniques that draw on religiosity to be applied in everyday life.

# Defenders

Chaplains, unlike the soldiers they counsel, do not carry weapons, but they wear a soldier's uniform and usually a large, visible insignia to signal their status as chaplains. One of their key contributions is crafting an understanding of how to respond to armed aggression, some of which is Russian-backed but some of which draws on grievances Ukrainians have with other Ukrainians. Military chaplains begin with soldiers themselves. The sin of murder and forgiveness are topics that soldiers raise in conversation with chaplains. Aware of the commandment, "Thou shall not kill," how should soldiers understand what they have done and how might God understand it? Many chaplains encourage soldiers to forgive themselves by differentiating the aggression that results from defending one's country from murder. One chaplain from the UOC-KP (which is now part of the OCU) explained to his soldiers that there is no murder in war.[11] There is only "deactivation of the enemy," and responding to that obligation is a choice the soldier did not initiate. Another military chaplain from the UGCC explains his position in similar terms by saying, "Yes, this is war and our soldiers need to react with dignity when defending our land. But we didn't go to a foreign country, the enemy came to us. They brought this war here and we must defend our land with dignity. Every war is an act of aggression. Although we didn't start it, it's our duty to stop it."[12] When chaplains encourage soldiers to see themselves as morally empowered defenders, fulfilling their duty to protect their rightful territory, this potentially absolves soldiers from having committed sin. The act of killing becomes a sacrifice the soldier makes on behalf of others, even a form of heroism. This is reaffirmed publicly when commemorative markers given to the Heavenly Hundred as martyrs extend to include ATO fighters as defenders. The implication is that all have made sacrifices for the betterment of Ukraine, some with their lives, some by sacrificing the lives of others. Heroic sacrifice is further highlighted on the local level when dead soldiers return for burial and people line the streets on their knees in homage as the hearse passes by.

Chaplains are also called on by the state to encourage the greater population to see soldiers as moral exemplars of the common good. A new commemorative holiday, Day of the Defender of Ukraine (*Den' Zakhysnyka Ukrainy* in Ukrainian) was established on October 14, after the war began. The gendered name of the holiday does not reflect the over 30,000 women serving the armed forces in various capacities as of 2019. Rather, the intention was to replace the February 23 Soviet holiday, Defenders of the Fatherland, which was equally as male gendered, and considered a counterpart to March 8, International Women's Day.

October 14 has religious and historical symbolism. It is not only an important Orthodox feast day, the Day of Protection of the Blessed Virgin (*Sviato Pokrovy Presviatoi Bohorodytsi* in Ukrainian), it is also the Day of Ukrainian Cossacks (*Den' Ukrains'koho Kozatstva* in Ukrainian). According to Eastern Christian liturgical tradition, Mary the Theotokos appeared to St. Andrew and his disciple Epiphanius in the tenth century on October 1 (Julian calendar) at the Blachernae Church in Constantinople, where relics of her robe, veil, and belt were venerated. At the time the city was in danger of invasion by pagan Rus, but the miracle of appearance saved them; thus the Feast of the Intercession became a feast day in the Byzantine Rite Orthodox churches. Lore has it that the Cossacks considered the Mother of God their patron and prayed to her before military campaigns saying, "We pray: cover us with your Holy Veil and deliver us from evil." The Ukrainian Insurgent Army (UPA) also declared the Mother of God to be their patron and chose October 14 as a commemorative anniversary.

**FIGURE 5.1.**  In 2019 a new monument to Defenders of Ukraine opened in Kharkiv with military chaplains in attendance. On the vertical columns the lines of the poem "Love Ukraine" by the Soviet-era poet Volodymyr Sosyura are engraved. The focal point of the monument reads, "Heroes do not die." Photo by the author.

In 2005 former President Viktor Yushchenko declared that this feast day would henceforth also be the Day of UPA. Thus, successive generations of defenders, motivated by protecting the Blessed Virgin Mary and Ukraine, are now commemorated with the participation of military chaplains on October 14. These commemorations increasingly occur at monuments, such as the one seen in figure 5.1, erected to honor defenders killed in Eastern Ukraine and the sacrifices they have made.

In addition to framing soldiers as defenders, other responsibilities that chaplains shoulder further illustrate the interpenetration of religion and national patriotism. According to the training military chaplains receive, they are tasked with developing "high patriotic feelings and the spirit of combat among servicemen" and are encouraged to do so by drawing on the "moral and spiritual potential of the religious and cultural heritage of the Ukrainian people" (Kalenychenko and Kokhanchuk 2017). This integrates a nondenominational religiosity, referred to as a universalism into understandings of the cultural heritage of the Ukrainian people. What's more, chaplains are expected to familiarize soldiers with the "history of the national, cultural and religious formation of Ukrainian statehood," which serves to integrate religion into the foundation of Ukrainian independence and cultural heritage. Finally, using the oft-repeated, Soviet-era brotherly trope to emphasize unbreakable, kin-like bonds, chaplains are expected to foster "brotherly relations among servicemen" that rest on "principles of solidarity, humanity and a sense of the sacredness of military duty." In other words, military chaplains are tasked with creating commitments to the country based on a shared heritage expressed in the idiom of kin that is worth defending.

Prominent chaplains are at times confronted with military leaders who interpret these instructions to mean that military chaplains serve as *politruki* (*politicheskie rukovoditeli* in Russian), or political managers of soldiers. A *politruk* was responsible for ideological indoctrination in the USSR and for ensuring the political reliability of troops. During World War II, the Soviet Red Army had *politruki* embedded in battalions to minimize defections. Some commanders see chaplains as a means to make soldiers obey orders. Others are not religious, and do not appreciate the work of chaplains but tolerate it nonetheless.

## Spiritual Gym

"Sweet" is how the name of one of the first military chaplains I met would be translated.[13] Given his dual credentials as a military man and as a clerical leader in two institutions known for patriarchy and chain-of-command approach to power, I was not prepared for how truly sweet he was. He was ordained in 2006 as a Greek-Catholic priest and right away became a military chaplain at the Lviv National Ground Forces Academy. Later his chaplaincy expanded to include students and orphans. In 2012, he became responsible for a parish in the center of historic Lviv that caters to believers and tourists of all ages, which was the site of the exhibit discussed in chapter 4. Known as the Garrison Church, it was built in the early seventeenth century by Jesuits to serve the Austrian and Polish troops stationed in Lviv. When Western Ukraine was annexed to the USSR, and the Ukrainian Greek-Catholic Church was outlawed in 1946, the church was turned into a book depository. Soviet authorities stored over two million volumes in floor-to-ceiling shelves there. After much dispute, in 2010 the church was finally handed over to the Ukrainian Greek Catholic Church. The books have been removed, but scaffolding remains throughout the nave of the church as restoration continues to remove the vestiges of the church's prior life as a book warehouse. In spite of the construction, the immense Baroque detail of the church's interior and its majestic icons are still visible. Given its history as a garrison church, it became the Center of the Military Chaplaincy for the UGCC. This is where Stepan Sus served, along with twenty other priests, from 2012 to 2019.

In January 2020, shortly after running a 10K race with Ukrainian war veterans as part of the Marines Marathon in Washington, DC, Stepan Sus learned that, at age thirty-eight, he would become the single youngest bishop to serve in the Catholic Church, joining seven other Ukrainian bishops ranging in age from thirty-eight to forty-three, who constitute the youngest bishops in the entire Catholic Church worldwide. The strong preference for young hierarchs within the UGCC bespeaks a commitment to catapult over generations whose thinking might be tainted by Soviet-era values and practices. Once the pope confirmed his new status on November 15, 2019, Sus claimed that for him, "a new marathon in the life of the Church" began.

We met for the first time one month before this happened in an outdoor café, not far from the Garrison Church, on an exceptionally warm fall day. He proposed to conduct the interview in English. I soon understood why. Here we were in an open, public place, highly visible to other patrons of the café as well as to numerous pedestrians who passed by. His priestly collar made him instantly identifiable as a member of the clergy. Many people know him, and he must have greeted or chatted with at least ten passersby during the course of our meeting. Yet by speaking in English in this public place, he gained a measure of privacy. Even those who did not know him could see a priest in the mundane act of having a coffee in a café with a woman. This made him approachably human, which, I learned, is a goal he consistently pursues.

Vibrant Parish (*Zhyva Parafiia* in Ukrainian) is an initiative that the UGCC developed after the Maidan in 2015 to reconsider what parish communities can do for parishioners. This initiative appealed to him because he never intended to be a parish priest. Given his strong commitment and active engagement in the community, I asked why he was initially so reticent to serve in a parish. He explained:

> As a seminarian, I wanted to be a chaplain for deaf children. Sign language. I studied at a special college for deaf children. I wanted to provide some kind of ministry that is totally different from parish ministry. Since Ukrainian independence, we have focused on the parish. You are going to be a parish priest. This was the only model. And it seemed to me to be a very small way to contribute. It is not the only way and not the best for the church. For the Ukrainian Greek Catholic Church, the chaplaincy was something that they knew about. At the very beginning we had a model of priests relating to the church like priests behind the iconostasis.

He went on to explain what he meant by that, and in the process, explained what a military chaplain's obligation to "be close by" means. People have been conditioned to "only come to the church, listen to the priest and obey him, and nothing more." Sus laments that "Church life for too many parishes now consists of liturgy, funerals, baptisms and nothing more. I didn't want to be in a parish like that. I started to think that we had to change our attitudes to the faithful. How can we provide our ministry? Now we started this project, 'Vibrant Parish 2020.' I always thought we had to do something more," he said.

This determination led him to work with soldiers. He explained how a military chaplain helps to establish comradeship and develop the ability to get along with others. Sometimes it takes a bit of convincing. Soldiers often ask him why they have to repeat such phrases as *"Hospodi pomylyi"* (Lord have mercy in Ukrainian) so many times. It seems senseless. Sus explains the value of prayer in terms they can relate to. "I say to them when you go to the gym you do exercises many times. Five, ten, fifteen repetitions. Why do you do that? They say, "To have results. To have muscles. To be strong." I explain that we have inner struggles too and we need to be strong." Religion, in this way, becomes a "spiritual gym," where one's conscience grows robust with the repetition of prayer. "In the Church, you are making your soul. You are examining your soul. You teach yourself how to survive, how to deal with challenges, how to look at many things," he says, which reveals the therapeutic qualities of religious practice as he understands and imparts them to soldiers. One of the most important intended results of repeatedly praying and other ritualized practices, Sus explains, is to hear a developed, strong voice of the soul in the form of a conscience. "We need to hear our soul to be ourselves. We need to hear what we want and what we need," he says. Fostering self-knowledge by promoting the development of a conscience, understood as the voice of the soul, through prayer and ritual participation is meant to help a soldier develop a more robust moral code and therefore become a better, stronger, and more decisive person.

Eastern Slavs often use the soul as a referent, claiming they do things for their soul. Correspondingly, a well-known proverb, *"chuzhaia dusha potiomki"* (Another's soul is darkness), reveals d*usha* as the force that animates a person's inner world—emotions, intuitions, values, sensations, and dreams (Pesman 2000). Sharing one's *dusha* is a form of intimacy because it makes a person vulnerable. Even in a secular therapeutic context, *dusha*, or soul, is used to orient a person to their lifeworld and to use the soul to make beneficial decisions.[14] The soul was often evoked in the Soviet period to refer to the moral aspects of personality and the righteousness of will. A strong soul allowed a person to remain true and uncompromising (Matza 2018, 267).

To use the soul as a source of commonality and solidarity, hearing the voice of one's conscience through prayer is only the first step. One must also learn to obey that voice. A key aspect of a chaplain's service, much like a therapist's, is building an ongoing relationship with soldiers to help them use the voice of their soul to regulate behavior. The difference is that chaplains add religious ritual and prayer to talk therapy to do so. Via analogy to walking down a road, Sus explains to his soldiers how to use their souls to live a moral life.

> Between a sidewalk and a road there is a line. This is a sign to show us that one part is no longer the sidewalk. Although the road looks like a sidewalk, it is not any more a sidewalk. It is so wide. You can walk on the road but it's very dangerous. You can be crushed, destroyed and many things can happen to you. This line between sidewalk and road is the locus of morality. God says that those who are following the narrow ways of life—it can be so narrow—but this line shows the path to success. Some want to walk on the wide road, thinking that it is their sidewalk. Nowadays some people are thinking and saying, "Why can't I choose to walk on the wide road?" They don't think about their life. They can lose their life on the road. The purpose of the church is to explain to people where the line of life is, where the line leading to salvation and safety is. That's morality. In the US so many people use cars so maybe you can't imagine what I mean.

I think even car-loving Americans can imagine this. The analogy is clear and readily understandable and one of the many ways he prioritizes explaining church teachings in terms of everyday life to make a connection with his soldiers, many of whom might be among the Just Orthodox and only have a tenuous connection to religion. Sus applauds the decision of Christian missionaries in Asia to substitute rice for bread when they taught the phrase, "Give us our daily rice," as an example of how clergy should meet a person on their own terms. This principle governs the way he approaches his duties as a military chaplain. In sum, his goal, which was also repeated to me by other chaplains, is for chaplains to prevent a broken relationship with God from developing during fighting on the front or while processing its aftermath on the home front. If this pairing between God and soldier can endure, this relationship can be the foundation for building others. One successful pairing can lead to others.

The second part of a military chaplain's job is to speak of war, to recognize those who fought, and especially those who died, and the suffering their sacrifice has brought to their families and friends. Sus insists, if there is no recognition of their sacrifice, no empathy for their suffering, there will be little support for veterans when they return home. This becomes doubly important when soldiers return disfigured, disabled, and still without a clear victory. If the recognition of sacrificial death on the Maidan began with spontaneous shrines, which were later coopted and amplified by the state, the job of obliging the public to recognize the death due to war falls to chaplains, many of whom are now state employees.

## Religiosity as a Therapeutic Strategy

Julia Lerner (2020) uses the term "therapeutic religiosity" in studying the rise of "therapeutic culture" and how a "psychological logic" affects the discourse of religiously observant migrants from the former Soviet Union to Israel. Even when they are from a variety of faith traditions, in their quest for "happiness," she argues, a blending of a religious way of life and a neoliberal subjectivity emerges, at once therapeutic and religious. This cultivates a specific emotional palette, which is reflected in narratives that inform "communal, public and collective realms." (2020, 1–13) Unlike Lerner's interlocutors, here the focus is not happiness, nor on serving a neoliberal order. Rather, the goal of therapeutic religiosity is enduring and healing from the experiences of war. Religiosity as a therapeutic strategy is marshaled to help people who are wounded in different ways return to some productive capacity as committed citizens capable of contributing to society. Military chaplains offer religiously infused talk therapy to soldiers as they transition to civilian life and a form of empathic care that centers on dialogue and existential engagement, which often begins on the battlefield or in a hospital and extends beyond. The work of military chaplains normativizes a spiritual dimension to care and the therapeutic capacities of religion by injecting religiosity into social institutions to restore and maintain the social fabric.

Techniques grounded in religious worldviews and spiritual practices have long been applied in a variety of contexts to therapeutically bring about a desired transformation of an emotional, bodily, or psychic nature. Religiosity as a therapeutic strategy contrasts with secular therapeutics, meaning credentialed medical expertise, in that it validates religious expertise as a means to empowerment, protection, and transformation thanks to religious practices and religious actors' ability to access the intervention of otherworldly forces. When military chaplains serve on the home front, they use religious concepts and spiritualized practices, some of which are site specific, to instrumentally solve problems. Secular therapists and counselors, who also use talk therapy, might invoke concepts with religious underpinnings, such as the soul. However, they cannot pivot to ritual, ritualized behaviors, and an array of other non-verbal vernacular religious practices to evoke the transcendent.

To aid soldiers during the processes of resocialization and re-entry into civilian life, which mandates learning to trust, forgive, and accept the rights of others in a pluralist society, as well as freeing oneself of anger and the urge to violence, chaplains must develop an empathic understanding for the difficulties soldiers, their families and communities might be experiencing. Perhaps even more challenging, they need to help soldiers cultivate empathy for those living among them whose values and visions are different from their own. Othering one's compatriots, or an enemy aggressor, forecloses on the possibility of imagining a relationship by denying empathy, by denying their very humanity. This perpetuates hostility and is a dynamic frequently found in divided societies. Although empathy can advance reconciliation and peace, it can also be used to intensify recognition of one's own suffering and thereby heighten hostility toward others, which compounds obstacles to reconciliation and recovery. This is more likely to happen when tropes of victimhood, martyrdom, and sacrifice are mobilized, as they are here, to alter understandings of who is a "brother" and who is a "neighbor."

We now turn to the work of chaplaincies that address the psychic and emotional pain of grieving family members as well as soldiers and veterans in distress. For many reasons, both cultural and economic, a one-child family became and remains the norm in Ukraine. Therefore, when a child is killed in combat, for parents this means the end of family life. The loss has ramifications not only in the present in terms of grief but in the future in terms of economic well-being. There's an old saying: Better to have one hundred friends than one hundred rubles. Children are valuable on many levels. Aloneness heightens the vulnerability of an already precarious life. Given the current state of social service provision and economic instability in Ukraine, most people count on their children to provide post-retirement elderly care, which is shattered when a son dies. There are status categories in English to identify loss through death. An orphan is a child who does not have parents. A widow/widower has lost a spouse to death. In Ukrainian, there are words for parents who have lost a child, even at different stages. *Mama anhela*, angel mother, is a woman who has lost a small child or a child during labor. "Parents who have been orphaned" (*bat'ki osirotily*) is an expression that indicates parents who, like an orphaned child, have no one to take care of them.

For family members in mourning, military chaplains arrange monthly services at the Lychakivs'kyi Cemetery, Lviv's most historic cemetery, where soldiers from this region killed in combat are buried in a special section dedicated to them. The first time I went to this part of the cemetery, I was awestruck by the endless sea of graves. They were undeniable evidence of the staggering number of deaths in the Donbas. The plethora of standardized gravestone memorials communicates the war's mass dimensions and illustrates the state's own abilities to effectively render space sacred. The tremendous personalization of those same identical grave sites marks each soldier as a son, husband, father, or all of the above. This form of material commemoration, of clearly marking each person as part of a collective, and yet depicting their individuality, continues the Maidan trend of both knowing the victim and recognizing their sacrifice of life for a cause greater than themselves. We know the dead through photographs and the familiar material objects that personify their lives. This facilitates the bonds of attachment by moving the viewer beyond an imagined realm into a lived reality of solidarity.

Once a month, people meet at the cemetery for a *panakhyda*, or memorial ceremony for the dead, followed by prayers and the incessant repetition of chants of *vichna yomu pam'iat'* (eternal memory to him). Each *panakhyda* is open to all, and I attended several (see figure 5.2). Nearly everyone present was there because they had a connection to a dead soldier. These ceremonies were comforting for

**FIGURE 5.2.**   After the memorial service led by a UGCC priest at a cemetery in Lviv. Burial in this part of the cemetery is uniquely reserved for war veterans. There were five new graves on the day this photo was taken. Photo by the author.

people who could not articulate the loss they had sustained—and therefore could not engage in dialogue. Nonetheless, they can recite prayers memorized in childhood and perform scripted gestures on cue collectively. This can become a bonding form of communication. For some, they are the only way to articulate the pain of loss. Because these forms of discourse are ritualized and scripted, they are effective in staving off the morphing of grief into rage. These families might gather at the cemetery over prayer and other ritualized acts, but they remain long after. Some women pull up a chair and as grieving mothers wait for others to stop by to chat and mourn together. Others tend graves by placing flowers, photos, and incense, much as they do at shrines and monuments. Tending a grave is a way to feel the presence of someone departed by "doing something" for them. Even though each tends their own relatives' grave, and often in silence, they do it at the same time, making this a collective endeavor. This coordinated practice serves to stave off a "patriotism of despair," which Serguei Oushakine (2009) argues descends on families in Russia in the early 2000s when soldiers' deaths from the first Chechen war were unacknowledged and their sacrifices unrecognized.

This gathering of family and friends is a manifestation of Olga Berggolts' famous World War II axiom of "No one is forgotten. Nothing is forgotten." The value of these gatherings, which function as something of a therapeutic support group, is in evidence for the priest responsible for the Center for Military Chaplaincy by the fact that three families that lost a son have decided to adopt a child. Adoption is fairly stigmatized in Ukraine, thanks to unexamined stereotypes that only alcoholics or other dishonorable people would abandon a child. So deciding to recreate a family through adoption is bold. Other parents, who cannot make that step, have volunteered to provide backup care for the new parents. These are the exceptions; the majority mourn in silence. Yet, exceptions serve the purpose of illustrating that rage is not the only available response to grief and that relatedness can be remade too.

# To Live with Dignity

Another domain where chaplains are active is providing humanitarian aid to the poor and those in need. Serhii is the head of the Synodal Department for the Medical Chaplaincy of the Orthodox Church of Ukraine. He began as a priest with the UOC-MP, switched to the UOC-KP quite publicly, and now is with the OCU. A former medical-turned-military chaplain and now a medical chaplain once again, Serhii served in a parish for many years in southern Ukraine. He is tall, lanky, chain-smoking, and fast-talking. He was a "chaplain of the Maidan," and after serving in Eastern Ukraine, he has become quite active in peacebuilding initiatives, among other endeavors, and this is the reason I initially contacted him in July 2018. I called at around 8 p.m. on a Saturday evening. He said I should come over right away. His daughter was out on a date and for sure he would not go to bed before 1 a.m. Plus, he was putting in a proposal for funding, and he was having trouble with the Americans. Perhaps you could help, he asked. I have learned to go with the flow, and so I arrived at St. Michael's Monastery about an hour later to interview him. He offered me raspberries that an older woman had brought him and honey made by veterans. He had been to the Chernobyl Zone the day before, and pinned to his army green jacket were several Soviet-era pins (*znachki* in Russian). He instantly handed them over. "Take them," he said, "they're probably still radioactive."

I asked him about a photographic portrait hung at the front of the room. He was seated in clerical robes with soldiers in uniform, six on either side of him, Last Supper-like. The photo was taken in a combat zone in the early phases of the war. This prompted him to launch into a tirade about how the UOC-MP does everything categorically against Ukraine. "It's just a political-religious organization right out of the Middle Ages," he said. "In fact, the Moscow Patriarch blesses the killing of its own believers." He claims to have switched his parish to the Kyiv Patriarchate for one reason: "We didn't want to participate in the killing of Ukrainian citizens." Kyiv Patriarch Filaret provided financing for Serhii to create a network of social services, which now has grown to include twelve subsidiaries, that address various social problems, from HIV/AIDS discrimination to refugee resettlement.

Before we could even begin the interview, the Americans called. An Evangelical group in the United States was considering sponsoring one of these projects. But they wanted details. Knowing that his NGO helps the sick and poor, volunteers, displaced persons, the military, and anyone else in need was not enough. They wanted background on stakeholders, transparency, and financial reporting. Exasperated that they failed to see that there was a war going on in Ukraine, Serhii said he was about to send them to hell. A young Ukrainian woman with limited English had been attempting to assist. He cursed his fate that he had to deal with these types and lamented that major foundations prefer to give to NGOs, not churches. "Here churches are like social organizations," he said.

I offered to translate the requests and responses while Serhii went out for a smoke. Having acted as a peacekeeper myself in this brewing conflict, just as the interaction with the Americans was ending, three Lithuanians and a Pole arrived with a bottle of cognac in hand at about 10:30 p.m. They had just given an interview on Ukrainian television on how the people in their countries were militarily preparing for the Russian threat, and they were eager to talk to a military chaplain who frequently went behind the front lines in Eastern Ukraine. After much lamenting about the Russians and their accursed geographic fate, they left and it was possible to resume speaking about the organization he had helped found and now leads.

Among his many duties, he is the chairperson of the Eleos-Ukraine Network. The Greek name translates as mercy, compassion, and kindness. This name was chosen because it represents the core values of the organization. Their mission is to "help everyone live with dignity." Notably, Eleos sponsors programs that address highly stigmatized groups, such as street children, drug addicts, and the mentally ill. One of the reasons why foreign funders might have had difficulty understanding the exact nature of this network is because their activities are wide ranging and involve numerous partners. The chaplains and other supporters of Eleos interface with NGOs, religious communities, governmental organizations, and basically anyone who can help facilitate solving social problems, some of which are unanticipated and episodic, while others are chronic. There is nonetheless an emphasis on assistance to people with disabilities, people suffering from chronic illnesses, such as cancer and hepatitis, as well as designing responses to the global pandemic.

Their programs are also targeted toward mitigating the negative consequences of war. The multitude of social problems that have arisen since the outbreak of the war are reflected in the wide spectrum of programs the Network offers. More specifically, they aim to provide consistent, professional training for medical chaplains, especially those who serve soldiers. A second goal is to improve the consistency and quality of pastoral care for patients, their families, and healthcare workers. They serve displaced people, families of mobilized soldiers, volunteers serving in Eastern Ukraine, demobilized soldiers and volunteers. They are also involved in peacebuilding initiatives and spiritual and patriotic education for young people. All these factors contributed to Eleos becoming active in working to institutionalize the medical chaplaincy in Ukraine. A closer look at the conditions under which medical chaplains currently work illustrates the need for such efforts as they are currently provided by military chaplains.

## Spiritualized Healing of the Injured

Ivan is an energetic, passionate supporter of the chaplaincy. He became an ardent enough believer during his participation in the Maidan protests to decide to break with his past life and become a priest with the UOC-KP. After the war began in 2014, his clerical life became oriented toward the military chaplaincy almost right away, and this is where he continues to serve. He reaffiliated to the OCU after the *tomos* was granted. When asked why he chose this particular church, he stated flatly, "The proper development of correct Christian values is a question of national security." In other words, it was a political decision and a means to "securitize" religion. He has a wife but no children and she agreed to support him, which is what allowed him to volunteer as a military chaplain for three years.

Like so many other current believers and even clergy, he did not come from a religious family and was for a long time not an active believer. However, a revelation of sorts during the Maidan, which he describes as a "calling from God," changed everything. "I understood there was a different path," he said unequivocally. This moment prompted him to make a break with his former life as a "businessman." Not everyone is willing to share the details of a life they once lived and now disavow. He was not interested in discussing aspects of his past and repeatedly insisted that his conversion "is a long story." Before becoming a priest, he acknowledged having worked as a "representative" of a Swedish company in Eastern Ukraine. His front teeth had been knocked out and the deep circles under his eyes and leathery tone of his skin betrayed hard living. His persistent avoidance of probing questions about his past was the polar opposite reaction to those I had encountered among converts to evangelical Protestantism. They used a morally compromised past as a foil to illustrate the difference between a life with God and one without. Conversion redeemed a "fallen" past by making it instrumental for inspiring others and measuring spiritual progress, which could be used to enhance one's moral credentials. In Eastern Christianity, the same sweeping transformation as a result of going from being nominally Orthodox to no longer so is not expected. Therefore, prior lifeworlds that could be construed as unbecoming to a priest were best avoided.

When Ivan began to serve, there were no official military chaplains. He said,

> There was no sense that becoming a military chaplain was even possible. I just went myself to the soldiers on Tuesdays and Thursdays. That's why, when an official chaplaincy was developed, they offered me a full-time ongoing post and I accepted. But I never thought about it. An official chaplaincy? We couldn't even dream that such a thing would become possible. But that's what happened. Gradually, gradually, since 2017 my status has become official. Why? Because a law, rather than an order (*prikaz* in Russian), in January 2017 came out. I began my duties as a military chaplain. Where my career started, is where I think it will end.

He insists on the need for chaplains to be better prepared. Although he received a brief theological education, his biggest regret is his lack of training in psychology given the therapeutic qualities of religiosity he tries to harness. Convinced of the tight connection between spiritual and physical healing, he now serves on another front line of sorts, in a large military hospital in Kharkiv. The hospital is the first stop outside the conflict zone where the wounded are taken. Access to the hospital is strictly controlled. All visitors must show their passports, and foreigners are prohibited from entering. So, I could not see for myself how visits with soldiers in the hospital unfolded. Discharged soldiers also cannot enter the hospital. Therefore, as part of his quest to build an ongoing relationship with soldiers and veterans, Ivan often met with them in the café across the street from the hospital, where I was able to participate in their meetings and conversations.

Ivan has specific ideas as to how the medical chaplaincy should develop. These ideas were sharpened after he was hospitalized. He noticed that volunteer clergy rarely made it to the hospital chapel to provide spiritual care to patients. He confirmed this with a nurse, who in twenty years of working at the hospital never had seen a priest. The Minister of Health from 2016 until 2019 was Dr. Uliana Suprun, an American member of the Ukrainian diaspora. She advocated the placement of dedicated chaplains in hospitals when tasked with reforming the health-care sector under President Poroshenko. After the collapse of the USSR in 1991, some medical establishments began to include a small chapel on their grounds. Most priests served there in addition to their parish duties, as they did in other public institutions including the military, on an ad hoc basis. The result, as Ivan's experience reflects, was that chapels were rarely used. Dr. Suprun initiated legislation that began to change that. Increasingly, even rehab centers, assisted living facilities, and other health-care centers now have prayer spaces that are used by people who work in these facilities every bit as much as by patients.

The practice of including chapels in health-care facilities is receding in parts of Europe. In the UK, for example, even when a chapel is maintained in a hospital, it is often used as a multipurpose room (Beckford 1998). In the United States, the practice of including prayer space in hospitals and health-care facilities continues, but these places strive to be interfaith, capable of serving people of different or no faith simultaneously. Chapels in public facilities, such as the Veterans Administration, go a step further. They aim to strike a tone of religious neutrality, which often renders them bland and nondescript. Many hospitals in the United States have clear religious affiliations; therefore, their chapels openly appeal to an aesthetic of that faith tradition. [15]

Chapels in Ukraine represent another model. It is becoming more and more common to build or convert space in hospitals and rehabilitation centers into chapels. These worship spaces, by and large, do not reflect a particular patriarch-bound Orthodox jurisdiction nor exclude Byzantine Catholics. They achieve a certain universalism by incorporating a Ukrainian folklore aesthetic, which is characterized by *rushnyky*, or traditional embroidered cloths, draped around the icons as well as decorative naïve depictions of Ukrainian folk elements, such as

sunflowers and *kalyna*, a native berry. The sacredness of the space is communi-
cated by stylized icons, Byzantine crosses, candles, something of an altar in front,
and ample room to sit quietly in prayer or meditation. In this way a generalized
atmosphere of religiosity mixed with national folk elements caters to people who
see themselves as Just Orthodox. At the same time, it reaffirms the indissoluble
links between a national and religious essence and attaches them to healing
properties in a public institution.

## Healing the Soul

Ivan offers therapeutic religiosity in the form of talk therapy during visits to
wounded soldiers in the hospital. He clearly delineates the forms of medicalized
assistance psychotherapists and psychiatrists can offer from what he and other
chaplains provide. A psychotherapist, in his view, handles logistical matters, such
as how to get along with others and build relationships, whereas a chaplain engages the fundamental meaning of life questions. In his view, a different kind of
expertise is needed to address such questions prior to the work psychotherapists
do. He explains,

> A doctor heals the body. A priest heals the soul. Medicine doesn't ad-
> dress the soul on the level of science. A doctor can help a psychologist
> solve worldly, day to day problems. But that's not always what a person
> needs. You need to understand the person. Where is he coming from
> and where is he going? He needs understanding. Not just one or two
> years in the future. But fundamental questions: why am I alive? What
> will happen later? If I'm at the front and they kill me, what will happen
> to me then? When the body dies, is anything left or not? Can a psycholo-
> gist help with that? No. That's the answer. These are the fundamental
> questions that trouble people. You can give someone calming meds and
> he'll come back as himself. That's also necessary. But that's the body.
> And then there is the soul.

The topics Ivan discusses are often mystical, existential, and even philosophical. Abstract philosophical talk becomes talk therapy when it provides an indirect
route to exposing fears and anxieties, which, along with contemplation and intro-
spection, assist in recovery from physical pain and emotional distress. Some of the
most common questions that arise are whether there is life after death, if hell exists, and if everyone answers to a higher power. Such existential questions might
sound lofty and abstract, but they have a certain urgency for men who might have

killed. Ivan views such dialogue as therapeutic, as a means to heal, because it brings mystical searching into everyday life and promotes a release from despair.

There was not a developed tradition of turning to psychoanalysis or psychotherapy during times of anguish in the former Soviet Union. Psychiatry played a rather punitive role in Soviet society. It was a weapon the state used against dissidents, critics, and other nonconformists who refused to comply with ideologically accepted behavior. Psychiatry to this day is more known for its restrictive capacities than healing or managing chronic mental illnesses. It is against such a backdrop that chaplains step into the healing process. Much like psychoanalysts, chaplains derive their authority and perhaps even the legitimacy of their expertise by having shared (or having imagined they shared) some of the experiences of those they counsel.[16] Ivan's healing of the soul lacks a specific scientific ontology and methodology. If Sus tries to help soldiers hear their conscience as the voice of their soul, Ivan tries to help their souls heal so that they have a voice. He relies heavily on building a relationship through dialogue to allow the soldier to uncover self-knowledge with the goal of bringing forth the desired transformation to a healthier state, however that might be understood.

# Liminal Atmosphere of the Monastery

I mentioned to Ivan that in the United States, veterans struggle with problems of suicide and domestic violence, two issues not covered in the existential themes he mentioned. He responded by saying that they have yet to effectively address such issues in Ukraine. He advocates that each exiting soldier should be given a transition period of six months in a monastery, reviving a tradition of monastic medicine when healers of the soul were also healers of the body. Such a proposition trades on the assumption that soldiers have neither confessionally specific nor denominationally specific allegiances and that a Just Orthodox orientation to Eastern Christianity is prevalent enough to make this proposal viable.

The plan is not farfetched. Ivan works primarily in Kharkiv, where in the nineteenth century, a wealthy family bequeathed their estate to the Orthodox Church and built a psychiatric hospital there in honor of their daughter who was mentally ill. During the Soviet period, the religious buildings were repurposed, and the estate became the main regional psychiatric hospital. There has been much discussion as to whether the hospital should be returned to the church or not. There is already a UOC-MP church on the grounds (see figure 5.3). Ivan thinks not only should they be returned but that they should be used for the therapeutic rehabilitation of veterans based on a program of contemplation. This

**FIGURE 5.3.**   Church of the UOC-MP on hospital grounds. Along with a list of the rules of behavior just inside the front door, words of caution urge visitors to mind their personal belongings because people STEAL (all in capital letters). Next to the church is a small kiosk where religious goods are sold. Photo by the author.

is vastly different from the medicalized care that relies on drug therapy that is now provided, according to the director of the psychiatric hospital who, predictably, is against all efforts to turn the hospital over to the church (Wanner 2021). There are already two groups of volunteers at the hospital, one connected to the UOC-MP and another small group of highly dedicated women, who provide food and clothing to the patients every week. While he considers the assistance offered by the volunteers from the UOC-MP negligible, he applauds the efforts of the other nonchurch affiliated volunteers for their reliable care and attention to patients as well as the tangible material assistance they provide.

Many people in Orthodox countries believe monasteries are the sites of spiritual energy that heal and rejuvenate. As a result, they visit monasteries to address emotional, psychic, and physical pain, as we saw in chapter two. In that spirit, some Orthodox monasteries offer something of a halfway house for drug addicts who are "working on themselves" (*pratsiuvaty nad soboiu* in Ukrainian; *rabotat' nad soboi* in Russian) with the help of spiritual advisers and medical personnel (Wanner 2007 and Zigon 2010). Ivan explains how a monastery, as sacred ground with healing properties, is particularly well suited to returning soldiers. When I ask if he advocates this because he sees a monastery as a space apart, a place to experience some inner peace, he counters with the opposite.

> It creates confusion (*smushchenie* in Russian). That is what is created when we change something. He [a soldier] was at the front. He had specific goals. He knew what to do. He comes back and he sees that now everything is not like that. Why did he do that? It loses meaning. He needs to substitute one thing for another. He needs a new life in the social world. For that he needs most of all calmness and to accept this new life. To want to live. It begins with deep spiritual problems.

Ivan believes that a monastery creates ideal conditions for soldiers to mobilize themselves, as they did in combat, to adapt to civilian life by recreating themselves (*perestraivat'sia* in Russian). Precisely the liminal atmosphere of the monastery, the not-of-this-world but not-yet-of-the-next in-betweenness, makes it a fundamentally creative place. The confusion a monasterial eye-of-the-storm period could potentially dislodge developed instincts, impulses, and propensities related to combat. This would allow the soldier to reorient to another set of circumstances by engaging in contemplation to gain self-knowledge and develop skills for a new working life in a postcombat world.

Just as monks do physical labor in the monastery, Ivan advocates that the returning soldiers should too. "Not hard labor," he quickly adds. Rather, he envisions soldiers growing food and then consuming it themselves. The cycle of creative production and consumption is extremely important because, as Ivan says, "war means destruction and murder. One needs to understand that it is not right. It was necessary to fight. He [a soldier] needs to be born again, to do something productive again." As a microcosm of the greater society, the prescribed environment of the monastery, with its liminal atmosphere and religious supports in place, could offer a healing and reorientation process that would allow each person to develop their potential (*realizovat'sia normal'no* in Russian).

The kind of therapeutic religiosity Ivan proposes is meant to yield the discovery of a new purpose through dialogue, use labor to begin to fulfill that purpose, and contemplation to give that purpose and new life meaning. Self-knowledge through labor rehabilitation is meant to create a sense of empowerment by allowing the soldier to demonstrate that he is capable of meaningfully contributing to society and finding social meaning in work (*sotsial'noe znachenie* in Russian). Clerical expertise in a monasterial setting that draws on the military chaplain's empathic understanding of the trauma the soldier has experienced would be key to ensuring a successful transition. This is all a far cry from what is currently offered to soldiers returning to civilian life. They are now given cash compensation, which most use to buy a home or a car.

In the United States, the Battlemind program is offered to discharged soldiers (Finley 2011,1 05–6). It is a twofold program that gears up soldiers for combat in the beginning and psychologically prepares them for reentry at the end of a tour. Military chaplains run the workshop for returning soldiers, which rarely lasts more than one day. The primary focus is on interpersonal relationships and marital counseling. In both Ukraine and the United States, the difficulties of reentry range from the challenges of learning to relax vigilance to reckoning with how much of a stranger a soldier has become to his or her family. It is not difficult to imagine that there are soldiers who could benefit from a more gradual transition, surrounded by people who understand the difficulties of rewiring actions and reactions, emotions, and behavior.

After acknowledging that his proposals for a six-month transition period might elude implementation in Ukraine for quite some time, with the intensity of a warrior on the front, Ivan continues to insist on the necessity of working with men and women who come out of the army and with their families:

> We didn't think about it before, but it has now become necessary for us too. Even our Afghan veterans, to this day they live in Afghanistan. They remember it. They didn't adapt after that. And now those problems are not disappearing. In fact, they are growing. . . . Military chaplains should not only be close by to active duty soldiers, they should also do postservice adaptation. That is the most important aspect of their service. Chaplains need to continue serving, supporting, and accompanying soldiers. Not just on the front. What comes after is also an important moment. We have to want that. The government needs to take up such questions. They should see the importance of that.

Whether the government does or not, the Greek Catholic Church has declared its commitment to working with veterans. In 2019 the church announced an intention—albeit with no details—to have every diocese have a rehabilitation center for veterans.[17] So slowly, whether it is medical chaplains working in state-run hospitals and rehabilitation centers or collaborating with NGOs to improve the level of treatment or churches establishing their own medical facilities and staffing them with medical chaplains, care of the soul and care of the body conflate.

## Building the Country We Want to Live In

"The war doesn't mean the end of Ukraine. It is the beginning of a Ukraine that we don't know yet."[18] This was one of the opening salvos of the first military chaplain to serve in the Donbas as he gave a lecture at Kyiv-Mohyla Academy, one of Ukraine's flagship universities and where the chaplain himself studied political science. The perspective one takes determines the vista one has. Zelins'kyi is a priest in the Ukrainian Greek Catholic Church. He has made a name for himself by virtue of the novel perspectives he takes and, as a result, the inspiring visions he offers. In the process, he has become a well-known public intellectual and author of two books about his experiences on the front (Zelins'kyi 2015, 2016). Some military chaplains return from the front and counsel those grieving. Others engage in social assistance and healing. Zelins'kyi uses his military experience to inspire leadership in the next generation to rekindle a vision that draws on radical hope for the country's future.

He expands the military chaplain mandate to "be close by" to include the goal of creating "humans for humanity." Humanity for him means the ability to appreciate justice, truth, beauty, and the ability to do good. During combat on the front, he saw his job as "provoking a soldier into his/her own humanity" in the face of circumstances that threatened to destroy it. On the home front, he works to ensure that "people have the capacity to do good, to fight for justice, to seek truth, and to contemplate beauty."[19] The qualities he tries to foster are necessary to not only win the war but to win the peace too.

Zelins'kyi's broad pursuit of justice, truth, beauty, and goodness has made him active in many spheres of public life, but especially in policy initiatives concerning cultural politics, nationbuilding, and increasing leadership capacity in Ukraine. He was born in Lviv in 1989, but he left Galicia to study philosophy in the United States for four years, theology in Italy for five, and spent two years in a monastery in Siberia before returning to Kyiv to study political science at Kyiv Mohyla Academy. In between it all, he worked at the National Academy of Land Forces in Lviv and was instrumental in 2007 in setting up the military chaplaincy there. He currently has multiple titles that reflect the wide spectrum of the domains in which he is actively engaged: co-founder of the Ukrainian Leadership Academy; Instructor at the Institute of Leadership and Administration of the Ukrainian Catholic University; a priest in the Ukrainian Greek Catholic Church and Deputy Director of the Military Chaplaincy of the UGCC; political scientist, and author of several books.

The mandate to "be close by" motivated him to participate in the Maidan from the very first day. Once the war started, he was the first to serve at ATO headquarters in June 2014 as a military chaplain. As he said to me, and repeated in many interviews and in his writings, he became the first military chaplain to serve in a combat situation because "40 percent of my friends were there." The war was one of the biggest surprises of his life and a possibility he, like almost everyone else, never considered during the Maidan.

He served two years in Eastern Ukraine during the early stages of the war when fighting was particularly intense, and Ukrainian forces were woefully ill-equipped and unprepared. He witnessed bloodshed and death, courage and fear, all in heavy doses. During this time, he heard confessions alongside the steady fire of grenade launchers and administered communion in trenches with rubble and shrapnel strewn about. In a combat situation, he maintains that it is the human heart that is the "final fortress" that must be defended from the enemy at all costs. Unlike others who witnessed combat, he managed to chronicle his impressions and experiences in two books, numerous articles, and many interviews. In the process, he has made known the unknown horrors of war, given face to the young men and women who comprise the staggering number of war causalities, and offered radical hope in the form of a way to think about the past such that a path to a future of peace, reconciliation, and well-being seems possible.

This has made Zelins'kyi an inspirational speaker, something of a life coach, especially for the youth of Ukraine. Although based at the main Ukrainian Greek Catholic Cathedral in the capital, he keeps a furious travel schedule that would exhaust the most seasoned traveler. His trips to soldiers, churches, and various chapters of the Ukrainian Leadership Academy are chronicled on social media with daily smiling selfies of Zelins'kyi together with young people making his signature thumbs-up gesture. He is often wearing a navy sweatshirt with the mantra of the Ukrainian Leadership Academy, "I am Ukraine. I love Freedom."

He communicates unbounded energy and optimism with his slightly crooked smile and athleticism. He jogs every morning at 6:30, regardless of weather, even as he crisscrosses the country. I interviewed him in Lviv under the single worst conditions I have ever interviewed anyone in the thirty years I have conducted ethnographic research. He had been a speaker at a conference on "Populism and Responsibility" at the Ukrainian Catholic University. Unbeknownst to either of us, we chose a place to talk right beside where a children's dance performance was about to be staged. A small army of parents arrived and surrounded us, cell phones in hand to photograph their twirling children, as the music began blaring out to accompany the tiny dancers. It was bearable until the music shifted from classical to the pop hit "Despacito," which played at full volume. As one might expect from a man who has been in combat, he was entirely undaunted. He simply raised his voice over the music and forged on, explaining his visions and dreams for the youth of Ukraine as members of that very youth danced all around us.

## Increasing Leadership Capacity

One year after the Maidan ended in 2015, he cofounded the Ukrainian Leadership Academy (ULA). The ULA is something of a highly selective, structured gap year. It offers a ten-month, six-day-a-week residential program of physical, emotional, and intellectual challenge to Ukrainians and members of the Ukrainian diaspora from ages sixteen to twenty. Entrance is competitive, and participants receive a stipend. The program has grown steadily since its inception and now includes about 240 participants each year. The ULA is modeled on the Israeli Shnat Sherut program of post-high school community service, which strives to strengthen Jewish-Israeli identity while helping participants develop certain values and skills that will make them assimilated and productive citizens of Israel.[20]

The ULA has a two-fold goal of developing national awareness and the values and skills conducive to leading initiatives for social improvement in a post-Maidan world. The ULA aims to encourage responsibility, creative thinking, and the confidence among youth to implement their own visions so they can "create the country they would like to live in," as Zelins'kyi says. It has branches in six Ukrainian cities (Kyiv, Lviv, Mykolaiv, Poltava, Kharkiv, and Chernivtsi) and participants usually go to a city outside the region they are from during their tenure at the Academy, which allows them to get to know other regions of their own country. Few Ukrainians vacation in country other than going to their dacha summer home. Those who can travel usually go abroad. This leaves Ukraine a terra incognita for most Ukrainians, which is why a premium is placed on serving beyond one's hometown and region. It becomes a means to fortify national awareness and identification.

During the ten-month period, participants attend lectures, volunteer for various community projects, play sports, and organize "Impact Days," where members of the greater community come to the Ukrainian Leadership Academy's campus to participate in outreach events and programs. I attended an Impact Day at the ULA in Kharkiv that coincided with the Day of Defenders of Ukraine. Maria, a young woman from Lviv, gave us a tour of the ULA campus. She spoke Ukrainian, as did the other participants. The ULA is located in a renovated, well-furnished two-story building, with large meeting rooms and a kitchen downstairs and dormitory-style rooms upstairs where the participants, along with local leaders, live. The Kharkiv ULA gained some notoriety when one of the local leaders of the program, a young man in his early thirties, committed suicide. Another leader before him had attempted to do the same. For some Kharkivites, the "total institution" aspect of a ULA gap year and the suicide make the ULA suspect, especially when combined with the ever-present suspicion of cults and the steadfast assumption that organized endeavors are inherently coercive.

None of this was apparent or seemed to dampen spirits on Impact Day. On a day when school was not in session because of the Day of Defenders holiday, the ULA participants offered free patriotic activities for neighborhood kids. They staged a historically themed play, organized craft activities that incorporated national symbolism, offered meals, games, and other outdoor activities. In the evening parents joined in the festivities with their kids. In essence, ULA participants provided free childcare and creative, educational activities, all with a distinctly national flavor, for kids who otherwise would probably have been indoors before a screen. Such activities are part of a greater initiative to promote "self-organization" (*sama-organitsiia* in Ukrainian), a concept that flourished during the Maidan and aims to create a more vibrant civil society by encouraging civic involvement on the local level. Zelins'kyi visited the ULA in Kharkiv and met with the participants the day before, timing his visit to coincide with the consecration of the new monument to the Defenders of Ukraine in Kharkiv.

## Lessons Learned in War

There are several insights Zelins'kyi shares, based on his experiences as a member of the clergy and military, publicly in seminars, speeches, and in meetings he holds with ULA participants. I focus on only two here that relate to the therapeutic qualities of religiosity that can be made part of everyday life. The first lesson is the importance of facing, not evading, fears, even in a combat situation when fears are particularly intense. In an article he wrote about serving on the front over Christmas after he received the "People's Hero of Ukraine" award, he stated, "Fear coerces us into hatred, forces us into despair and hopelessness, to distrust, and a hardening of our own sense of self-confidence, finally wrecking the entire construct of our individuality. We must never allow ourselves to become prisoners of our fears."[21] The essence of faith, he insists, is that it allows a person to endure fear and still maintain humanity. By detailing his own prayerful supplications, devotional practices, and collective participation in the liturgy on the front, he explains how the therapeutic qualities of religiosity work to dispel fear by diminishing feelings of loneliness and vulnerability.

On the home front, religiosity serves to increase, what he calls "psychological resilience" and self-knowledge as a means to empower a positive transformation in one's life. He speaks of the "mental mattresses" people carry with them, so that if they fall, they will not be injured. He seeks to make the church a place of trust to counter the widespread distrust people have of one another and of institutions as a result of "national traumas" experienced over generations. Both a reduction of fear and an augmentation of psychological resilience are necessary for soldiers, and even for all Ukrainians, to retain a sense of humanity and an ability to recognize and pursue "justice, truth, beauty, and goodness."

A second lesson that he offers, which was the gist of one of our conversations and the subject of many of his interviews elsewhere, relates to how the past should be reinterpreted to provide a path forward. The various churches offer different interpretations of the Ukrainian historical experience to distinguish each other, given their common roots in Eastern Christianity. Rather than using history to situate Ukraine in relation to Russia, as most do, the vision Zelins'kyi offers is targeted toward bridging regional differences in Ukraine and reconciling the tensions that contributed to the war in the first place. He returns to the Maidan as an example of a way forward. This event was a creative driving force that demonstrated the ability to unite Ukrainian citizens around what I have called "radical hope." Zelins'kyi notes that an insistence on justice and human dignity and vowing not to back down until they were realized united a broad cross section of the population on the Maidan. People of different faith traditions speaking a variety of languages did not seek to advance a particular aspect of identity politics that hinged on language, religious affiliation, or any other standard identity markers. Rather, he sees the Maidan as evidence of the possibility and power of a civic, value-oriented understanding of what it means to be Ukrainian.

Years later Zelins'kyi's own optimism prompts him to interpret this moment as one that reveals that Ukrainians are on the cusp of a new beginning. He hardly discounts the chaos and destruction in Eastern Ukraine and the overall instability the war has wrought. Rather than focusing on that, the endless inter-church squabbles, the failures of the Ukrainian government, or other potentially demoralizing topics, he insists that uncertainty and instability open up possibilities. To prove the point, he noted that in the United States, for example, the chaplaincy is an established institution. This makes it far more difficult to introduce change. In Ukraine, in contrast, legislators and clerical leaders are in the process of creating the chaplaincy, which means that the possibilities for innovation and shaping this profession are almost endless. The same is true of how he assesses the prospect of reunifying Ukraine after its territory has been truncated by annexation and war, and its population pummeled and divided by hardship. How these events are interpreted, especially given their freshness and magnitude, will lay the groundwork as to how the country will develop in the future, he insists. His reaction to this precarity and instability is to insist, "We live in a world we don't understand, in an uncertain world, a world that is unstable. But this is not the end, this is a new beginning. It is our own ability to reinterpret events that we depend on to define how we will live."[22] This is radical hope. The future is neither visible nor legible, but the guiding light Zelins'kyi uses to build leadership capacity is his recall of the common, unified pursuit of justice that was achieved on the Maidan.

# Naming the Affective Atmosphere

The 2019 election slogan of President Poroshenko was "Army, Language, Faith!" It epitomized his nationalist ideological vision forward. Zelins'kyi criticizes such efforts, claiming that "hovering over the nineteenth century trying to rehabilitate in the twenty-first century ideas that were embraced in Europe two hundred years ago" was never successful in the past. It is unlikely to be effective now. He cautions against scouring history for a viable national story with a universal appeal or struggling to articulate a "national idea" based on the Ukrainian language, a literary canon, or a Ukrainian Church. Durable allegiances are forged on what he calls "social ontologies." This refers to the values that inform personal decisions, collective priorities, and civilizational aesthetics. A national idea cannot be a text or a cultural trait. It must be a "verbalization of social ontology," or of a lifeworld that depicts a way of being in the world. He looks to diverse, multicultural countries, such as Israel, that have espoused concepts like a "promised land," which are laden with hope, to effectively absorb and assimilate a diverse group of Jewish immigrants into Israeli citizens sharing a common social ontology. Just as Israel draws on Judaism in all its varieties, the orienting values Zelins'kyi sees are tied to an Eastern Christian faith tradition.

The use of a conceptual national-emotional register is a more promising avenue to generate a commitment to people and place, Zelins'kyi argues, than privileging certain cultural traits, such as language or a particular denomination, which inevitably will create minorities. Indeed, a nationalized emotional register embodied in the arts has defined a certain ontology for other countries. The tango is emblematic of Argentina, samba of Brazil, reggae of Jamaica, fado of the Portuguese, and gospel, blues, and jazz of African Americans. Maria Sonevytsky suggests that "wild music" is a trope that allows Ukrainians to imagine a unifying vision of sovereignty (2019, 177). She sees "discursive wildness" reflected in a variety of music styles, from the Hutsul Wild Dances of the pop performer Ruslana to the sounds of Eastern, Orientalizing Crimean music, as amounting to a form of "acoustic citizenship" because of the common aural sphere it creates.[23]

Ukraine, as a borderland, has always been caught between multiple state structures, ideological systems, and aesthetic styles. The city of Chernivtsi has used "nostalgic cosmopolitanism" as something of a social ontology to rebrand itself and renovate public space (Wanner 2016). Zelins'kyi believes that, rather than seeing this diversity of experiences as a weakness, it can also bequeath a versatility, openness, and tolerance that could be considered a strength. From Byzantium, Russia took the idea of itself as a third Rome because Russia interpreted its roots in terms of power. In contrast, he offers that Ukrainians could interpret their legacy and distinctiveness in terms of *sofia*, "wisdom" in Greek, specifically a "wisdom of being." Rather than seeing religious pluralism as a source of divided loyalties and interpreting the lack of a single dominant national church as a sign of a weak national identity, these dynamics are a source of freedom and tolerance, opening an ecumenical vista forward.[24] The "wisdom of being" has yielded the "Kyiv tradition," an ecumenical union of Orthodoxy and Catholicism. A concept that draws on a broad Eastern Christian faith tradition, such as *sofia* is a potentially unifying rubric. This is a social ontology with world-making capacities, including winning the peace. This is the radical hope he offers his compatriots.

Such hope is radical because the world-breaking capacities of religion and the possibility for prolonged tensions and violence are on the horizon. Religious leaders, and especially military chaplains, are engaged in bringing along the next generation of patriotic leaders, meaning someone who cares about the country, who cares about something greater than him or herself. Such a designation is meaningful in a county where there is a significant degree of cynicism, indifference, and suspicion toward people in power. Even if the affective atmosphere on the Maidan can be revived to reflect an inclusive and universal religious idiom, Ukraine already shares with neighboring Russia the rise of a military-patriotic culture that fosters "militarized masculinity" (Knorre 2015; Knorre and Zygmont 2020). Victoria Fomina writes of a "new culture of war patriotism" that is promoted in Russia as a path forward for the country to reclaim its rightful place on the world stage. (2018). This militarized culture of patriotism involves the Russian Orthodox Church. Initiatives to popularize soldier-heroes in Russia, such as Evgenii Rodionov, a soldier beheaded in Chechnya during the First Chechen War when he refused to renounce his faith, have now morphed into church-state efforts to memorialize and even canonize such figures as saints worthy of veneration. There are now icons depicting Rodionov and pilgrims come to his gravesite to offer devotions (Fomina 2018; Kormina 2014). The massive new Cathedral of the Armed Forces in Moscow, built to mark the 75th anniversary of the Soviet victory in the Great Patriotic War, finds a counterpart in Kyiv where discussions are ongoing to build a special chapel dedicated to defenders who fought and died in Eastern Ukraine.

The emphasis I have placed on military chaplains as drivers of social change and the enhanced affective atmosphere of religiosity after the Maidan and the start of the war could also easily combine to endorse a morally validated militarized masculine defense of the home front. As participants in the war and in the war recovery effort, military chaplains have a dual perspective on hate, indifference, and the violence they fuel as well as on the empathetic processes involving verbal and nonverbal forms of communication that can potentially yield healing and eventual reconciliation. Although violence rages on in Eastern

Ukraine in a contained uncontrolled zone, chaplains are already changing the emotional tenor of public domains. The work of winning the peace and engendering patriotism falls to them in either condemning or legitimating violence. Even as the Just Orthodox refuse an institutional affiliation, the institutions remain robust in as much as they sponsor spiritual ambassadors in the form of chaplains who serve in spaces made sacred in nonreligious settings. Given the populist age of hatred and resentment in which we live, they play a pivotal role in either using religiosity to cultivate empathy and healing or using their moral authority to validate simmering tensions and animosities.

# CONCLUSION
## The New Politics of Belonging

In 1982, a monumental complex was built on one end of Khreshchatyk, the main boulevard in the capital Kyiv, in the lower part of Mariïns'kyi Park, once known as the Merchants Garden. A giant titanium arch resembling a silver rainbow was officially declared the "Arch of Peoples Friendship," although it was popularly called the "yoke." The arch stood over a monument to Russian and Ukrainian workers holding the Soviet Order of Friendship of Peoples and a granite rendition of the Pereiaslav Council (1654), which in the official Soviet historical interpretation marked the reunification of Ukraine with Russia. Below the arch, there is a stage and amphitheater, which is now usually filled with skateboarders, gaming machines, and food kiosks.

Although monuments and other signs in the urban landscape have a history, their meanings change over time in tandem with the normative and political functions they perform. The post-Maidan remake of monuments and aesthetics uses concepts of the sacred, the moral, and the political to reenchant public space to purge the urban landscape of fallen idols and articulate new ones. The passage of decommunization laws in 2015 slated the Arch of People's Friendship for demolition because the Soviet political message of relatedness no longer applied. In its place, a new monument dedicated to the heroes of the Donbas War was planned.

In the interim, activists were allowed to paint a black crack on the arch in 2018 as part of a campaign to agitate for the release of Ukrainian political prisoners held in Russia (Kaidan 2018). The addition of a black crack to symbolize shattering of the People's Friendship between Russia and Ukraine, was so well

**FIGURE C.1.**    The People's Friendship Arch now includes a crack as symbolic commentary.

received that the mayor of Kyiv, boxing heavyweight champion Vitalii Klitschko, shifted the money earmarked for destroying the monument to building an addition to it (see figure C.1). In May 2019, the cracked arch became the gateway to a new complex that featured a transparent sightseeing platform on the cliffs high above the banks of the Dnipro River. The platform connects the cracked arch to a monument erected in 1853 to Prince Volodymyr holding a cross. He is credited with bringing Christianity to Kyiv.

The bridge is considered an ideal place for taking selfies because of its dramatic background. As a result, going under the cracked arch to the viewing platform over the open river has become popular among tourists and locals alike. This has made the arch a focal point, albeit one that depicts a message that is antithetical to what was originally intended. The permanency of the massive steel arch carries an impressive degree of flexibility in its semiotic forms. Michael Herzfeld writes, "Architectural arrangements, in which physical permanence easily overshadows the significance of variable use, share with the idiom of morality the semiotic illusion of invariance: constant signifiers mask shifting signified. The more fixed the semiotic forms, the greater is the play of ambiguity and the more surprising are the possibilities for violating the code itself" (2005, 20). The

Soviet-era trope of People's Friendship has not only been violated, it has also been irretrievably transformed. First, in the minds of some, by acts of annexation and armed aggression and, as a response to that from others, with acts of desecration. With the addition of a black crack, the moral message of this immense arch is crystal clear and seemingly invariable once again.

Monuments are iconic representations of immutable power. As tools of statecraft, ideological instruction, and contributors to an atmosphere, they are infused with a mystical aura of omnipotence and designed to prompt feelings of awe. Many Soviet monuments were metaphorically designed to illustrate supernatural state power, ideal-type gendered citizens, and the glories of socialism. Conflated as Soviet ideology was with a sacred vision of worldly salvation, urban life featured an ongoing presence of the sacred in Soviet political ritual, lived domestic space, and in everyday social and cultural practices.

Altered monuments, new shrines, and a new aesthetic adorning public space reject the rigid confines a socialist realist aesthetic imposed but retain the practice of enchanting public space. They articulate new forms of transcendence that link multi-generations in bonds of solidarity and validate new understandings of relatedness. If familial bonds between fraternal nations have cracked and if geographically dispersed familial networks are strained, some to the breaking point, how might bonds be prevented from breaking on other levels? How can the sharp divisions, tensions, and fighting one finds on the Korean peninsula, in Northern Ireland, as well as in the former Yugoslavia and elsewhere, over sovereignty and divergent political futures be prevented from overtaking Ukraine?

George Bernard Shaw is quoted as saying that "England and America are two countries separated by a common language."[1] Differences in political visions between Russia and Ukraine are increasingly manifest in terms of a common faith. The creation of an independent Orthodox Church of Ukraine was an institutional manifestation of these divergent visions and a move to reinforce the different trajectories the two countries are on. As such, it signals, along with the war itself, an end to the post-Soviet era. New social and cultural differences in the sphere of religion and how it relates to governance now characterize peoples who have for the most part shared a common historical experience and common faith tradition. By seeping into public and private spaces and exerting influences far beyond established institutions, religiosity shapes subjectivities, lifeworlds, and everyday experiences of the transcendent. Compared to the Soviet period, Russian and Ukrainian societies and the politics that regulate them, with their recourse to vernacular religious practices and institutional religion to fulfill transactional and transcendent needs, have become even more secular and even more religious simultaneously, but in different ways.

The means employed to achieve a church independent from Moscow had the byproduct of muddying the lines of separation, which were already thin, between state and religious institutions. Although there was significant support for the creation of a "new local church" and a wide recognition that jurisdictional lines could fortify state boundaries, far fewer than expected have reaffiliated to the church because they prefer to remain Just Orthodox. There are a multitude of reasons for this. For one, the analysis I have provided of the pervasiveness of popular piety expressed in vernacular religious practices in public and private spaces, when embedded in an affective atmosphere of religiosity that increasingly pervades public space and public institutions, shows that there is not much need. Vernacular religious practices, the ambient atmosphere of religiosity, and Orthodox understandings of belonging rooted in place weaken allegiances to specific denominations. However, those same dynamics contribute to a heartfelt attachment to an Eastern Christian faith tradition that can be exercised in multiple sites, including monasteries, healthcare centers, cemeteries, and within the armed forces. In a word, individuals have seized a great deal of agency from religious institutions. Their experiences of transcendence, as they engage in religious practices to suit their needs and proclivities, occur in sites that are often related to, but not always within, religious institutions.

Second, a nationalized understanding of belonging and religious affiliation fuels the appeal of a generalized identity that is manifest in the category Just Orthodox. By birthright, the sympathizers, casual believers, agnostics, doubters, indifferent, and atheists with traditions can claim to be Orthodox. This is an identity they have inherited, but how they interpret it is up to them. Something very sharply defined, such as citizenship, turns out to be very elastic when it comes to religious affiliation. With its multiple Orthodox churches in a single state, Ukraine continues to challenge the accepted model of ecclesiastical organization in the Eastern Christian world. Yet, the prevalence of a deinstitutionalized general Just Orthodox form of allegiance contributes to religious tolerance and facilitates the creation of sacred spaces beyond institutional confines, thereby creating attachments to place over denomination.

Third, and related to issues of belonging, is that there is little sense of membership in a particular Orthodox parish or denomination, which mutes local exclusionary tendencies. The church serves the people in a broad sense, which yields a rather open understanding of access to religious buildings and sites. An affective atmosphere of religiosity and a sense of being Just Orthodox further allows individuals to unproblematically frequent churches, monasteries, and other religious sites of different jurisdictions.

However, such mobile and versatile forms of practice mean that it has proven difficult to implement a legal mechanism to allow property to change jurisdiction to strengthen the OCU. In the 1990s the attempts to return religious buildings to the denomination that owned them prior to Soviet confiscation were enormously disruptive on the local level, souring relationships in villages and small towns across Western Ukraine, where it was especially difficult to disentangle who owned what. Prolonged and contested conflicts over reallocation of church properties yielded little political gain for anyone at any level. Vlad Naumescu posited at the time that there was an "Orthodox imaginary," meaning a willingness among individual believers to imagine the competing Eastern Christian churches at the time (UOC-MP, UOC-KP, UAOC, and UGCC) into one, which allowed believers to separate out sincere religious practice from the jockeying of religious institutions for power and privilege (2006). This imagined unity allowed churchgoing Western Ukrainians in Sykhiv, where he conducted fieldwork, to skirt political divisions and visit churches of different denominations interchangeably by imagining them as one.[2]

The limits of an Orthodox imaginary quickly became readily apparent though. Unity on an institutional level was not imagined when it came to property, authority structures, or ambitions to be *the* dominant Ukrainian Orthodox church. Disentangling what belongs to whom was then, and remains today, exceptionally difficult given the all-national inclusive understanding of who a religious institution serves and amorphous understandings of parish membership, all of which the Just Orthodox carry forward. Existing legislation regulates reaffiliation based on the will of the members of individual religious communities, which creates a complicated process of reaffiliation that is incessantly open to dispute. These difficulties are further compounded by, as we have seen in this book, low levels of institutional commitment, but high levels of religious commitment, and high levels of belief that are manifest in high levels of vernacular forms of practice.

The dynamic nature of everyday religiosity among the Just Orthodox is reflected in law and legislation that includes, what Oxana Shevel refers to as "multilevel ambiguity," in her study of micro-level analyses of disputes over parish transfers (2021). The ambient affective atmosphere of religiosity and dexterity of vernacular religious practices find their counterparts in state legislation and church statues that allow for flexibility and interpretation in terms of membership. Inevitably, this breeds contested reaffiliations that play out in court. This has thwarted the prospect of strengthening the OCU through securing reaffiliations from the UOC-MP and has fueled the propensity to simply build new churches to buttress the OCU.

In 2019 Ukraine became the first country with a predominantly Eastern Christian population with at least two canonically recognized Orthodox churches. The Just Orthodox phenomenon is an expression of an ability, and even preference,

to subscribe to an overarching faith tradition over a particular institutional structure, and to use individual agency to reduce the political instrumentalization of
religion. And yet, being Just Orthodox still allows for meaningful attachments to
one's patrimony, kin group, and country.

Perhaps it should not be surprising that the multiplex forms of ecclesiastical
pluralism and elastic allegiance that have taken root in a single faith tradition in
a borderland country among the Just Orthodox are having difficulty surviving
a war among brotherly nations. The constant pressure to shore up state sovereignty makes religious affiliation a resource, a political response to circumstances beyond their control. As swing voters in the intensifying conflict between
Russia and Ukraine, which finds a parallel, a proxy war if you will, in the competition for adherents between the OCU and the UOC-MP, the Just Orthodox
are increasingly motivated to trade in their generalized allegiance to a faith
tradition in favor of a firm declaration of denominational affiliation as a statement of national solidarity and an intention to protect state sovereignty with
whatever means are available. If politics made them Just Orthodox and allowed
them not to choose, it is political struggle that has risen to the level of prolonged
armed combat that is making them choose sides now. In November 2021, for the
first time, the Just Orthodox were not the largest group among those who claim
to be Orthodox in Ukraine. Just one month shy of the anniversary of its three-
year formation, the OCU claimed 39.8 percent of Orthodox sympathizers and
the Just Orthodox 36.2 percent. Affiliations to the UOC-MP fell to 21.9 percent,
or nearly half the level of the OCU, among those who consider themselves
Orthodox. Of the total Ukrainian population, only 13.3 percent now claim affiliation with the UOC-MP.[3] This is the result of escalating political tensions,
and the weaponization and even securitization of religion as a weapon.

My goal in writing this book has been to analyze seemingly innocuous appeals for assistance from otherworldly forces that reflect institutional disaffection and anticlericalism, a trend that is on the rise far beyond Ukraine and
Europe. Such forms of religiosity offer insulation against moral judgments and
the retention of autonomy against communal obligations. Yet such vernacular
practices are symbiotic to religious institutions and to their political agendas and
preferences. This suggests that it is no longer feasible, if it ever was, to consider
religion as something outside political and public life, even in highly secular
societies. Is there still such a thing as secular public space and secular power?
As long as there are vernacular religious practices that are widely shared and
visible, should they prompt ritualized practices to take root in certain sites, these
practices can make sacred spaces and feed an affective atmosphere of religiosity. Therefore, it is the secularization of space and limits to the sacralization of

state power that must be imposed. When an affective atmosphere of religiosity cultivates an ever-present potential to pivot to the sacred, analytical distinctions are perhaps more accurately rendered as religious and nonreligious rather than sacred and secular. The forms of religiosity analyzed here merge with the secular, with profane transactional interests as well as transcendent yearnings to belong, to such an extent that, ultimately, distinctions between the secular and the religious, even in terms of categorizing public space or the nature of agents of power, become heuristic tools for the purposes of knowledge production rather than any kind of dichotomy that is borne out in lived experiences and the ethnographic data that record them.

This signals that, even in the face of institutional disaffection and disparagement, should individuals engage in extra-institutional practices as Just Orthodox, nones, or any other purposefully unmarked category, the significant potential remains for religiosity to become a political resource and retain a prominent presence in public space and public institutions. Such religiosity offers an instrumentally effective way for individuals to get what they need. When this is done in relation to religious institutions that claim to be part of a dominant cultural tradition with site-specific practices, this can yield powerful attachments to place, to the people who have lived there, and to the political authorities and other institutional structures that claim to be their protectors. Analyzing the presence of unmarked religiosity underlines the social and political stakes of a public religiosity and allows us to refine comparative concepts for analyzing mainstream religious institutions that might be hiding in plain sight and quietly, pervasively exercising influence that goes largely unnoticed and, by extension, unchecked.

An affective atmosphere of religiosity is an essential first step for religious nationalism, a confessional state, or the use of political theologies to develop in a secular society. Thinking comparatively to other armed conflicts of long duration in Europe, such as Northern Ireland or the former Yugoslavia, we see that lingering resentment and ongoing grief often have a tenacious afterlife, enduring long after the fighting has ceased but always keeping rage within reach. The undeclared, war of words and weapons that continues to produce casualties and displaced persons in Ukraine is unlikely to be an exception to these established patterns. The mounting cultural boundaries to reinforce political borders and state sovereignty multiply far beyond the frontiers of war. The world making and world breaking capacities of religiosity to evoke or withhold empathy for others are likely to determine if relatedness and attachments to places, which vernacular religious practices are so exquisitely capable of forming, will fortify boundaries or break them down. Therein lies the true political power of religion.

# Notes

## INTRODUCTION

1. This essay repeats many of the same points Putin raised in an earlier address after the results of a referendum on the status of the Crimean Peninsula, which was boycotted by pro-Ukrainian groups, showed an overwhelming majority of Crimean residents supporting Crimean succession from Ukraine in favor of joining the Russian Federation. "Address by the President of the Russian Federation, March 18, 2014," President of Russia, March 18, 2014, http://en.kremlin.ru/events/president/news/20603.

2. The essay was translated into multiple languages, including Ukrainian, and released on July 12, 2021. For the English text, see "Article by Vladimir Putin 'On the Historical Unity of Russians and Ukrainians,'" President of Russia, July 12, 2021, http://en.kremlin.ru/events/president/news/66181.

3. "Social and Political Mood of the Population, 23–25 July 2021," Rating Sociological Group, July 27, 2014, https://ratinggroup.ua/research/ukraine/obschestvenno-politicheskie_nastroeniya_naseleniya_23-25_iyulya_2021.html. The poll was conducted after the release of Putin's article and was based on 2,500 respondents to computer-assisted randomized telephone interviews across the country.

4. The Ecumenical Patriarchate (EP) in October 2018 annulled a 1686 edit that placed religious life in what is today Ukraine under the jurisdiction of the Moscow Patriarchate. This reversed the "annulment of the canonical sanctions," or excommunication, imposed by the Moscow Patriarch on "schismatics," meaning the clergy and laity of the UOC-KP, which was created in 1992 following Ukrainian independence, and the UAOC, which was created in 1921, outlawed in the USSR, and reestablished in Ukraine in 1990. On December 15, 2018, at a Unification Council attended by representatives of three Orthodox jurisdictions in Ukraine (UOC-KP, UAOC, and two bishops who left the UOC-MP) the Orthodox Church of Ukraine formed.

5. Along with granting a *tomos*, the EP dissolved the Russian Exarchate of Western Europe, thereby obliging Orthodox churches in Europe to merge under the EP. The ROC rebuked this act, cut ties with the EP, the symbolic leader of all of Eastern Christianity, and obliged Orthodox communities in Europe to choose allegiance either to hierarchical authority structures in Constantinople or in Moscow (Clark and Vovk 2020). Kormina and Naumescu (2020, 8) assert that this alignment of theopolitics and geopolitics was an attempt to realign forces on the political and religious levels far beyond Ukraine.

6. The billionaire Viktor Nusenkis alone sponsored the construction of over 650 churches in the first twenty years of Ukrainian independence.

7. Byriukov is a controversial figure. After his activism on the Maidan, in March 2014 he founded Phoenix Wings, an NGO that fundraises to purchase uniforms, weapons, and other necessities for volunteers fighting alongside the Ukrainian Army in Eastern Ukraine. The group also provides humanitarian aid and sponsors various commemorative events for fallen soldiers, such as the Memory Tree project. The group's ideology leans right-wing nationalist and uses a skull and bones as its emblem.

8. "Ukrainian Civil Society Outlines 'Red Lines' President Zelenskyi Can't Cross," Euromaidan Press, May 23, 2019, http://euromaidanpress.com/2019/05/23/ukrainian-civil-society-outlines-red-lines-president-zelenskyi-cant-cross/.

9. There is an enormous literature on the history of religious institutions and popular Orthodoxy. Citing only those studies of religious institutions set comparatively or within Ukraine, see Bociurkiw 2003; Sysyn and Plokhy 2003; Hurkina 2014; Shlikhta 2014; Denysenko 2018; Metreveli 2020. For studies of popular Orthodoxy, see Zayarnyuk and Himka 2006; Hann and Goltz 2010; Adams and Shevzov 2018; Luehrmann 2018; Merdjanova 2021. (See Freeze 2015 and Smolkin 2018 for exceptions.) A one-sided focus on either institutional religion or popular practices is understandable in that each is substantial in its own right. My point is that the two are mutually constituting. Institutions tolerate, and in some instances even encourage, such informal practices at the same time that these vernacular religious practices form in tandem with institutionally-accepted practices. It is the interrelational nature of the two that I depict here.

10. I understand secularism to be a political principle that aims to limit the presence of religion in the public sphere via disestablishment of a state church or other means. My point is that the sites of religious practices are multiplying. Increasingly, they can be found in mundane places, which changes the tenor of those places and contributes to a particular atmosphere.

11. As low as the percentage of regular churchgoers in Ukraine is, it is nearly double the number in Russia. "Orthodox Christianity in the 21st Century," Pew Research Center, November 8, 2017, https://www.pewforum.org/2017/11/08/orthodox-christians-are -highly-religious-in-ethiopia-much-less-so-in-former-soviet-union/. I was an adviser to the Pew Research Center for questions regarding Ukraine on its 2017 Eastern European survey.

12. The next level of such categorization, *gorozhane*, indicates urban secularists who care deeply about religious buildings for historical and cultural reasons (Kormina 2020). Pious Orthodox practitioners who wanted St. Isaac's Cathedral to be returned to the ROC were pitted against *gorozhane*, the secular experts, or professionals dedicated to preserving historic architecture in a contest of who would be more devoted and capable of effectively caring for the church, art, and objects that are part of this important St. Petersburg landmark. See chapter 1.

13. "Religious Affiliation: Religious Pluralism in Ukraine," MAPA: Digital Atlas of Ukraine, https://harvard-cga.maps.arcgis.com/apps/MapSeries/index.html?appid=9d716 0c9e77a4f7bbd0384fe60eb3e2a. These data were gathered as part of a research project in which I participated, "Region, Nation and Beyond: An Interdisciplinary and Transcultural Reconceptualization of Ukraine, 2012–2015," University of St. Gallen, https://www.uaregio .org/en/about/stage-1/.

14. "Osoblyvosti relihiinoho i tserkovno-relihiinoho somavyznachennia hromadian Ukrainy: Tendentsii 2000–2020," Razumkov Center Survey, November 25, 2020, https:// razumkov.org.ua/uploads/article/2020_religiya.pdf. For a recent historical comparison, see Sysyn 2005. He details the growth of the UOC-KP, which became part of the OCU in 2018, at the expense of the UOC-MP in the early post-Soviet period and the extent of regional variation in the number and types of religious communities across Ukraine.

15. "Jewish Americans in 2020," Pew Research Center, May 11, 2021, https://www .pewforum.org/2021/05/11/jewish-americans-in-2020/.

16. All statistics on the number of parish communities are from the State Service of Ukraine for Ethnopolicy and Freedom of Conscience. "Zvit pro merezhu relihiinykh orhanizatii v Ukraini stanom na 1 sichnia 2021 roku," January 1, 2021, https://dess.gov.ua /statistics-2020.

17. The primate of the UGCC, Cardinal Liubomyr Huzar, flatly said, "We are not a provincial church somewhere on the edge of Ukraine . . . We are one of the four branches of the Kyivan Church—an all-Ukrainian Church, a Church of the entire Ukrainian nation" (Vysokyi zamok 2011). See Wanner and Yelensky 2019. Indeed, the visibility and

influence of the UGCC in national politics is significant as evidenced by its growing presence in Kyiv. Nonetheless, its stronghold remains in Western Ukraine.

18. See Luehrmann 2018 for an insightful collection of articles on how the material accoutrements of Orthodoxy make for sensational experiences that often lead to conversion or enhanced religious practice. See Meyer 2011 for a compelling analysis of how sensational forms intersect with semiotic ideologies to produce religious experiences that are "ultimately real and immediate," persuasive, and foundational to the formation of worldviews (2011, 31).

19. It is common for individuals or groups to engage in spiritualized practices and simultaneously deny them as religion. This is why I focus on feelings and experiences of transcendence rather than religion in a narrow, institutional sense. One of the most notable examples of this phenomenon are the plethora of twelve-step programs that steadfastly maintain their nonreligious nature even though, Alcoholics Anonymous, for example, counts among its steps such practices as admitting powerlessness, believing in a power greater than oneself, turning over individual will and one's life to God, admitting to God the nature of the wrongs committed, using prayer and meditation to improve contact with God, and so on. See "The Twelve Steps of Alcoholics Anonymous," Alcoholics Anonymous, https://www.aa.org/assets/en_US/smf-121_en.pdf.

## 1. FREEDOM IS OUR RELIGION

1. By early 2021, the number of causalities exceeded 13,000. "Update on the Human Rights Situation in Ukraine," United Nations Office of the High Commissioner on Human Rights, May 1, 2021, https://www.ohchr.org/Documents/Countries/UA/HRMMU_Update 02_2021-05-01_EN.pdf. See also "Global Conflict Tracker," Council on Foreign Relations, December 22, 2021, https://www.cfr.org/global-conflict-tracker/conflict/conflict-ukraine.

2. There is burgeoning literature on how religious institutions are shaping national narratives and memories of the past. For analyses of the role of churches in Ukraine, see Kravchuk and Bremer 2016; Wanner and Yelensky 2019; Fert 2020; and Bogumil and Yurchuk 2021, especially the contributions by Yurchuk, Muratova, and Marchenko.

3. For analyses of the intersection of religion and politics in Ukraine, see Timoshenko 2002; Yelensky 2002; Plokhy and Sysyn 2003; Naumescu 2006; Maierchuk 2011; Gordeev 2014; Kolodnii 2014; Wawrzonek 2014; Krawchuk and Bremer 2016; Denysenko 2018; and Hovorun 2018. For identity politics more generally, see Kulyk 2017 and Onuch, Hale, and Sasse 2018.

4. For studies of church-state relations in Russia, see Knox 2004 and 2008; Papkova 2011; Richters 2013; Agadjanian 2014; Stoeckl 2014; Burgess 2017; Bernstein 2019 and Kenworthy and Agadjanian 2021.

5. In my opinion, "transcendent" social would be a more accurate translation than "transcendental" social.

6. I focus on the vernacular religious practices of individuals that engage the transcendent rather than religious institutions' use of performative, extra-institutional means of mobilizing commemorations of these two historical events. For studies of how religious institutions try to influence understandings of these two particularly contested events, see Yurchuk 2021. For similar efforts in the Russian context, see Fomina 2017.

7. Protestants are the most numerous minority confessional group in the Donbas. Prior to 2014, Donetsk hosted a Protestant Christian University, publishing houses that specialize in Christian literature, and a concentration of Soviet-era underground dissident and registered Protestant communities. See Wanner 2007.

8. "Address by President of the Russian Federation," President of Russia, March 18, 2014, http://en.kremlin.ru/events/president/news/20603 for a complete rendition of the speech in English translation. In the same speech Putin states quite forthrightly, "Crimea

is historically Russian land and Sevastopol is a Russian city. Yes, we all knew this in our hearts and minds, but we had to proceed from the existing reality and build our good-neighborly relations with independent Ukraine on a new basis. Meanwhile, our relations with Ukraine, with the fraternal Ukrainian people have always been and will remain of foremost importance for us." This last phrase elicited resounding applause.

9. Yanukovych's spiritual adviser (*dukhovnyk* in Ukrainian), Schema-Archimandrite Zosima Sokur (1944–2002), posthumously became a regional religious leader when his "Spiritual Testament" was made public. He was opposed to Ukrainian autocephaly and used his Testament to insist on continued allegiance to the Moscow Patriarchate.

10. A plethora of American, Caribbean, and Nigerian Pentecostal, Charismatic, and Baptist preachers opened churches across the former USSR in storefronts, hotels, former Soviet Houses of Culture, and even tents (Coleman 2000; Pelkmans 2009; Wanner 2007). By contrast, even when migration has resulted in the spread of Orthodoxy beyond Eastern Europe and the Middle East, religious communities usually retain an ethnic cast. Consider the Syrian Orthodox Church in Kerala, India (Naumescu 2019), or the Russian Orthodox Church in America and the Ukrainian Orthodox Church of the United States. This is one factor that explains why Orthodox-inspired visions of a global order remain understudied (Rupprecht 2018).

11. Karpov, Lisovskaya, and Barry (2012) refer to the fusion of religious and ethnic ideologies as "ethnodoxy" using Russia as a case study to signal a rigid connection between ethnic identity its dominant faith tradition. They argue for the pervasiveness and coherence of ethnodoxy, as I do for atmosphere, but they add an additional component in the form of ramifications for fostering religious and ethnic intolerance. This last is not inherent to an affective atmosphere of religiosity, although it is possible for an atmosphere to become laden with an emotional tone of intolerance and aggression targeted toward specific others.

12. Dr. Martin Luther King, Jr. and Archbishop Desmond Tutu are examples of clergy who have used religiosity to advance racial reconciliation, human rights and bring forth positive social change. The list of clergy who have done the reverse is extensive. One need only think of political conflicts with prominent religious dimensions that have simmered for decades, such as between Israel and Palestine, the former Yugoslavia, and Northern Ireland.

## 2. GOLD DOMED KYIV

1. Writing of attitudes toward Orthodoxy in Russia, John Burgess calls it an "affective affiliation" (2017).

2. Kharkiv is a Russian-speaking city in eastern Ukraine near the Russian border. It currently acts as a fence containing the armed conflict, but it has the potential to be a bridge reconnecting zones. Therein lies its strategic value in an undeclared, albeit omnipresent war. It also lies in one of the most secular regions of Ukraine, where the ratio of population to the number of religious organizations is among the highest. Most of the ethnography presented in this chapter was conducted in Kharkiv, one of the least religious regions of Ukraine.

3. "Idov. Garros. Evdokimov . . . ," Vestochka, www.vws.lv/article/147369.

4. For specific examples of the role of aesthetics in creating a particular atmosphere during the Maidan protests, see Sonnevytsky (2019) for music and "wildness"; Zychowicz (2020) and Musienko (2015) for art; and Stepnisky (2018) for politics. In a related study, Stephens (2015) explores what it would mean to understand nationalism as an atmosphere through an analysis of the "happy atmosphere" at the London 2012 Olympic Games.

5. It used to be common for men in Ukraine to remove their hats when passing before a church (Kononenko 2019).

6. A plethora of recent anthropological studies have engaged the various artistic and aesthetic sensational forms of Orthodoxy. See Bandak and Boylston 2014; Engelhardt 2015; Kellogg 2017; Luehrmann 2018; and Antonhin 2019.

7. Paul Stoller (1994, 157) suggests that the mimetic faculty operates, like a sixth sense, as "embodied imagination." It dispels the divide between subject and object by representing the endless new vistas that emerge along the fine line between imitating and creating a presence. Imitating the experiences of others creates new experiences for the performer that often culminate in a shift in their perspective and behavior.

8. Many Eastern Slavs consider religious objects works of art and can be moved by then, less for their religious content and more because the objects have been secularized into cultural heritage. Elayne Oliphant analyzes how the Catholic Church in France organizes art exhibits of religiously themed works in their buildings, positioning art as the form, religion as the content, and cultural heritage as the experience (2021). Nonbelievers might not enter a church, but they might attend an art exhibit. Art exhibits keep the Church present in public space and create the possibility that viewers could interpret the art in a religious register.

9. In Russia, a spate of artistic happenings used religious symbolism to make political statements and fell prey to charges of blasphemy (*bogokhul'stvo, koshchunstvo*). Artwork juxtaposed traditional signs of Orthodoxy with commercial brands to highlight the Church's controversial financial activities. The prosecutor claimed the artists "humiliated the national dignity of a great number of believers" (Knox 2008). Pussy Riot's performance of a "punk prayer" imploring "Mother of God, take Putin away!" in Moscow's Cathedral of Christ the Savior brought charges of "hooliganism motivated by religious hatred" (Bernstein 2014). Erasing the divisions between religious and worldly aesthetics can court perils, depending on the political implications of how the signs are read (see Asad et al. 2009; Keane 2018).

10. See Wanner (2007), especially chapters 1 and 2 and the Hidden Galleries Project, http://hiddengalleries.eu, for photographic, archival, and material evidence of underground religious communities that depict how vibrant and meaningful these communities were to their members, and how vigorously they were pursued by the secret police in multiple socialist countries in Eastern Europe.

11. In the spirit of laïcité, the Québec government introduced legislation banning the public display of religious symbolism. This was challenged by objections to a crucifix hanging over the Speaker's chair in the legislative chamber of the National Assembly of Québec. Defenders of the crucifix claimed it represented Québec's "cultural heritage" (Klassen 2015). Catholicism, they said, like the French language, was reflective of "nos valeurs" and a distinguishing national feature that separated Québec from the rest of Anglophone, Protestant Canada. Through these national tropes, secular state power in Québec used religious signs to articulate who belongs and to what they belong, and this made it compatible with laws banning the public display of religious symbolism. This line of reasoning was overturned in 2019.

12. Brazilian Evangelicals used to lambast the immorality of Carnival, a public festival with Catholic roots that begins before the asceticism of Lent. They criticized the blatant sexuality of samba, a dance rooted in African religiosity and an integral element in Carnival parades. (Oosterbaan 2018) After encountering resistance from their own believers, they declared Carnival a "national tradition" and samba a "nationalized form of dance." By appropriating the "spiritual energy" (*axé* in Portuguese) of samba as Brazilian, Evangelicals rendered these practices permissible for a pious evangelical. Oosterbaan argues

that even when secular state policies try to protect religious pluralism by delineating religion from culture, heritage regimes do the reverse (2017, 701). They fuse national culture with religious traditions for added affect. Secularism can thus be undermined when competing actors combine religion and popular culture to advance identity politics.

13. Of the hundreds of Confederate monuments across cities and towns, most were erected after Reconstruction from 1890 to 1930 or during the rise of the Civil Rights movement in the 1950s and 1960s. In other words, these monuments were erected during pivotal moments when the rights of African Americans were expanding. These Confederate monuments were meant to slow the impetus for change.

14. Proposals to remove a monument to Confederate General Robert E. Lee in military regalia sitting atop a horse on a seventy-foot pedestal in Charlottesville, Virginia provoked radical rightwing groups to organize a "Unite the Right" rally there in 2017. They countered that this monument was symbolic of Southern heritage.

15. See the interview with one of the fiercest critics of decommunization policies, the historian Heorhii Kas'ianov. "Istoryk Heorhii Kas'ianov: Sposoby sdiisnennia dekomunizatsii nahaduiut' komunistychni praktyky," *Zhyttia*, May 7, 2016, https://life.pravda.com.ua/society/2016/05/7/211912/. He, along with others, argues that these laws limit historical debate. Other criticisms centered on the costs involved or fears that such changes to public space would alienate residents of eastern and southern Ukraine, who were disproportionately affected by this legislation. There have been no significant public protests to removing the remaining communist-era monuments nor to renaming streets and the names of 877 cities, towns, and villages that fall under this legislation.

## 3. RADICAL HOPE

1. The main square in Kyiv was renamed *Maidan Nezalezhnosti* (Independence Square) after 1991 and has been the site of all major protests in independent Ukraine. Some use the term EuroMaidan to refer to the 2013–14 protests. I follow Ukrainian convention and simply refer to the "Maidan."

2. There is already an enormous literature on the Maidan, including many books in Ukrainian that focus specifically on the role of religion. This is the first monograph in English that considers the role of religiosity in connection with the Maidan and its aftermath. For an overview of the intersection of religion and politics during the Maidan, see Gorgeev (2014); Kolodnyi, Sahan, and Shevchenko (2014); Feinberg and Holovach (2016); Krawchuk and Bremmer (2016); Dymyd (2018); and Clark and Vovk (2020); on the unfolding of Maidan protests, see Philipps (2014); Stepanenko and Pylynskyi, (2014); Wanner (2014); Wilson (2014); Marples and Millis (2015); Raabe and Sapper (2015); Yekelchyk (2015); Portnov (2016); Snyder (2016); Shore (2017); and Carroll (2019). For works that consider how aesthetics contributed to the affective atmosphere on the Maidan, see Musienko (2015); Sonevytsky (2019); and Zychowicz (2020).

3. "A Year of Disaster and Triumph," *Day*, January 15, 2015, https://day.kyiv.ua/en/article/topic-day/year-disaster-and-triumph.

4. "Expert: Religion is Woven into the Landscape of the Maidan as it is in all of Ukrainian Society," Religion Information Service of Ukraine, https://risu.ua/ekspert-religiya-vpletena-v-landschaft-maydanu-tak-yak-i-v-use-ukrajinske-suspilstva_n66472.

5. Shoshana Felman and Dori Laub (1991) define trauma as an event or series of events that elude articulation. While working with Holocaust survivors and their relatives, those who had firsthand experience could not narrate what they lived through. Their children or grandchildren, by contrast, felt impelled to articulate what happened, to publicly recognize the experiences of survivors, so as to move beyond the trauma and no longer be possessed by it.

6. Other Indian chieftains also had dream-visions. Sitting Bull responded to the dev-astation that had befallen the Sioux in terms of an apocalyptic revival movement that centered on summoning a messiah to bring back their former way of life. In other words, whereas the Crow chieftain plunged forward into an unknown future, Sitting Bull took a restorative approach and tried to reconstruct aspects of the Sioux's past life. Sitting Bull was killed at Standing Rock after the Sioux did the Ghost Dance for three months to re-vive the coherence of their former lives and the satisfaction they once felt. Authorities justified their violence against the Sioux as preemptive, fearing that the emotions stim-ulated by the Sioux dance were a prelude to violence.

7. Jennifer Carroll (2019) notes the limits of Maidan inclusivity. Individuals with addic-tion problems and HIV were actively turned away from protesting or participating in other capacities. Philipps (2014) and Martsenyuk and Grytsenko (2017) note gender-based limits on participation and Channel-Justice (2019) addresses issues of unity and inclusion.

8. For the use of history in nation-building, see Wanner 1998; Portnov 2015; Wanner 2016; Schmid and Myshlovska 2019; Wylegala and Glowacka-Grajper 2020; for language, see Kulyk 2018; Bilaniuk 2020; for religion, see Denysenko 2018; Wanner and Yelensky 2019.

9. The name Bohdan literally means "God given" (*Boh-dan*). This can be a last name and is a traditional and very popular Ukrainian first name.

10. Such nuances have very significant relevance for social scientists who conduct sur-vey research on ethnonational identifications and religious affiliation. Many associa-tions that are part and parcel of how such concepts are understood locally on the ground are counterintuitive to Western analysts and yet they inform the fluidity of how and where a person places themselves on a continuum of possibilities at any given moment and in any given context. See Hale (2004, 464); Onuch 2016; and Kulyk 2018.

11. These Facebook posts, which early on achieved notoriety, later became part of a semipermanent commemorative exhibit on the Maidan. This post, in particular, has been recognized as the first official spark that ignited the Maidan protests.

12. Many of these statements have been compiled in Fylypovych, Horkusha, and Ty-tarenko 2014 as well as Finberg and Holovach 2016.

13. Other estimates of the number of protesters by November 24, 2013, in Kyiv are as high as 100,000 (Mukhars'kii 2015, 13).

14. Gray (2016) analyzes how an affective atmosphere of street protests cannot only be studied but also experienced via virtual ethnography.

15. Stepan Bandera led the Organization of Ukrainian Nationalists (OUN) under the protection of Nazi German forces during World War II against the Soviet Red Army in an attempt to achieve Ukrainian state independence. As a figure accused of collabora-tion with Nazi forces and committing atrocities, Viktor Yushchenko's decision to make Bandera a "Hero of Ukraine" is controversial, even in Ukraine. (Drapac and Pritchard 2015; Mick 2011).

16. "Night of Open Doors," ZN, UA, December 6, 2013, https://zn.ua/internal/noch -otkrytyh-dverey-_.html.

17. "Interconfessional Prayer Tent," Religious Information Service of Ukraine, December 6, 2013, https://risu.ua/vid-uchora-na-maydani-diye-molitovniy-mizhkonfe siyniy-namet_n66119. See also Hryhorenko (2018, 36–55) for a profile of the schedule of liturgies and prayer requests.

18. See Buyskykh (2018) for background on why this mythic image of a female guard-ian arose along with the independence movement.

19. Not all Protestant communities embraced this activist responsibility. Some pre-ferred to maintain what they called "neutrality." This led to serious splits and lasting

divisions among the spectrum of Protestant groups in Ukraine and great discord between Protestant groups in Ukraine and their Russian "brethren."

20. "Confrontations in the Center of Kyiv," Religious Information Service of Ukraine, December 11, 2013, https://risu.ua/v-centri-kiyeva-trivaye-protistoyannya-na-maydani-nezalezhnosti-perebuvayut-svyashchennosluzhiteli-riznih-konfesiy-onovlyuyetsya_n66211.

21. "Confrontations in the Center of Kyiv."

22. "Odesa Metropolitan Agafangel Calls the EuroMaidan a Place of Disorder," Religion in Ukraine, https://religion.in.ua/news/ukrainian_news/24271-odesskij-mitropolit-agafangel-nazval-evromaidan-smutoj-kuda-sobiraetsya-sil.

23. For a discussion of how Russia became the third largest supplier of global migrants after India and Mexico and the efforts of the Russian state to capitalize on the geopolitical advantages this diaspora might offer, see Suslov (2018).

24. Suslov (2018) notes how some conservative intellectuals explain the Russian World metaphorically in terms of a magnificent cathedral, which previously had "side chapels" (*pridely* in Russian), such as Crimea and Novorossiia, the southern flank of Ukraine, which are now being reintegrated into the cathedral once again.

25. The UCCRO was created in 1996 as an interconfessional advisory body. It is charged with promoting interconfessional dialogue, church-state relations, and charitable activities. It also supported European integration.

26. Multilingual versions of Hovorun's statement can be found on the blog of Kievskaia Rus', "Bohoslovye Maidana," Kievskaia Rus', December 12, 2013, http://www.kiev-orthodox.org/site/churchlife/4975/.

27. For two fascinating ethnographies that engage the concept of dignity as it relates to law and social morality in entirely different contexts, see Osanloo 2020 and Willen 2019.

28. Earlier still were references to human dignity, without using the word per se, in the United States Declaration of Independence, signed on July 4, 1776. The Declaration firmly asserts the "self-evident" truths that all people are created equal, and all have certain unalienable rights to "Life, Liberty and the pursuit of Happiness."

29. The Soviet representatives to the UN Council objected to the use of multinational organizations to guarantee human rights. They argued that this would pit the protection of dignity and human rights against the sovereignty of individual nation-states. Taking a Marxist position that has historically informed socialist movements, they argued that human dignity could only be assured by a just social and economic order, which, in turn, could only be realized on the individual state level. Therefore, they disagreed with assigning the task to the UN because it authorized a supranational model of jurisdiction capable of infringing on state sovereignty. They countered with the proposal that individual states implement their own measures to protect human dignity. This set the stage for a confrontation between what has been called "sovereignist vs. dignitarian politics," which utilizes different modes of reasoning to determine the objects of state power.

At the time, the American Anthropological Association (AAA) reasoned that by putting limits on "cultural practices" states were effectively limiting tolerance. The AAA essentially supported a position of Boasian cultural relativism to the extreme, thereby denying the possibility to make political judgments. The AAA retracted such pronouncements in 1999, which are increasingly seen as an embarrassing moment of misjudgment (Engle 2001; Bennett 2015).

30. A direct outgrowth of the UN Declaration of Human Rights is the supranational European Court of Human Rights, which was established in 1959, to guarantee the protection of a range of civil and political rights should individual sovereign states fail to do

so. This made the commitment to protect human dignity a central element in the political and legal policies that now govern the forty-seven signatories to the European Convention on Human Rights (Costa 2013: 402).

31. A commitment to dignity subsequently underwrote a range of initiatives from the teachings of Liberation Theology to moral pronouncements on the sanctity of human life, which led to the condemnation of abortion, euthanasia, and other practices. The 2008 *Dignitas Personae*, which addresses the church's position on a variety of bioethical questions, opens with, "The dignity of a person must be recognized in every human being from conception to natural death." "Instruction Dignitas Personae," Vatican, http://www.vatican.va/roman_curia/congregations/cfaith/documents/rc_con_cfaith_doc_20081208_dignitas-personae_en.html.

32. "The Russian Orthodox Church's Basic Teaching on Human Dignity, Freedom, and Rights," Russian Orthodox Church, Department for External Church Relations, https://old.mospat.ru/en/documents/dignity-freedom-rights/ All citations from this document are found here.

33. "The Russian Orthodox Church's Basic Teaching on Human Dignity, Freedom, and Rights."

34. "The Russian Orthodox Church's Basic Teaching on Human Dignity, Freedom, and Rights" and "The Basis of the Social Concept," Russian Orthodox Church, Department for External Church Relations, https://mospat.ru/en/documents/dignity-freedom-rights/ and https://mospat.ru/en/documents/social-concepts/.

35. Nawara Najem, "Egyptian Dignity in the Face of Death," *Guardian*, February 20, 2011.

36. "Vstavai," Okean Elzy, December 15, 2013, https://www.youtube.com/watch?v=R0KvzXWO9RE.

37. "Ukrains'ki Tserkvi 2014-ho," *Day*, December 24, 2014, http://www.day.kiev.ua/uk/blog/suspilstvo/ukrayinski-cerkvy-2014-go.

38. Alexei Yurchak (2014) refers to the designation "little green men" as evoking the image of leprechauns. Most Ukrainians I spoke to, however, understood the reference to "little" as a dismissive insult and the assertion of their "greenness" as not only reflective of their uniforms but of their alien qualities as well.

39. It became an issue in 2017 when Ukraine and the EU were in negotiations to create a visa-free regime for Ukrainian citizens. EU officials insisted that Ukraine's eastern border be secured and administered according to Schengen standards.

40. Fredric Jameson claimed that the political form of postmodernism would include "global cognitive mapping," the purpose of which will be to "grasp our positioning as individual and collective subjects and regain a capacity to act and struggle which is at present neutralized by our spatial as well as our social confusion" (1984, 54).

## 4. THE AESTHETICS OF RELATEDNESS

1. The tryzub dates back to Kyivan Rus'. The black and red flag was used by the Ukrainian Insurgent Army (UPA), a fighting force that forged an alliance with Nazi forces against the Soviet Red Army during World War II. After having been stigmatized during the Soviet period as partisans, UPA soldiers are now also recognized as heroic defenders of the homeland, as forerunners of ATO fighters in Eastern Ukraine. This is one of the many elements that makes World War II commemorations so politicized and laden with religious symbolism. Since the fall of the USSR, nationalist groups that unite religious, militarized, and Cossack symbolism have been among the fighters not just in Eastern Ukraine but in the armed conflicts that preceded it in Transnistria, Moldova and South Ossetia and Abkhazia, Georgia.

2. A perspective that privileges the body and moral impulses diverges from those asserted by other scholars, such as Anthony Giddens (2013), who see the capacity to engage in moral reasoning as located in reflexivity and rational thought. For Giddens, unlike Bauman (1992), there is no moral impulse, no universal moral truths, just secular claims to moral authority, which always reserve the right to change. For Giddens, bodily sensory responses to situations only have significant meaning after there has been a breakdown in the cognitive ability to understand. For Baumann, it is the other way around.

3. Maintaining the visibility of Lenin's dead body on Red Square underscores that the "revolution lives," as one of the old slogans proclaimed. Mausoleums, columbarium, and other shrine-like structures allow for a continued presence of the dead in public space (Bernstein 2019; Todorova 2006; Verdery 2000). Elaborate, ongoing death rituals sustain the active social afterlife of revolutionary heroes. Death and burial rituals were some of the most tenacious forms of religious practice that Soviet antireligious campaigns had to confront. In the end, the Soviet state coopted these instincts into its own political cult of the dead (Luehrmann 2011; Smolkin 2018; Wanner 2012).

4. This phrase was also used when commemorating the murder of the opposition leader Boris Nemtsov after he was shot and killed in Moscow in 2011.

5. Robert Hertz recognized the importance of materiality for religiosity long ago ([1907] 1960). He theorized that material objects create a relationship with the deceased through strategies of curation, destruction, or gradual decay. "Flesh-type" objects, like the body itself, slip away and become reconstituted in the Beyond. They serve as a metaphor for the soul, which after forty days should have passed into heaven. "Bone-type" objects, or relics, which are more permanent, mediate the relationship between the living and the dead over time. Robben (2004, 9) maintains that Hertz's essay "endures as the single most influential text in the anthropology of death." See Metcalf and Huntington (1991, 83) for a critique of Hertz.

6. In instances of bad death, the usual funerary rites were not always practiced. Corpses were usually buried along roads or at the site of death, not in the cemetery, a practice symbolically maintained on the Maidan. Some believe the souls of those who die in unfortunate circumstances wander the earth and can harm the living (Kukharenko 2011, 65–67).

7. Both the gold loaf of bread and Vladimir Lukyanenko came to a sordid end. Lukyanenko was arrested on charges of child sexual exploitation in Monaco in 2016. One year earlier, the golden loaf was stolen from its display in Yanukovych's Mezhyhirya residence, which opened to the public as the Museum of Corruption.

8. I thank Julia Buyskykh for bringing this poem to my attention and Adrian Wanner for his assistance in translating it.

9. Elsewhere in the same speech, Putin states forthrightly, "Crimea is historically Russian land and Sevastopol is a Russian city. Yes, we all knew this in our hearts and minds, but we had to proceed from the existing reality and build our good-neighborly relations with independent Ukraine on a new basis. Meanwhile, our relations with Ukraine, with the fraternal Ukrainian people have always been and will remain of foremost importance for us." This last phrase elicited resounding applause. "Address by the President of the Russian Federation," President of Russia, http://en.kremlin.ru/events/president/news/20603.

10. AKIpress News Agency, May 8, 2014, https://link.glae.com/apps/doc/A367415051/GIC?u=psucic&sid=GIC&xid=487e9ac6.

11. "Teritoriia Hidnosti: Yak Hromadiany Rozrobliaiut' Pravyla Rekonstruktsii Maidanu," The Insider, November 28, 2014, http://www.theinsider.ua/rus/lifestyle/teritoriya-gidnosti-yak-gromadyani-rozroblyayut-pravila-rekonstruktsiyi-maidanu/.

12. The interruption of individual dialogue and exchange is compounded by the cut in rail and aerial routes connecting the two countries. Road connections are now heavily monitored. There is a suspension of imported goods, especially of printed material, in both directions.

## 5. SERVING ON THE FRONT AND THE HOME FRONT

1. Crimea was an autonomous republic within Soviet Russia until 1945 when it became an oblast. The oblast was transferred to Soviet Ukraine in 1954 largely for administrative reasons. When the treaty of annexation was signed on March 8, 2014, Crimea became one of the twenty-two republics of the Russian Federation.

2. There is burgeoning literature on the military chaplaincy in Ukraine and an established scholarly record on the significance of chaplaincy and religion in war. An extensive oral history archive on the war, including many interviews with military chaplains, is available at https://ui.uinp.gov.ua/uk/fondi/fond-1-ukrayinskiy-institut-nacionalnoyi-pamyati. See also Kalenychenko and Kokhanchuk 2017; Kovtunovych and Pryvalko 2019, as well as Elisabeth Sieca-Kozlowski, "Oral History: The Russo-Ukrainian War through the Eyes of Ukrainian Military Chaplains," *Journal of Power Institutions in Post-Soviet Societies*. http://journals.openedition.org/pipss/6344, DOI: https://doi.org/10.4000/pipss.6344; See also special issues of *Faith & International Affairs* 7, no. 4 (2009) and *Religion State and Society* 39, no. 1 (2011) devoted to the changing role of the military chaplaincy, the latter specifically in countries of the former USSR. For studies of the significance of the military chaplaincy in a variety of contexts and periods, see Cox 1972; Loveland 2004; Krebs 2005; Werkner 2008; and Hassner 2014.

3. See Kalenychenko and Kokhanchuk 2017 for an extensive manual prepared for soldiers and volunteer fighters about the military chaplaincy. This manual was sponsored by the Christians of Evangelical Faith and Pentecostals, confessional groups that previously espoused an Anabaptist advocacy of pacificism. This was one of the many points of contention that has emerged to divide Ukrainian evangelical religious groups from their counterparts in Russia. https://risu.ua/php_uploads/files/articles/ArticleFiles_64910_Buty-poruch-kapelany.

4. See "Pro Mystetstvo buty poruch, ateistiv v okopakh ta pankovi probizhky—rozmova z kapelanom Zelins'kym" *Hromadske*. January 14, 2020, https://hromadske.ua/posts/pro-mistectvo-buti-poruch-ateyistiv-v-okopah-ta-rankovi-probizhki-rozmova-z-kapelanom-zelinskim.

5. This ad hoc status was not always the case. As recently as World War II, western Ukrainian military units had chaplains attached to them (Hunczak, 2000; Dats'ko and Horiacha, 2014: 146). I thank Kathryn David for bringing this to my attention.

6. This was the number of chaplains reported to me by other chaplains in the course of interviews.

7. US religious organizations have been particularly influential. The US Army Chaplain Corps was officially established in 1775. Chaplains have participated in wars ever since. To become a chaplain in the United States, one must be endorsed by a religious organization, meet mental and physical training standards, have a postgraduate degree in theology or a related field, and have at least two years of service in a parish community. Endorsement suffices in Ukraine. US military chaplains have the rank of a commissioned officer, whereas Ukrainian chaplains do not have ranks (Loveland 2004). For a comparative study of chaplains, see Hassner (2014).

8. "Dva Kapelany," *Hromadske*, April 27, 2019. https://hromadske.ua/posts/dva-kapelani-chastina-12-l-hromadskedoc. This is a three-part film series that illustrates the dual nature of serving on the front and the home front and the vastly different services military chaplains are asked to provide.

9. "World-Low 9% of Ukrainians Confident in Government," Gallup, March 21, 2019, https://news.gallup.com/poll/247976/world-low-ukrainians-confident-government.aspx.

10. "Otsinka Gromadianamy Diialnosti Vlady," Razumkov Center, February 24, 2020, http://razumkov.org.ua/napriamky/sotsiologichni-doslidzhennia/otsinka-gromadianamy-diialnosti-vlady-riven-doviry-do-sotsialnykh-instytutiv-ta-politykiv-elektoralni-oriientatsii-gromadian-liutyi-2020r; "Volunteer Organizations Most Trusted Institution in Ukraine," Ukrinform, December 11, 2018, https://www.ukrinform.net/rubric-society/2598710-volunteer-organizations-most-trusted-institution-in-ukraine.html.

11. Synodal'ne Upravlinnia Viis'kovoho Dukhovenstva. "Rozlohe Interv'iu Kapelana," Synodal Administration of Military Clergy, November 17, 2017, https://www.suvd.com.ua/uk/articles/rozloge-interv-ju-kapelana/show.

12. "Interv'iu z ottsem Stepanom Sysom: Cherez agresiiu Rosii Tserkva v Ukraini Otrymala Novii Dosvid—Tse Viis'kove Kapelanstvo," Kapelanstvo.info, July 30, 2019, https://kapelanstvo.info/garnizonnyj-hram/interv-yu-z-ottsem-stepanom-susom-cherez-agresiyu-rosiyi-tserkva-v-ukrayini-otrymala-novyj-dosvid-tse-vijskove-kapelanstvo/.

13. I use the actual names of chaplains, and all others interviewed for this book, that are public figures. For all others, I follow the standard convention in ethnographic research of using pseudonyms.

14. Tomas Matza's study of psychotherapeutic techniques in Russia reveals how a religious concept can become a life skill technique (2018). Matza observed a counselor in St. Petersburg encourage clients to rely on *dusha* during periods of uncertainty to make life changing decisions This counselor affirms, "We can't understand our path because we look from the mind—only our dusha can point the way to happiness" (2018, 182). Dusha keys into the totality of one's lifeworld. Matza argues that psychosocial explorations of *dusha* not only are intended to result in greater self-knowledge, but also in "a kind of social communion" that can result in "harmonious relations" (2018, 183, 196). See Wanner 2021 or a fuller analysis of the differences between psychotherapy and other secular healing techniques and the talk therapy chaplains aim to provide.

15. See Wendy Cadge (2012) for a profile of the medical chaplaincy and interfaith hospitals chapels.

16. Psychoanalysis obliges its practitioners to undergo their own analysis so as to more fully appreciate the experience of their patients who often will only reluctantly divulge private information. The same is true of chaplains who also have been in or near combat situations.

17. "U Kozhnii Eparxii Ukrains'koi Hreko-katolyts'koi Tserkvy Stvoriat' Reabilitatsiini Tsentry dlia Uchasnykiv Boiovykh Dii," ArmiiaInform, November 7, 2019, https://armyinform.com.ua/2019/11/u-kozhnij-yeparhiyi-ukrayinskoyi-greko-katolyczkoyi-czerkvy-stvoryat-reabilitaczijni-czentry-dlya-uchasnykiv-bojovyh-dij/?fbclid=IwAR27-VPxsPFL4RSGKtswiK0Fm22sYNQu41h5noWEROv_4_mHJ706mdZ2TaE.

18. "Lektsiia Andriia Zelins'koho u NaUKMA," Soundcloud, September 2, 2016, https://soundcloud.com/user-504638903/lektsya-andrya-zelnskogo-u-naukma.

19. "Pro Mystetstvo buty Poruch, ateistiv v okopakh ta Rankovi Probizhky—Rozmova z Kapelanom Zelins'kym," Hromadske, January 14, 2020, https://hromadske.ua/posts/pro-mistectvo-buti-poruch-ateyistiv-v-okopah-ta-rankovi-probizhki-rozmova-z-kapelanom-zelinskim.

20. Bar-Tura and Fleischer (2004) analyze the extent to which the national youth service in Israel actually creates a "common civic denominator," as it promises, rather than ultimately segregating by experience non-Jewish citizens of Israel, who are mostly Palestinian, from their Jewish Israeli counterparts.

21. "A Ukrainian Military Chaplain's Candid Reflections on Christmas," EuroMaidan Press, January 6, 2016, http://euromaidanpress.com/2016/01/06/a-ukrainian-military-chaplains-candid-reflections-on-christmas/.

22. "Lektsiia Andriia Zelins'koho u NaUKMA," Soundcloud, September 2, 2016, https://soundcloud.com/user-504638903/lektsya-andrya-zelnskogo-u-naukma.

23. Sonevytsky contrasts the pragmatic form of patriotism she sees emerging in Ukraine in the immediate aftermath of the Maidan as displacing "ethno-nationalism in favor of a sovereign imaginary predicated on civic inclusivity and incremental change" (2019, 57). This contrasts with a from a patriotism that draws on a sense of inevitability, which breeds despair and alienation (Oushakine 2009).

24. "Kapelan Andrii Zelins'kyi: Ukrains'ka Natsional'na Ideia-Sofiinist," Glavkom, January 27, 2020, https://glavcom.ua/interviews/kapelan-andriy-zelinskiy-ukrajinska-nacionalna-ideya-sofiynist-655408.html.

## CONCLUSION

1. This quote is usually attributed to Shaw, although another Irish writer, Oscar Wilde, wrote the following in *The Canterville Ghost* in 1887: "We have really everything in common with America nowadays except, of course, language."

2. In some ways, the "Orthodox imaginary" that Naumescu depicts is a local response to the Russian World, which also rests on an imagined unity among all Eastern Slavic Orthodox believers that places them in a single institutional configuration under the Moscow patriarchate.

3. These are the results of a survey conducted by the Razumkov Center from November 12–19, 2021. "Kil'kist' Virian PTsU Maizhe Vdvichi Perevishchyla Chyslo Prykhyl'nykiv UPTs MP" Religious Information Service of Ukraine, February 2, 2022. An earlier survey from June 2021 also found a reduction in the number of Just Orthodox, although different questions and categories were used. "Relihiina Samoidentyfikatsiia Naselennia i Stavlennia do Ocnovnykh Tserkov Ukrainy: Cherven' 2021 Roku" Kiev International Institute of Sociology, July 6, 2021, http://kiis.com.ua/?lang=ukr&cat=reports&id=1052&page=1&t=9. I am grateful to Oxana Shevel and Frank Sysyn for discussing interpretations of these data.

# References

Adams, Amy Singleton, and Vera Shevzoz, eds. 2018. *Framing Mary: The Mother of God in Modern, Revolutionary and Post-Soviet Russian Culture*. DeKalb: Northern Illinois Press.

Adamsky, Dmitry. 2019. *Russian Nuclear Orthodoxy: Religion, Politics and Strategy*. Palo Alto, CA: Stanford University Press.

Agadjanian, Alexander. 2014. "The New Age of Russia: Occult and Esoteric Dimensions." *Nova Religio* 17, no. 3: 136–38. doi:10.1525/nr.2014.17.3.136.

——. 2019. "Religion's Claims of Space, Power, and Culture: the secular, challenged, fragile, but enduring" Working Group on Lived Religion Annual Conference, September 20, Lviv, Ukraine.

Akhutin, Anatoly V., and Irina E. Berlyland. 2016. "Maidan as Event." *Russian Studies in Philosophy* 54, no. 3: 239–51.

Alexander, Jeffrey, Dominik Bartmanski, and Bernhard Giesen, eds. 2012. *Iconic Power: Materiality and Meaning in Social Life*. New York: Palgrave Macmillan.

Ammerman, Nancy, ed. 2007. *Everyday Religion: Observing Modern Religious Lives*. New York: Oxford University Press.

Ammerman, Nancy. 2013. "Spiritual But Not Religious? Beyond Binary Choices in the Study of Religion." *Journal for the Scientific Study of Religion* 52, no. 2: 258–78. https://doi.org/10.1111/jssr.12024.

Anderson, Benedict R. 2006. *Imagined Communities: Reflections on the Origin and Spread of Nationalism*. London: Verso.

Anderson, J. 2010. *Understanding Cultural Geography: Places and Traces*. Abingdon: Routledge.

Antohin, Alexandra S. 2019. "Preserving the Intangible: Orthodox Christian Approaches to Spiritual Heritage." *Religions* 10, no. 5: 336. https://doi.org/10.3390/rel10050336.

Appadurai, Arjun. 1996. *Modernity at Large: Cultural Dimensions of Globalization*. Minneapolis: University of Minnesota Press.

Asad, Talal. 2003. *Formations of the Secular: Christianity, Islam, Modernity*. Redwood City, CA: Stanford University Press.

——. 2006. "Trying to Understand French Secularism." In *Political Theologies*, edited by Hent de Vries, 494–526. New York: Fordham University Press.

——. 2009. "Free Speech, Blasphemy, and Secular Criticism." In *Is Critique Secular? Blasphemy, Injury, and Free Speech*, edited by Talal Asad, Wendy Brown, Judith Butler, and Saba Mahmood, 20–63. Berkeley: University of California Press.

Bakker, H. P. S. 2013. "Desire in Eastern Orthodox Praxis." In *City of Desires-A Place for God?: Practical Theological Perspectives*, edited by Bonnie J. Miller-McLemore, Rein Brouwer, and Reinder Ruard Ganzevoort, 163–72. Zurich: I IT Verlag.

Bandak, Andreas, and Tom Boylston. 2014. "The Orthodoxy of Orthodoxy: On Moral Imperfection, Correctness, and Deferral in Religious Worlds." *Religion and Society* 5, no. 1: 25–46. doi:10.3167/arrs.2014.050103.

Barilan, Yechiel Michael. 2012. *Human Dignity, Human Rights and Responsibility: The New Language of Global Bioethics and Biolaw*. Boston: MIT Press.

Bar-Tura, Maggie, and Nicole Fleischer. 2004. "Civic Service in Israel." *Nonprofit and Voluntary Sector Quarterly* 33, no. 4. 51S–63S. https://doi.org/10.1177/0899764004269742.

Bateson, Gregory. 1972. *Steps to an Ecology of Mind.* New York: Ballantine Books.

Baudrillard, Jean. 1976. *L'Echange symbolique et la mort* [Symbolic Exchange and Death]. Paris: Gallimard.

Bauman, Zygmunt. 1992. *Mortality, Immortality, and Other Life Strategies.* Palo Alto, CA: Stanford University Press.

Beckford, James A. 1998. "Ethnic and Religious Diversity among Prisoners: The Politics of Prison Chaplaincy." *Social Compass* 45, no. 2: 265–77.

Benedict, Ruth 1934. *Patterns of Culture.* New York: Houghton Mifflin.

Bennett, Gaymon. 2015. *Technicians of Human Dignity: Bodies, Souls, and the Making of Intrinsic Worth.* New York: Fordham University Press.

Bennett, Jill. "Stigmata and Sense Memory: St Francis and The Affective Image." *Art History* 24, no. 1: 1–16.

Bennett, Michael. 2001. "From Wide Open Spaces to Metropolitan Places: The Urban Challenge to Ecocriticism." *Interdisciplinary Studies in Literature and Environment* 9, no. 1: 31–52.

Bernstein, Anya. 2013. *Religious Bodies Politic: Rituals of Sovereignty in Buryat Buddhism.* Chicago: University of Chicago Press.

——. 2014. "Caution, Religion!: Iconoclasm, Secularism, and Ways of Seeing in Post-Soviet Art Wars." *Public Culture* 26 (3): 419–48.

——. 2019. *The Future of Immortality: Remaking Life and Death in Contemporary Russia.* Princeton: Princeton University Press.

Bernstein, Seth. 2016. "Remembering War, Remaining Soviet: Digital Commemoration of World War II in Putin's Russia." *Memory Studies* 9, no. 4: 422–36. doi:10.1177/1750698015605573.

Bilianiuk, Laada. 2020. "Linguistic Conversions: Nation-Building on the Self." *Journal of Soviet and Post-Soviet Politics and Societies* 6, no. 1: 59–82.

Billig, Michael. 1995. *Banal Nationalism.* Los Angeles: Sage.

Billington, J. H. "Orthodoxy and Democracy." *Journal of Church and State* 49, no. 1 (2007): 19–26. doi:10.1093/jcs/49.1.19.

Bloch, Maurice. 2008. "Why Religion Is Nothing Special but Is Central." *Philosophical Transactions of the Royal Society of Biological Sciences* 363, no. 1: 2055–61.

Bloch, Maurice, and Jonathan Parry, eds. 1982. *Death and the Regeneration of Life.* Cambridge: Cambridge University Press.

Bociurkiw, Bohdan R. 1996. *The Ukrainian Greek Catholic Church and the Soviet State (1939–50).* Edmonton: Canadian Institute of Ukrainian Studies Press.

Bogumil, Zuzanna, and Yuliya Yurchuk, eds. 2021. *Memory and Religion from a Post-secular Perspective.* New York: Routledge.

Böhme, Gernot, and Jean-Paul Thibaud. 2017. *The Aesthetics of Atmospheres.* New York: Routledge.

Bowman, Marian, and Ülo Valk, eds. 2014. *Vernacular Religion in Everyday Life: Expressions of Belief.* New York: Routledge.

Boylston, Tom. 2018. *The Stranger at the Feast: Prohibition and Mediation in an Ethiopian Orthodox Christian Community.* Santa Barbara: University of California Press.

Brennan, Teresa. 2004. *The Transmission of Affect.* Ithaca: Cornell University Press.

Burgess, John P. 2017. *Holy Rus': The Rebirth of Orthodoxy in the New Russia.* New Haven: Yale University Press.

Buyskykh, Yuliya. 2018. "Berehynia: Sproba dekonstruktsii odnoho 'kabinetnoho' mifa." *Ukraina Moderna,* May 24. https://uamoderna.com/md/buyskykh-berehynia-myth.

Cadge, Wendy. 2012. "Negotiating Religious Differences in Secular Organizations: The Case of Hospital Chaplains." In *Religion on the Edge: De-Centering and Re-Centering the Sociology of Religion*, edited by Courtney Bender, Wendy Cadge, Peggy Levitt, and David Smilde. New York: Oxford University Press.

Caldwell, Melissa. 2004. *Not by Bread Alone: Social Support in the New Russia*. Berkeley: University of California Press.

Carroll, Timothy. 2018. *Orthodox Christian Material Culture: Of People and Things in the Making of Heaven*. London: Routledge Press.

Carroll, Jennifer J. 2019. *Narkomania: Drugs, HIV, and Citizenship in Ukraine*. Ithaca, NY: Cornell University Press.

Casanova, José. 2013. "Exploring the Postsecular: Three Meanings of the 'Secular' and their Possible Transcendence." In *Habermas and Religion*, edited by Craig Calhoun, Eduardo Mendieta, and Jonathan VanAntwerpen. Boston: Polity Press.

——. 1996. *Public Religions in the Modern World*. Chicago: University of Chicago Press.

——. 2006. "Secularization Revisited: A Reply to Talal Asad." In *Powers of the Secular Modern*, edited by David Scott and Charles Hirschkind, 12–30. Stanford: Stanford University Press.

——. 2020. "Revisiting Religious Pluralism in Ukraine." YouTube. https://www.youtube.com/watch?v=HwJwDH5wsmc&ab_channel=UkrainianResearchInstituteHarvard University.

Channel-Justice, Emily S. 2016. "Left of Maidan: Self-Organization and the Ukrainian State on the Edge of Europe." PhD diss., City University of New York.

Channel-Justice, Emily. 2019. "'We Made a Contribution to the Revolution': Shifting Scales of Politics and Unity in Ukraine." *City and Society* 31, no. 3: 462–83. https://doi.org/10.1111/ciso.12236.

Cherenkov, Mykhailo. 2015. "Protestant Churches after the Maidan." *Euxeinos* 17: 42–48.

Chua, Liana. 2011. "Conversion, Continuity, and Moral Dilemmas among Christian Bidayuhs in Malaysian Borneo." *American Ethnologist* 39, no. 3: 511–26.

Chulos, Chris J. 2003. *Converging Worlds: Religion and Community in Peasant Russia, 1861–1917*. DeKalb: Northern Illinois University Press.

Coleman, Simon. 2000. *The Globalization of Charismatic Christianity: Spreading the Gospel of Prosperity*. Cambridge: University of Cambridge Press.

Coleman, Simon, and J. Eade, eds. 2004. *Reframing Pilgrimage: Cultures in Motion*. London: Routledge.

Collins, Randall. 2004. *Interaction Ritual Chains*. Princeton: Princeton University Press.

Costa, Jean-Paul. 2013. "Human Dignity in the Jurisprudence of the European Court of Human Rights." In *Understanding Human Dignity*, edited by Christopher McCrudden, 393–402. Oxford: Oxford University Press.

Cox, Harvey G. 1972. *Military Chaplains: From Religious Military to a Military Religion*. New York: American Report Press.

Darieva, Tsypylma, Florian Mühlfried, and Kevin Tuite. 2018. *Sacred Places, Emerging Spaces: Religious Pluralism in the Post-Soviet Caucasus*. New York: Berghahn Books.

Das, Veena. 2007. *Life and Words: Violence and the Descent into the Ordinary*. Berkeley: University of California Press.

Das, V., A. Kleinman, M. Lock, M. Ramphele, and P. Reynolds. 2001. *Remaking a World: Violence, Social Suffering and Recovery*. Berkeley: University of California Press.

Dats'ko, Ivan, and Mariia Horiacha, eds. 2014. *Josyf Slipy. Spomyny*. Lviv: Ukrainian Catholic University Press.

de Vries, Hent, ed. 2008. *Religion beyond a Concept*. New York: Fordham University Press.

Desjarlais, Robert, and C. Jason Throop. 2011. "Phenomenological Approaches in Anthropology." *Annual Review of Anthropology* 40, no. 1: 87–102. doi:10.1146/annurev-anthro-092010-153345.

Denysenko, Nicholas. 2018. *The Orthodox Church in Ukraine: A Century of Separation.* DeKalb: Northern Illinois Press.

Dragadze, Tamara. 1993. "The Domestication of Religion under Soviet Communism." In *Socialism: Ideals, Ideologies, and Local Practice*, edited by Chris M. Hann, 148–56. London: Routledge.

Drapac, Vesna, and Gareth Pritchard. 2015. "Beyond Resistance and Collaboration: Towards a Social History of Politics in Hitler's Empire." *Journal of Social History* 48, no. 4: 865–91.

Durkheim, Emile. 1995. *The Elementary Forms of the Religious Life*. Translated by Karen Fields. New York: Free Press.

Dymyd, Mykailo. 2014. *Kaminnia Maidanu*. Lviv: Ukrainian Catholic University Press.

El Bernoussi, Zaynab. 2015. "The Postcolonial Politics of Dignity: From the 1956 Suez Nationalization to the 2011 Revolution in Egypt." *International Sociology* 30, no. 4: 367–82.

Engelhardt, Jeffers. 2015. *Singing the Right Way: Orthodox Christians and Secular Enchantment in Estonia*. New York: Oxford University Press.

Engelke, Matthew. 2007. *A Problem of Presence: Beyond Scripture in an African Church*. Berkley: University of California Press.

Engelke, Matthew E. 2012. "Angels in Swindon: Public Religion and Ambient Faith in England." *American Ethnologist* 39, no. 1: 155–70.

——. 2013. *God's Agents: Biblical Publicity in Contemporary England*. Berkeley: University of California Press.

Engle, Karen. 2001. "From Skepticism to Embrace: Human Rights and the American Anthropological Association from 1947–1999." *Human Rights Quarterly* 23, no. 3: 536–59.

Epstein, Mikhail, Aleksandr Genis, and Slobodanka Vladiv-Glover. 1999. *Russian Postmodernism: New Perspectives on Post-Soviet Culture*. New York: Berghahn Books.

Etkind, Alexander. 2013. *Warped Mourning: Stories of the Undead from the Land of the Unburied*. Stanford: Stanford University Press.

Evans-Pritchard, Edward E. 1937. *Witchcraft, Oracles, and Magic among the Azande*. London: Oxford University Press.

Eyadat, Zaid. 2012"The Arab Revolutions of 2011: Revolutions of Dignity." *Mediterranean Academy of Diplomatic Studies*. University of Malta. https://www.um.edu.mt/library/oar/bitstream/123456789/39502/1/The_Arab_revolutions_of_2011_revolutions_of_dignity_2012.pdf.

Fagan, Geraldine. "Ukraine's Rebels Worship the Past, Not God." *Moscow Times*, August 13, 2014. https://www.themoscowtimes.com/2014/08/13/ukraines-rebels-worship-the-past-not-god-a38317.

Fedele, Anna. 2014. "Energy and Transformation in Alternative Pilgrimages to Catholic Shrines: Deconstructing the Tourist/Pilgrim Divide. *Journal of Tourism and Cultural Change* 12, no. 2: 150–65. https://doi.org/10.1080/14766825.2014.915091.

Felman, Shoshana, and Dori Laub, MD. 1992. *Testimony: Crises of Witnessing in Literature, Psychoanalysis, and History*. New York: Routledge.

Fert, Andriy. 2020. "Between Mourning and Veneration: Churches Commemorate Victims of the Holodomor in Ukraine (2014–19)." Paper presented at the Association for Slavic, Eastern Europe and Eurasian Studies Annual Conference, November 15, 2020.

——. 2021. "From Martyrs to Secular Martyrs and Back: Churches Commemorate Holodomor Victims in Ukraine." Paper presented at the Working Group on Lived Religion Seminar, October 28, 2021.

Fylypovych, L. O., and O. V. Horkusha eds. 2014. *Maidan i Tserkva: Khronika podii ta ekspertna otsinka*. Kyiv: Sammit-Kniha.

Finberg, Leonid, and Uliana Holovach. 2016. *Maidan Svidchennia: Kyiv, 2013–14*. Kyiv: Dukh i Litera.

Finley, Erin P. 2011. *Fields of Combat: Understanding PTSD among Veterans of Iraq and Afghanistan*. Ithaca: Cornell University Press.

Flatley, Jonathan. 2008. *Affective Mapping: Melancholia and the Politics of Modernism*. Cambridge, MA: Harvard University Press.

Fomina, Victoria. 2018. "Between Heroism and Sainthood: New Martyr Evgenii Rodionov as a Moral Model in Contemporary Russia." *History and Anthropology* 29, no. 1: 101–20.

Foucault, Michel, and Jay Miskowiec. 1986. "Of Other Spaces." *Diacritics* 16, no. 1: 22–27.

Freeze, Gregory L. 1998. "Policing Piety: The Church and Popular Religion in Russia, 1750–1850." In *Rethinking Imperial Russia*, edited by David L. Ransel and Jane Burbank, 210–50. Bloomington: Indiana University Press.

Gaidai, Oleksandra. 2021. "Leninfall in Ukraine: How Did the Lenin Statues Disappear? *Harvard Ukrainian Studies* 38, no. 1–2: 45–70.

Gebauer, Gunter, and Christoph Wulf. 1995. *Mimesis: Culture, Art, Society*. Translated by Don Reneau. Berkeley: University of California Press, 1995.

Geertz, Clifford. 1973. *The Interpretation of Cultures: Selected Essays*. New York: Basic Books.

Giddens, Anthony, and Christopher Pierson. 2013. *Conversations with Anthony Giddens: Making Sense of Modernity*. Cambridge: Polity.

Gobodo-Madikizela, Pumla. 2008. "Empathetic Repair after Mass Trauma: When Vengeance Is Arrested." *European Journal of Social Theory* 11, no. 3: 331–50.

Golovneva, Elena, and Irina Shmidt. 2015. "Religious Conversion, Utopia and Sacred Space (Okunevo Village in Western Siberia)." *State, Religion and Church* 2, no. 2: 54–76.

Gordeev, Aleksei. 2014. *Tserkov' na Maidane*. Kyiv: Knihonosha

Gray, Patricia A. 2016. "Memory, Body, and the Online Researcher: Following Russian Street Demonstrations via Social Media." *American Ethnologist* 43, no. 3: 500–10. https://doi.org/10.1111/amet.12342.

Grzymała-Busse, Anna. 2015. *Nations under God: How Churches Use Moral Authority to Influence Policy*. Princeton: Princeton University Press.

Gupta, Akhil, and Ferguson, James. 1992. "Beyond Culture: Space, Identity and the Politics of Difference." *Cultural Anthropology* 7, no. 1: 6–23.

Hale, Henry E. 2004. "Explaining Ethnicity." *Comparative Political Studies* 37, no. 4: 458–85. doi:10.1177/0010414003262906.

Halfin, Igal. 2000. *From Darkness to Light: Class, Consciousness, and Salvation in Revolutionary Russia*. Pittsburgh, PA: University of Pittsburgh Press.

Harding, Susan Friend. 2001. *The Book of Jerry Falwell: Fundamentalist Language and Politics*. Princeton: Princeton University Press.

Hassner, Ron E., ed., 2014. *Religion in the Military Worldwide*. New York: Cambridge University Press.

Heelas, Paul, and Linda Woodhead. 2005. *The Spiritual Revolution: Why Religion is Giving Way to Spirituality*. Malden, MA: Blackwell.

Henig, David. 2020. *Remaking Muslim Lives: Everyday Islam in Postwar Bosnia and Herzegovina*. Urbana: University of Illinois Press.

Heo, Angie. 2018. *The Political Lives of Saints: Christian-Muslim Mediation in Egypt*. Berkley: University of California Press.

Hertz, Robert. [1907] 1960. "A Contribution to the Study of the Collective Representation of Death." In *Death and the Right Hand*. Translated by R. Needham and C. Needham, 28–87. Glencoe, IL: Free Press.

Hervieu-Léger, Danièle. 2000. *Religion as a Chain of Memory*. New Brunswick, NJ: Rutgers University Press.

Herzfeld, Michael. 2005. *Cultural Intimacy: Social Poetics in the Nation-Sate*. New York: Routledge.

Hirschkind, Charles. 2006. *The Ethical Soundscape: Cassette Sermons and Islamic Counterpublics*. New York: Columbia University Press.

Horkusha, O.V. 2014. "Evromaidan iak indicator transformatsii relihiinoi funktsional'nosti abo revoliutsiia hidnosti iak situatsiia spovidi pered Bohom." In *Maidan i Tserkva*, edited by L. O. Fylypovych and O. V. Horkusha, 61–75. Kyiv: Sammit-Kniha.

Hovorun, Cyril. 2017. *Scaffolds of the Church: Towards Poststructural Ecclesiology*. Eugene, OR: Cascade Books.

Hovorun, Cyril. 2018. *Political Orthodoxies: The Unorthodoxies of the Church Coerced*. Minneapolis: Fortress Press.

Hurkina, Svitlana. 2014. *Do Svitla Voskresinnia Kriz' Merni Katakomb*. Lviv: Ukrainian Catholic University Press.

Ingold, Timothy. 1993. "The Temporality of Landscape." *World Archaeology* 25, no. 2: 152–53.

Interfax. 2014. "West Is Moving Away from Russia Due to Its Return to Orthodoxy, Lavrov Said." June 5, 2014. http://interfax-religion.ru/?act=news&div=55525.

Jackson, Michael. 2005. "Preface: The Struggle for Being." In *Existential Anthropology: Events, Exigencies and Effects*, ix–xxxii. New York: Berghahn Books.

——. 2017. *How Lifeworlds Work: Emotionality, Sociality & the Ambiguity of Being*. Chicago: University of Chicago Press.

Jameson, Fredric. 1984. "The Politics of Theory: Ideological Positions in the Postmodernism Debate." *New German Critique* 12, no. 33: 53–65.

Kaell, Hillary. 2021. "Religious Heritage and Nation in Post-Vatican II Catholicism: A View from Quebec" *Religions*, 12, no. 4: 259. https://doi.org/10.3390/rel12040259.

Kalenychenko, Tetiana, and Ruslan Kokhanchuk. 2017. "Buty Poruch: Osnovy Viis'kovoho Kapelanstva dlia Viis'kovykh i Volonteriv." Kyiv: Skyniia

Kaliuzhnii, Anatolii. 2014. "Yabi buv Boh y sertsi ta rozumi—chi khtos' biv vi ditei?" In *Maidan i Tserkva*, edited by L. O. Fylypovych and O. V. Horkushi, 33–37. Kyiv: Sammit-Kniha.

Kant, Immanuel. 1983. *Perpetual Peace and Other Essays*. New York: Hackett.

Karácsonyi, Dávid, Konstyantyn Mezentsev, Grygorii Pidgrusnyi, and Zoltán Dövényi. 2014. "From Global Economic Crisis to Armed Crisis: Changing Regional Inequalities in Ukraine." *Regional Statistics* 4, no. 2: 18–39.

Karpov, Vyacheslav, Elena Lisovskaya, and David Barry. 2012. "Ethnodoxy: How Popular Ideologies Fuse Religious and Ethnic Identities." *Journal for the Scientific Study of Religion* 51, no. 4: 638–55. doi:10.1111/j.1468-5906.2012.01678.x.

Kasianov, Georgiy, Oleksii Tolochko and Marta D. Olynyk. 2015–16. "National Histories and Contemporary Historiography: The Challenges and Risks of Writing a New History of Ukraine." *Harvard Ukrainian Studies* 34, no. 1/4: 79–104.

Keane, Webb. 2018. "On Semiotic Ideology." *Signs and Society* 6, no. 1: 64–87. doi:10.1086/695387.

Kenworthy, Scott, and Alexander Agadjanian. 2021. *Understanding World Christianity: Russia*. Minneapolis: Fortress Press.

Kertzer, David I. 1988. *Ritual, Politics, and Power*. New Haven: Yale University Press.

Kirmayer, Laurence. 2008."Empathy and Alterity in Cultural Psychiatry." *Ethos* 36, no. 4: 457–74.

Kivelson, Valerie A., and Robert H. Greene. 2003. *Orthodox Russia: Belief and Practice under the Tsars*. University Park: Pennsylvania State University Press.

Klassen, Pamela E. 2015. "Fantasies of Sovereignty: Civic Secularism in Canada." *Critical Research on Religion* 3, no. 1: 41–56. doi:10.1177/2050303215584230.

Klumbytė, Neringa. 2019. "Sovereign Uncertainty and the Dangers to Liberalism at the Baltic Frontier." *Slavic Review* 78, no. 2: 12–23.

Knibbe, Kim, and Helena Kupari. 2020. "Theorizing Lived Religion: Introduction." *Journal of Contemporary Religion* 35, no. 2: 157–76. https://doi.org/10.1080/13537903.2020.1759897.

Knorre, B. 2015. "Contemporary Russian Orthodoxy: From the Social Paradoxes to the Cultural Model," In *Culture Matters in Russia and Everywhere. Backdrop to the Russian-Ukrainian Conflict*, edited by L. Harrison and E. Yasin, 127–44. Lanham, MD: Lexington Books.

Knorre, Boris, and Aleksei Zygmont. 2020. "'Militant Piety' in 21st-Century Orthodox Christianity: Return to Classical Traditions or Formation of a New Theology of War." *Religions* 11, no. 1: 2. https://doi.org/10.3390/rel11010002.

Knox, Zoe. 2004. *Russian Society and the Orthodox Church*. London: Curzon.

——. 2008. "Religious Freedom in Russia: The Putin Years." In *Religion, Morality, and Community in Post-Soviet Societies*, edited by Mark D. Steinberg and Catherine Wanner, 281–314. Bloomington: Indiana University Press.

Kolstø, Pål, and Aleksander Rusetskii. 2012. "Power Differentials and IdentityFormation: Images of Self and Other on the Russian-Georgian Boundary." *National Identities* 14, no. 2: 139–55.

Kononenko, Natalie O. 2019. *Ukrainian Epic and Historical Song: Folklore in Context*. Toronto: University of Toronto Press.

Kormina, J. 2010. "Avtobusniki: Russian Orthodox Pilgrims' Longing for Authenticity." In *Eastern Christians in Anthropological Perspective*, edited by C. Hann and H. Golz, 267–86. Berkley: University of California Press.

Kormina, Jeanne. 2021. "'The Church Should Know Its Place': The Passions and the Interests of Urban Struggle in Post-Atheist Russia." *History and Anthropology* 32, no. 5: 574–595. https://doi.org/10.1080/02757206.2020.1848822.

Kormina, Jeanne, and Sonja Luehrmann. 2018. "The Social Nature of Prayer in a Church of the Unchurched: Russian Orthodox Christianity from its Edges," *American Academy of Religion* 86, no. 2: 394–424.

Kormina, Zh.B. 2019. *Palomniki: Etnograficheskie ocherki pravoslavnogo momadizma* [Pilgrims: Ethnographic essays of Orthodox nomadism]. Moscow: Izdatel'skii Dom Vysshei Shkoly Ekonomiki.

Krawchuk, Andrii, and Thomas Bremer, eds. 2016. *Churches in the Ukrainian Crisis*. New York: Palgrave Macmillan.

Kukharenko, Svitlana. 2011. "Traditional Ukrainian Folk Beliefs about Death and the Afterlife," *Folklorica* 16, no. 1: 65–86.

Kulyk, Volodmyr. 2018. "Shedding Russianness, Recasting Ukrainianness: The Post-Euromaidan Dynamics of Ethnonational Identifications in Ukraine." *Post-Soviet Affairs* 34, no. 2–3: 119–38. https://doi.org/10.1080/1060586X.2018.1451232

Langer, Susanne K. 1967. *Mind: An Essay on Human Feeling*. Baltimore: Johns Hopkins Press.

Laruelle, Marlene. 2015. "Russia as a 'Divided Nation,' from Compatriots to Crimea: A Contribution to the Discussion on Nationalism and Foreign Policy." *Problems of Post-Communism* 62, no. 2: 88–97.

Latour, Bruno. 1993. *We Have Never Been Modern*. Cambridge, MA: Harvard University Press.

Lear, Jonathan. 2006. *Radical Hope: Ethics in the Face of Cultural Devastation*. Cambridge, MA: Harvard University Press.

Lerner, Julia. 2020. "Saving the Post-Soviet Soul: Religion as Therapy in the Narratives of Russian-speaking Migrant Woman." In *Assembling Therapeutics: Cultures Politics, and Materiality*, edited by S. Salmenniemi, J. Nurmi, H. Bergroth, and I. Perheentupa, 74–91. London: Routledge.

Lesiv, Mariya. 2013. *The Return of Ancestral Gods: Modern Ukrainian Paganism as an Alternative Vision for a Nation*. Montreal: McGill-Queen's Press.

Lindquist, Galina. 2005. "Healers, Leaders and Entrepreneurs: Shamanic Revival in Southern Siberia." *Culture and Religion* 6, no. 2: 263–85.

Litonjua, M. D. 2016. "Spiritual, but Not Religious: Untangling a Seeming Paradox." *International Review of Modern Sociology* 42, no. 1: 21–22.

Loveland, Anne C. 2004. "From Morale Builders to Moral Advocates: US Army Chaplains in the Second Half of the Twentieth Century." in *The Sword of the Lord: Military Chaplains from the First to the Twenty-First Century*, edited by Doris L. Bergen, 233–50. Notre Dame: University of Notre Dame Press.

Luehrmann, Sonja. 2011. *Secularism Soviet Style: Teaching Atheism and Religion in a Volga Republic*. Bloomington: Indiana University Press.

——, ed., 2018. *Praying with the Senses: Contemporary Orthodox Christianity Spirituality in Practice*. Bloomington: Indiana University Press.

Luhrmann, Tanya. 2012. *When God Talks Back: Understanding the American Evangelical Relationship with God*. New York: Alfred A. Knopf.

Luhrmann, T. M. 2020. *How God Becomes Real: Kindling the Presence of Invisible Others*. Princeton: Princeton University Press.

Maierchuk, Maria. 2011. *Ritual i tilo*. Kyiv: Krytyka.

Marples, David R., and Frederick V. Millis, eds. 2015. *Ukraine's Euromaidan: Analyses of a Civil Revolution*. Stuttgart: Ibidem.

Marsden, Magnus, Diana Ibañez-Tirado, and David Henig. 2016. "Everyday Diplomacy: Introduction to Special Issue." *Cambridge Journal of Anthropology* 34, no. 2: 2–22.

Martsenyuk, Tamara, and Ganna Grytsenko. 2017. "Women and Military in Ukraine: Voices of the Invisible Battalion." *Ukraine Analytica* 1, no. 7: 29–37.

Marynovych, Myroslav. 2015. "'Being a Church' during Times of Crisis." *Euxeinos* 17: 55–59.

——. 2019. "Religious Aspects of the Three Ukrainian Revolutions." In *Three Revolutions: Mobilization and Change in Contemporary Ukraine I: Theoretical Aspects and Analyses on Religion, Memory, and Identity*, edited by Pawel Kowal, Andreas Umland, Iwona Reichardt, and Georges Mink,553–565. Stuttgart: Ibidem Verlag.

——. 2019. *Metropolyt Andrei Sheptyts'kyi i Pryntsyp "Posytivnoi Sumi."* Lviv: Staroho Leva.

Matza, Tomas. 2018. *Shock Therapy: Psychology, Precarity, and Well-Being in Postsocialist Russia*. Durham, NC: Duke University Press.

Merdjanova, Ina, ed. 2021. *Women and Religiosity in Orthodox Christian Contexts*. New York: Fordham University Press.

Metcalf, Peter, and Richard Huntington. 1991. *Celebrations of Death: The Anthropology of Mortuary Ritual*. Cambridge University Press.

Metreveli, Tornike. 2020. *Orthodox Christianity and the Politics of Transition: Ukraine, Serbia and Georgia*. London: Routledge.

Meyer, Birgit. 2011. "Mediation and immediacy: sensational forms, semiotic ideologies and the question of the medium." *Social Anthropology* 19, no. 1: 23–39.

——. 2020. "Religion as Mediation." *Entangled Religions* 11, no. 3. doi: 10.13154/er.11.2020.8444.

Meyer, Birgit, and Marleen De Witte. 2013. "Heritage and the Sacred: Introduction." *Material Religion* 9, no. 3: 274–80.

Mick, Christopher. 2011. "Incompatible Experiences: Poles, Ukrainians and Jews in Lviv under Soviet and German Occupation, 1939–44." *Journal of Contemporary History* 46, no. 2: 336–63.

Miller, A. I. 2003. *The Ukrainian Question: The Russian Empire and Nationalism in the Nineteenth Century*. Budapest: Central European University Press.

Morgan, David. 2005. "The Look of the Sacred." In *Between Heaven and Earth: The Religious Worlds People Make and the Scholars Who Study Them*, edited by Robert Orsi. Princeton: Princeton University Press.

Morgan, David, ed. 2010. "Introduction: The Matter of Belief." In *Religion and Material Culture*, 1–18. New York: Routledge.

Musienko, Nataliia. 2015. *Mistetstvo Maidanu* [Art of the Maidan]. Kyiv: R. K. Maister-Print.

Naumescu, Vlad. 2006. *Religious Pluralism and the Imagined Orthodoxy of Western Ukraine*. Leipzig: LIT Verlag.

——. 2019. "Pedagogies of Prayer: Teaching Orthodoxy in South India." *Comparative Studies in Society and History* 61, no. 2: 389–418. doi:10.1017/s0010417519000094.

Navaro-Yashin, Yael. 2002. *Faces of the State: Secularism and Public Life in Turkey*. Princeton: Princeton University Press.

——. 2012. *The Make-Believe Space: Affective Geography in a Post-War Polity*. Durham: Duke University Press.

Nikolayenko, Olena. 2020. "The Significance of human dignity for social movements: mass mobilisation in Ukraine." *East European Politics* 36, no. 3: 445–62.

Nuckolls, Charles W. 1995. "The Misplaced Legacy of Gregory Bateson: Toward a Cultural Dialectic of Knowledge and Desire." *Cultural Anthropology* 10, no. 3: 367–94.

Oliphant, Elayne. 2015. "Beyond Blasphemy or Devotion: Art, the Secular, and Catholicism in Paris." *Journal of the Royal Anthropological Institute* 21, no. 2: 352–73.

——. 2021. *The Privilege of Being Banal: Art, Secularism, and Catholicism in Paris*. Chicago: University of Chicago Press.

Onuch, Olga, and Gwendolyn Sasse. 2016. "The Maidan in Movement: Diversity and the Cycles of Protest." *Europe-Asia Studies* 68, no. 4: 556–87.

Onuch, Olga, Henry E. Hale, and Gwendolyn Sasse, eds. 2018. "Identity Politics in Times of Crisis: Ukraine as a Critical Case." Special Issue. *Post-Soviet Affairs* 34, no. 2–3.

Oosterbaan, Martijn. 2017. "Transposing Brazilian Carnival: Religion, Cultural Heritage, and Secularism in Rio De Janeiro." *American Anthropologist* 119, no. 4: 697–709. doi:10.1111/aman.12930.

Orlova, Yuliya. 2014. *111 Dnei Maidana: Zapiski Kievlianki*. Kyiv: Duliby.

O'Rourke, Diane. 2007. "Mourning Becomes Eclectic: Death of Communal Practice in a Greek Cemetery. *American Ethnologist* 34, no. 2: 387–402.

Orsi, R. 1997. "Everyday Miracles: The Study of Lived Religion" In *Lived Religion in America: Toward a History of Practice*, edited by David D. Hall, 3–21. Princeton: Princeton University Press.

Orsi, Robert Anthony. 2002. *The Madonna of 115th Street: Faith and Community in Italian Harlem, 1880–1950*. 2nd ed. New Haven: Yale University Press.

Orsi, Robert A. 2005. *Between Heaven and Earth: The Religious Worlds People Make and the Scholars Who Study Them*. Princeton, NJ: Princeton University Press.

——. 2016. *History and Presence*. Cambridge, MA: Belknap Press of Harvard University Press.

Osanloo, Arzoo. 2020. *Forgiveness Work: Mercy, Law, and Victims' Rights in Iran*. Princeton: Princeton University Press.

Oushakine, Serguei Alex. 2009. *The Patriotism of Despair: Nation, War and Loss in Russia*. Ithaca: Cornell University Press.

Ozolina, Liene. 2019. "Would You Flee or Would You Fight? Tracing the Tensions at the Russian-Latvian Border" *Slavic Review* 78, no. 2: 348–56.

Özyürek, Esra. 2006. *Nostalgia for the Modern State Secularism and Everyday Politics in Turkey*. Durham, NC: Duke University Press.

Panchenko, Alexander. 2012. "'Popular Orthodoxy and Identity in Soviet and Post-Soviet Russia: ideology, consumption and competition." In *Soviet and Post-Soviet Identities*, edited by Mark Bassin and Catriona Kelly, 321–40. Cambridge: Cambridge University Press.

Papkova, Irina. 2011. *The Orthodox Church and Russian Politics*. New York: Oxford University Press.

Pesman, Dale. 2000. *Russia and Soul: An Exploration*. Ithaca: Cornell University Press.

Philipps, Sarah. 2014. "The Woman's Squad in Ukraine's Protest: Feminism, Nationalism, and Militarism on the Maidan." *American Ethnologist* 41, no. 3: 414–26.

Pile, Steve. 2012. "Emotions and Affect in Recent Human Geography." *Transactions of the Institute of British Geographers* 35, no. 1: 5–20.

Plokhii, Serhii, and Frank Sysyn. 2003. *Religion and Nation in Modern Ukraine*. Edmonton: CIUS Press.

Portnov, Andrii. 2016. "Post-Maidan Ukraine and the New Ukrainian Studies." *Slavic Review* 74, no. 4: 723–31.

Rakowska-Harmstone, Teresa. 1977. "Ethnicity in the Soviet Union." *The Annals of the American Academy of Political and Social Science* 433: 73–87.

Rappaport, Roy A. 1999. *Ritual and Religion in the Making of Humanity*. Cambridge: Cambridge University Press.

Richters, Katja. 2013. *The Post-Soviet Russian Orthodox Church: Politics, Culture, and Greater Russia*. New York: Routledge.

Riedel, Friedlind. 2020. "Atmospheric Relations: Theorizing Music and Sound as Atmosphere." In *Music as Atmosphere: Collective Feelings and Affective Sounds*, edited by Friedlind Riedel and Juha Turvinen, 1–42. New York: Routledge.

Ries, Nancy. 2002. "Anthropology and the Everyday, from Comfort to Terror." *New Literary History* 33(4): 725–42.

Robbins, Joel. 2014. "The Anthropology of Christianity: Unity, Diversity, New Directions: An Introduction to Supplement 10." *Current Anthropology* 55, no. S10: S157–S171.

——. 2015. "On Happiness, Values, and Time: The Long and the Short of It." *HAU: Journal of Ethnographic Theory* 5, no. 3: 215–33.

Robben, Antonius C. G. M. 2004. *Death, Mourning, and Burial: A Cross-Cultural Reader*. Malden, MA: Blackwell.

Rosaldo, Michelle Z. 1984. "Toward an Anthropology of Self and Feeling." In *Culture Theory: Essays on Mind, Self, and Emotion*, edited by Richard A. Shweder and Robert A. LeVine, 137–58. Cambridge: Cambridge University Press.

Rosaldo, Renato. 1984. "Grief and Headhunter's Rage." In *Culture and Truth: The Remaking of Social Analysis*, 1–23. Boston: Beacon.

Rosen, Michael. 2012. *Dignity: Its History and Meaning*. Cambridge: Harvard University Press.

Rudeyko, Vasyl. 2016. "Tam panuvalo khristiianstvo nekonfeciine." In *Maidan: Svidchennia. Kyiv, 2013–14*. Kyiv: Dukh i Litera, 676–77.

Rupprecht, Tobias. 2018. "Orthodox Internationalism: State and Church in Modern Russia and Ethiopia." *Comparative Studies in Society and History* 60, no. 1: 212–35. doi:10.1017/s0010417517000469.

Sarbadhikary, Sukanya. 2015. *The Place of Devotion Siting and Experiencing Divinity in Bengal-Vaishnavism*. Berkley: University of California Press.

Schmoller, Andreas. 2020. "The Syriac Orthodox and Coptic Orthodox Churches in Austria: Inter-Church Relations and State Recognition." *Mashriq & Mahjar: Journal of Middle East and North African Migration Studies* 8, no. 1: 76–102. doi:10.24847/v8i12020.300.

Seigworth, Gregory J., and Melissa Gregg. 2010. *The Affect Theory Reader*. Durham, NC: Duke University Press.

Sewell, William H. 1996. "Historical Events as Transformations of Structures: Inventing Revolution at the Bastille." *Theory and Society* 25, no. 6: 841–81.

Shestopalets, Denys. 2021. "What Is God's and What Is Caesar's? Autocephaly, Schism and the Clash of Political Theologies in Ukrainian Orthodoxy." *Political Theology* 22, no. 3: 1–20. https://doi.org/10.1080/1462317X.2021.1925439.

Shevel, Oxana. 2021 "Unholy Wars: Understanding Intra-Orthodox Conflict in Ukraine Since the Granting of the *Tomos*." Paper presented at the Association of Slavic, East European, and Eurasian Studies Convention, December 2, 2021.

Shlikhta, Natalia. 2014. "'Ukrainian' as 'Non-Orthodox': How Greek-Catholics Were 'Reunited' with the Russian Orthodox Church, 1940s–60s." *Gosudarstvo religiia tserkov' v Rossii i za rubezhom* 32, no. 4: 208–34.

Shore, Marci. 2017. *The Ukrainian Night: An Intimate History of Revolution*. New Haven: Yale University Press.

Shotkina, Katerina. 2014. "Nepravda vid perestrakhu." In *Maidan i Tserkva*, ed. L. O. Fylypovych and O. V. Horkusha. Kyiv: Sammit-Kniha.

Slezkine, Yuri. 2017. *The House of Government: A Saga of the Russian Revolution*. Princeton: Princeton University Press.

Siegelbaum, Lewis H. 1997. "Freedom of Prices and the Price of Freedom: The Miners' Dilemmas in the Soviet Union and Its Successor States." *Journal of Communist Studies and Transition Politics* 13, no. 4: 1–27.

Slaby, Jan. 2020. "The Weight of History: From Heidegger to Afro-Pessimism." *Phenomenology as Performative Exercise*, 173–95. doi:10.1163/9789004420991_012.

Smith, Jonathan Z. 1978. *"Map Is Not Territory: Studies in the History of Religions*, edited by W.J. Hanegraaff. Chicago: University of Chicago Press.

——. 1980. "The Bare Facts of Ritual." *History of Religions* 20, no. 1/2: 112–27.

——. 1987. *To Take Place: Toward Theory in Ritual*. Chicago: University of Chicago Press.

Smolkin, Victoria. 2018. *A Sacred Space Is Never Empty: A History of Soviet Atheism*. Princeton: Princeton University Press.

Snyder, Timothy. 2010. *Bloodlands: Europe between Hitler and Stalin*. New York: Basic Books.

Sonevytsky, Maria. 2019. *Wild Music: Sound and Sovereignty in Ukraine*. Middletown, CT: Wesleyan University Press.

Stahl, Henrieke. 2015. "Poesie als politische Partizipation: Der virale poetopolitische Diskurs um Anastasija Dmitruks Videogedict 'Nikogda my ne budem brat'jami' auf 'YouTube': Virale politische Videoposie—ein neues Phänomen." *Zeitschrift für Slavische Philologie* 71, 441–77.

Stepanenko, Viktor, and Yaroslav Pylynskyi, eds. 2014. *Ukraine after the Euromaidan: Challenges and Hopes*. Bern: Peter Lang.

Stephens, Angharad Closs. 2015. "Urban Atmospheres: Feeling Like a City?" *International Political Sociology* 9, no. 1: 99–101. doi:10.1111/ips.12082.

Stepnisky, Jeffrey. 2018. "Staging Atmosphere on the Ukrainian Maidan. *Space and Culture* (May)." https://journals.sagepub.com/doi/abs/10.1177/1206331218773671? jour nalCode=saca.

Stewart, Charles, and Rosiland Shaw, eds. 1994. *Syncretism/Anti-Syncretism: The Politics of Religious Synthesis*. London: Routledge.

Stewart, Kathleen. 2007. *Ordinary Affects*. Durham: Duke University Press.

——. 2017. "In the World That Affect Proposed." *Cultural Anthropology* 32, no. 2: 192–98. doi:10.14506/ca32.2.03.

Stoeckl, Kristina. 2020. "The Rise of the Russian Christian Right: The Case of the World Congress of Families." *Religion, State and Society* 48(4): 223–38.

——. 2014. *The Russian Orthodox Church and Human Rights*. London: Routledge.

Stoeckl, Kristina, and Kseniya Medvedeva. 2018. "Double Bind at the UN: Western Actors, Russia and the Traditionalist Agenda." *Global Constitutionalism* 7, no. 3: 383–421. doi: 10.1017/S2045381718000163.

Stoler, Ann Laura. 2013. *Imperial Debris: On Ruins and Ruination*. Durham: Duke University Press.

Stoller, Paul. 1994. "Double Takes: Paul Stoller on Jay on Taussig." *Visual Anthropology Review* 10, no. 1: 155–62.

Storch, Leonid. 2013. "The Pussy Riot Case." *Russian Politics & Law* 51, no. 6: 8–44. doi:10.2753/rup1061-1940510601.

Sturken, Marita. 1997. *Tangled Memories: The Vietnam War, the AIDS Epidemic, and the Politics of Remembering*. Berkley: University of California Press.

Suslov, Mikhail. 2014. "'Holy Rus': the Geopolitical Imagination of the Contemporary Russian Orthodox Church." *Russian Politics and Law* 52, no. 3: 67–86.

——. 2016. "The Russian Orthodox Church and the Crisis in Ukraine." In *Churches in the Ukrainian Crisis*, edited by Andrii Kravchuk and Thomas Bremer, 133–62. New York: Palgrave Macmillan.

——. 2018. "'Russian World' Concept: Post-Soviet Geopolitical Ideology and the Logic of Influence." *Geopolitics* 23, no. 2: 330–53. https://doi.org/10.1080/14650045.2017 .1407921.

Sysyn, Frank E. 2005. "Politics and Orthodoxy in Independent Ukraine." *Harriman Review*. May 2005.

Taussig, Michael. 1993. *Mimesis and Alterity: A Particular History of the Senses*. New York: Routledge.

Taylor, Charles. 1994. *The Politics of Recognition*. Princeton: Princeton University Press.

——. 2007. *A Secular Age*. Cambridge: Harvard University Press.

Thrift, Nigel. 2004. "Intensities of Feeling: Towards a Spatial Politics of Affect." In *Human Geography* 86, no. 1: 57–78.

Throop, Jason C. 2010. *Suffering and Sentiment: Exploring the Vicissitudes of Experience and Pain in Yap*. Berkley: University of California Press.

Thuswaldner, Gregor. 2014. "A Conversation with Peter L. Berger: 'How My Views Have Changed.'" In *The Cresset* LXXVII, no. 3: 16–21.

Timoshenko, I. I., ed. 2002. *Derzhavno-tserkovkni vidnosini: Svitovii dosvid i Ukraina*. Kyiv: European University Press.

Todorova, Maria. 2006. "The Mausoleum of Georgi Dimitrov as lieu de mémoire." *Journal of Modern History* 78, no. 2: 377–411. doi:10.1086/505801.

Tweed, Thomas A. 2006. *Crossing and Dwelling: A Theory of Religion*. Cambridge: Harvard University Press.

———. 2015. "After the Quotidian Turn: Interpretive Categories and Scholarly Trajectories in the Study of Religion since the 1960s." *Journal of Religion* 95, no. 3: 361–85.

Ukrinform. 2020. "Volunteer Organizations Most Trusted Institution in Ukraine." Ukrinform, December 11, 2020. https://www.ukrinform.net/rubric-society/2598710-volunteer-organizations-most-trusted-institution-in-ukraine.html.

Umland, Andreas, and Yuliya Yurchuk, eds. 2017. "Issues in History and Memory of OUN." *Journal of Soviet and Post-Soviet Politics and Societies* 3, no. 2 115–28.

Verdery, Katherine. 1999. *The Political Lives of Dead Bodies: Reburial and Postsocialist Change.* New York: Columbia University Press.

Vovk, Dmytro, and Elizabeth Clark. 2021. *Religion during the Russian Ukrainian Conflict.* London: Routledge.

Vysokyi zamok. 2011. "Blazhennishyi Liubomyr Huzar: 'My ne ye provintsiina Tservka des na kraiu Ukrainy, kudy nas khotily vidipkhaty,' Rozmovlialy Olesia Pasternak ta otets Ihor Yatsiv." *Vysokyi zmok.* April 21.

Wanner, Catherine. 1998. *Burden of Dreams: History and Identity in Post-Soviet Ukraine.* University Park: Penn State University Press.

———. 2007. *Communities of the Converted: Ukrainians and Global Evangelism.* Ithaca, NY: Cornell University Press.

———. 2014. "'Fraternal Nations' and Challenges to Sovereignty in Ukraine: The Politics of Linguistic and Religious Ties." *American Ethnologist* 41, no. 3: 427–39.

———. 2016. "The Return of Czernowitz: Urban Affect, Nostalgia, and the Politics of Place-Making in a European Borderland City." *City and Society* 28, no. 2: 198–221.

———. 2020. "An Affective Atmosphere of Religiosity: Animated Places, Public Spaces and the Politics of Attachment in Ukraine and Beyond," *Comparative Studies in Society and History* 62, no. 1 (January 2020): 68–105, https://doi.org/10.1017/S0010417519000410.

———. 2021. "Empathic Care and Healing the Wounds of War in Ukraine," *Emotions and Society* 3, no. 1 (May 2021): 155–70, https://doi.org/10.1332/263169021X16139626598365.

———, ed. 2012. *State Secularism and Lived Religion in Russia and Ukraine.* New York: Oxford University Press.

Wanner, Catherine, and Viktor Yelensky. 2019. "Religion and the Cultural Geography of Ukraine." In *Regionalism without Regions: Reconceptualizing Ukraine's Heterogeneity,* edited by Ulrich Schmid and Oksana Myshlovska, 247–96. Budapest: Central European University Press.

Wawrzonek, Michal. 2014. *Religion and Politics in Ukraine: The Orthodox and Greek Catholic Churches as Elements of Ukraine's Political System.* Cambridge: Cambridge University Press.

Werkner, Ines-Jacqueline. 2008. "Military Chaplaincy in International Operations: A Comparison of Two Different Traditions." *Journal of Contemporary Religion* 23, no. 1: 47–62.

Willen, Sarah S. 2019. *Fighting for Dignity: Migrant Lives at Israel's Margins.* Philadelphia: University of Pennsylvania Press.

Willen, Sarah S., and Don Seeman. 2012. "Introduction: Experience and Inquiétude." *Ethos* 40, no. 1: 1–23. doi:10.1111/j.1548-1352.2011.01228.x.

Williams, Raymond. 1961. *The Long Revolution.* New York: Columbia University Press.

———. 1977. *Marxism and Literature.* Oxford: Oxford University Press.

Wilson, Andrew. 2014. *Ukraine Crisis: What It Means for the West.* New Haven: Yale University Press.

Wylegala, Anna, and Malgorzata Glowacka-Grajper, eds. 2020. *The Burden of the Past: History, Memory, and Identity in Contemporary Ukraine*. Bloomington: Indiana University Press.

Yekelchyk, Serhy. 2015. *The Conflict in Ukraine: What Everyone Needs to Know*. New York: Oxford University Press.

——. 2020. "The Ideological Park: How the Tsar's Garden in Kyiv Became a Modern Political Space." in *Postsocialist Landscapes: Real and Imaginary Spaces from Stalinstadt to Pyongyang*, ed. Thomas Lahusen and Schamma Schahadat, 25–46. Bielefeld: Transcript.

Yelensky, Viktor. 2002. *Relihiia pislia komunizmy*. Kyiv: NPU.

——. 2014. "Ukrains'ki tserkvi pid chas Evromaidanu stali na vik narody." in *Maidan i Tserkva*, ed. L. O. Fylypovych and O. V. Horkusha. Kyiv: Sammit-Kniha.

Yurchak, Alexei. 2014. "Little Green Men: Russia, Ukraine and Post-Soviet Sovereignty." *Anthropoliteia*, March 31, 2014. https://anthropoliteia.net/2014/03/31/little-green-men-russia-ukraine-and-post-soviet-sovereignty/.

——. 2017. "The Canon and the Mushroom: Lenin, Sacredness, and Soviet Collapse." *HAU: Journal of Ethnographic Theory* 7, no. 2: 165–98.

Yurchuk, Yuliya. 2021. "Historians as Activists: History Writing in Times of War: The Case of Ukraine in 2014–2018" *Nationalities Papers* 49, no. 4: 691–709. doi: https://doi.org/10.1017/nps.2020.38.

Zayamyuk, Andriy, and John-Paul Himka, eds. 2006. *Letters from Heaven: Popular Religion in Russia and Ukraine*. Toronto: University of Toronto Press.

Zelins'kyĭ, Andriĭ. 2016. *Na rikakh Vavylons'kykh . . . : Kil'ka dumok pro povernennīa*. Lviv: Vydavnytstvo "Svichado."

——. 2015. *Soniakhy: Dukhovnist'na chas viĭny*. Lviv: Vydavnytstvo Staroho Leva.

Zubrzycki, Geneviève. 2016. *Beheading the Saint: Nationalism, Religion, and Secularism in Quebec*. Chicago: University of Chicago Press.

Zychowicz, Jessica. 2020. *Superfluous Women: Art, Feminism, and Revolution in Twenty-First-Century Ukraine*. Toronto: University of Toronto Press.

# Index

Note: Page references in *italics* refer to illustrative matter.

CPSIA information can be obtained
at www.ICGtesting.com
Printed in the USA
LVHW031215131122
732933LV00003B/248